Tony White was born in 1964 in Farnham, Surrey. He is the author of a number of novels including most recently the critically acclaimed *Foxy-T* published by Faber and Faber. White's short stories have been published in numerous magazines and collections and his fiction is also published in translation within the former Yugoslavia. He co-edited *Croatian Nights*, a collection of new fiction from Croatia, Serbia and Great Britain. Tony White lives in London, where he also works for Arts Council England and is literary editor of the *Idler* magazine.

For Sarah

Another Fool in the Balkans

in the footsteps of
Rebecca West

Tony White

CADOGAN

Cadogan Guides
2ⁿᵈ Floor, 233 High Holborn
London WC1V 7DN
info@cadoganguides.co.uk
www.cadoganguides.com

The Globe Pequot Press
246 Goose Lane, PO Box 480, Guilford,
Connecticut 06437–0480

Typesetting by Mathew Lyons
Printed in Italy by Legoprint
A catalogue record for this book is available
from the British Library
ISBN 10: 1-86011-151-3
ISBN 13: 978-1-86011-151-8

Contents

Notes on pronunciation

Throughout this book I have used standard rather than anglicized spellings of names and place names in Serbian and Croatian, together with any 'accents'. One of the wonderful things about the Serbian and Croatian languages is that each letter has only one possible sound, unlike in English, so the reader need know no more than the following broad rules.

The letter 'c' gives a 'ts' sound.

Where a 'c' or an 's' appears with a diacritical mark (č, ć, š), English speakers should read this as a 'ch' or a 'sh'. So, for example, *ćevapčići* ('little kebabs') should be pronounced 'chevapchichi'. (There are subtle differences between 'č' and 'ć', but it is not necessary to know these for an approximate pronunciation.)

The letter 'j' reads like the letter 'y' in 'yacht' in English.

'Dj', as in the name of the late Serbian Prime Minister Zoran Djindjić, is a Roman alphabet version of the character 'Đ' or 'đ' and is pronounced like the 'g' in 'ginger', whereas 'g' is always pronounced as in the English word 'green'. 'Dž' is pronounced like the 'j' in 'jackpot', while 'ž' on its own gives a softer 'j' sound like the 'j' in the French *je t'aime*.

Chapter One
Slavonia, London, Zagreb
(1993–2001)

I'm writing this in September. I have the back door open and a warm breeze rustles the coloured plastic strips of a fly curtain that's hung across the doorway. At this moment I can hear the sound of a plane coming in to land, and as the sound of its engines fades I hear once more the distant traffic and the murmur of leaves, gentle sounds that are punctuated by an occasional sharp laugh or shout from some young men who are sitting on a wall nearby; by a train going along the viaduct; by the ring of a mobile phone or by footfalls and the light rattle of a pushchair's wheels.

Not so far away, although right now it feels as if it's on the other side of the world, the fields of Slavonia, north of the Sava River in Croatia, will be full of ripe maize, perhaps tall enough to get lost in, the leaves turning papery and brown. The corn is probably ready to harvest.

I know that sometimes corncobs are left on the plant to be dried out, then used for animal feed. I remember my father saying this once, and he grew up in rural Hampshire. We'd go to his parents' house in Bentley on Sunday afternoons. Maybe my uncles would be visiting too – Cyril, Dennis, Ray or Bob – or my Aunty Eileen who lived up the road and who'd married a German POW land worker just after the Second World War. My sister and I would be left to our own devices in the sitting room, watching the wrestling or reading back issues of *Titbits* magazine, drinking orange tea from a big pot that was kept warm on the stove, and waiting for the dreaded moment when dinner would be ready. My granny used to start boiling the runner beans before she put the joint in the oven. After lunch we'd go outside and play in the garden or in the fields. Actually there was a lot to do. This was a hop farm. Rows of huts in one of the fields by the main road would be home to the migrant workers who swamped the place for two weeks every summer to pick the hops. They probably still do, though these days migrant workers are less likely to be Londoners.

Once the hops had been picked and dried, loaded up and sent off to the breweries, the 'bines' – as the hop's long, viney stems are called and have been, indeed, since the days of William Cobbett – would be thrown on top of the pile that had been left there to rot since the year before, a practice that had been going on for donkey's years. When they were fresh, these heaps of bines were enormous – 15 or 20 feet high – and to us at the time they seemed like huge springy mountains that made death-defying stunts completely feasible. You could take a running leap into space, somersault across the chasm between mountains, and the natural springiness of the bines would cushion your fall. Sometimes we'd go and look at the dead crows that the gamekeeper had hung with orange nylon string from the fence next to the garden gate, where the pheasants were kept. Along the windowsill of the porch were some old horseshoes and a row of what looked like rusty pebbles, but were in fact fossilized sea urchins that had been turned up in the fields. They were all cobwebby.

The fields out at the back of the house were often planted with corn, and I remember picking some cobs one sunny Sunday afternoon in September. Our father laughed and said that it was past the point when it was good to eat as corn on the cob, and they were probably keeping it back for the animals.

Perhaps that's what's happening along the banks of the Sava in Slavonia too: the cobs are being left on the plant to dry out.

Passing through this landscape, past the maize fields of Croatia rather than Hampshire, though close up there's little difference, is a train that, like the river, has come from the west; from somewhere beyond the city of Ljubljana in what is now the independent republic of Slovenia.

Slavonia. Slovenia. It can be easy to mix them up. The presiding judge at the trial of Adolf Eichmann in Jerusalem in 1961, during a part of the proceedings that was concerned with the concentration camps set up across the former Yugoslavia during the Second World War, asked a common question:

Presiding Judge: Is there a difference between Slovenia and Slavonia?

Witness Arnon: Slavonia is part of Croatia. Slovenia is an independent province which was at that time under Italian control.[1]

At the time of writing, Slovenia, where this train has come from, is about to join the European Union. By the time this book is published it will be a member state, the first 'former Yugoslav', 'ex-Yugoslav' or 'Yugoslav successor' country to join.

Following the implosion of the Austro-Hungarian Empire, Slovenia came into being as part of the Kingdom of the Serbs, Croats and Slovenes (proto-Yugoslavia) in 1918, then of actual Yugoslavia, for much of the 20th century. It was also the first of the republics to leave the Yugoslav federation in 1991.

Most people in Slovenia would probably rankle at the idea of their country being in 'the Balkans'. However, if you were to draw a horizontal line across the map from the points, at west and east, where the coastlines of the Adriatic and Black Seas turn south to form the Balkan peninsula, that line would link Trieste and Odessa, and a substantial part of Slovenia would be beneath it. It's an observable fact that Slovenia is part of the peninsula. Yet there is a tendency all over the region to see the designation 'Balkan' as referring to the people further south than you are. At times the terms 'Balkan' and 'Oriental' are used almost interchangeably to describe the defining characteristics of those people who live further south. Many Croats share with the Slovenians an antipathy to any casual inclusion of their country in the category 'Balkan'. Maybe it's partly because 'Balkan' is a derivation from the Turkish word for 'mountain', 'mountain range' or even 'bare cliffs', which became attached, in the accounts of 16th- and 17th-century travellers from Germany, France and Britain, to a particular mountain in Bulgaria.

This usage led to what the academic and theorist Maria Todorova calls a 'grand error':[2] the mistaken use of the word 'Balkan' to describe what was (itself mistakenly) perceived as an unbroken mountain range stretching from the Black Sea to the Adriatic. It's easy to imagine the 19th-century German geographer August Zeune pointing at this mountain and asking what it was called through his interpreter, and his interlocutor, trying to be helpful but maybe a bit puzzled, saying 'It's called *a mountain*?!' It's a satisfying reversal of the apocryphal story of the 19th-century Russian railway engineers being taken to see Vauxhall Station in London and supposedly thinking that 'Vauxhall' was the generic word for 'station.' At the time of Zeune's visit, however, the convention was to name regions after their dominant physical characteristics, and his designation that this should therefore be known as 'the Balkan peninsula' stuck.

Since Ottoman rule didn't really extend to Slovenia, nor to the whole of Croatia, you can perhaps understand that the use of a Turkish word to describe them may not be very popular. Indeed, even Maria Todorova, who has done more than most to unpick the symbolisms and prejudices of and about the region, defines the *really* 'Balkan' countries as 'the ones that participated in the historical Ottoman sphere'.[3] Yet, just because this is a commonly held thought, and both Slovenia and Croatia more often looked west and north towards the twin capitals of the Austro-Hungarian Empire, Vienna and Budapest, that doesn't mean that these countries are not pretty squarely located on the Balkan peninsula, nor that you can discuss either of them without discussing their neighbours, especially given the fact that now, as in the past and very probably in the future, their circumstances are inextricably linked. This antipathy is perhaps also partly due to the fact that the naming of the peninsula coincides more or less with the global adoption into general usage of the term 'balkan' (small b) as an adjective meaning backward and inexplicably violent, or its use in a verb, 'to balkanize', meaning to divide some social entity – a country, a region, the house of a married couple who are separating – into mutually competitive or aggressive smaller units.

Of course, if you keep going south you end up in Greece, which takes up a huge proportion of the peninsula, but is usually referred to as a separate entity altogether.

It seems to be a minor convention that books about the Balkans begin with a train journey across Slavonia. That's as true of Leon Trotsky's war reportage as it is of the novels that make up Olivia Manning's brilliant *Balkan Trilogy* – even if, the beginning of the first novel in the series, *The Great Fortune*, sees the protagonists, Guy and Harriet Pringle, spending a long day travelling across 'the *Slovenian* Plain'[4] (my emphasis) on their way to the Romanian border.

Rebecca West's *Black Lamb and Grey Falcon* is an exception. She did travel across Slavonia to Belgrade, though when she made the journey it was at night, so there was little to see apart from flooded fields on either side of the track.

I too found myself travelling by train across the Slavonian plain from Zagreb to Belgrade in September 2001. The sheer novelty of travelling through the Slavonian maize fields, a few miles from the border of Bosnia-

Herzegovina on my way to Serbia – a journey that would not have been possible a short time before – meant that the landscape was nagging at the periphery of my vision, practically tapping on the window to get my attention, and I spent most of the journey watching it all go by. Never mind Antoine de St-Exupéry's pronouncements on train travel – that children with their noses pressed up against the glass are the only ones who know where they are going – I was simply excited to be finally making this journey, having wanted to for many years. More than anything, I was excited about the destination, Belgrade.

I'd travelled through the centre of the former Yugoslavia before, when there still was a Yugoslavia, but that was by coach in 1982. Four of us had saved up to buy tickets for a three-day bus ride to Greece, with enough left over to live there comfortably for a week or so. We had planned to somehow eke out this tiny budget for two months. I was a teenager and thought, correctly as it turned out, that it would be quite possible to live on sunshine and whatever else turned up. At one point during the journey, having gone to sleep somewhere in Austria, I woke in the early hours, and saw road signs pointing to Zagreb and to Belgrade. Seeing those names on motorway signs was thrilling and I pointed them out to my friends. These were mythic names at the time: we had arrived in 'Eastern Europe', but somehow we hadn't had to go by way of the Berlin Wall to get there. Ignorant as I was, it seemed astonishing.

By daylight we drove across what seemed like endless plains, between mountain-fringed horizons, which I now know were in southern Serbia, Kosovo and Macedonia, where strange and violent rainstorms appeared from nowhere and lashed the windows of the bus before disappearing equally quickly. We stopped in the main squares of small stone villages, and women (whom we imagined might be prostitutes) waved at us from upstairs windows.

Somewhere south of Belgrade we stopped at a service station, of modern glass and concrete construction. We walked through the swing doors into a smart bar and café. There was a high ceiling, and the tables and chairs were laid out to get the benefit of all the light that was streaming in through the windows. Once we'd bought our beers, though, we realised that there must have been a power cut. The refrigerators were not working. What I wasn't to know then, but recognise now, is that the Yugoslav economy was in pretty poor shape in the early 1980s, crippled by the 'shock therapy' imposed by both the International Monetary Fund and Ronald Reagan's 'National Security Division Directive "United States Policy Towards Yugoslavia"'.[5] This, by many accounts, was intended to destabilize the Communist regime, and did so, but it also resulted in drastic austerity measures, enormous and almost immediate unemployment, and the rationing of necessities such as electricity, petrol and basic foodstuffs.[6]

Nearer still to the Greek border, the drivers made a toilet stop. I was shocked at the time by the visible poverty, which seemed to be exemplified by the sight of an elderly woman dressed in shabby widow's weeds who was gathering up urine-soaked rags from the floor of the mens' toilet and hanging them up to dry on a washing line outside.

Once we reached Corfu we followed the advice of a woman we'd met on the ferry and travelled to a village called Marathias on the west coast of the island. We pitched camp on a beautiful and nearly deserted beach, and quickly got to know the only other people there, a group of German students who thought that, because we were English, we must be 'punk rockers'. The olive groves around Marathias were fragrant with fenugreek and oregano, but also swarming with nasty flies that looked like moths and would drop out of the trees and bite us.

Just beneath the cliff where the track from the village crested the hill and met the beach was a whitewashed fisherman's hut, about the size of a small shed. We'd sometimes see the people who lived there sitting on the bench outside, reading, squinting in the light. They didn't look very Greek. We met them in the local taverna a couple of days later. She was English, he was German: Harry and Elizabeth.

Harry's favourite subject of conversation, and his ambition at the time, was to open a restaurant that sold nothing but the breakfasts of the world, all day long. Nothing else would be on the menu: just bacon and eggs, porridge, pancakes and maple syrup, croissants and coffee. 'And best of all,' he'd say, nodding at the old men in straw hats playing backgammon in the shade, 'the Greek breakfast: Metaxa brandy, coffee and a cigarette.'

It transpired that Harry was an aspiring writer, which to me at the time – I was 18 – seemed as good as actually having written something. He'd already anglicized his surname in anticipation of publication, because he thought that his real name sounded like 'pots and pans', and that was no kind of name for a writer. At one point the conversation turned to our journey, and my excitement at travelling through Yugoslavia.

'Ah, Yugoslavia,' he said, grinning broadly. 'Yes, they are *real animals* there. *Very* backward.' I didn't know at the time that this casual, smiling racism, the expectation of complicity, would be something I'd encounter again and again over the years. Though Harry found Greece pretty 'backward' too: 'Can you imagine?' he asked me, with prurient horror in his voice, 'They put olive oil on their bread. Just olive oil!'

Nineteen years later, in 2001, it seems strange being back in the centre of what had been Yugoslavia, but was now an independent Croatia, travelling across the same countryside that I'd seen back then. The only obvious differences are that I'm on a train, rather than a barely legal 'magic bus', and that this time I'm not just passing through on my way to some rite-of-passage proto-backpacking adventure.

In the intervening years, however, I'd rehearsed this journey across Slavonia in my mind countless times, and visualized it from memories of what I'd seen from that bus window in 1982. All of this came flooding back as I watched the maize fields slipping past the train window.

In the early 1990s I'd instigated and run a programme of new art commissions at a small art gallery in the East End of London called the Showroom. It was an oddly shaped former furniture showroom that in turn had been adapted from what had originally been the Kent brush factory on Bonner Road in Bethnal Green. The last major exhibition that I'd commissioned, and one that seemed impossible to follow, was a month-long performance by a (then) Yugoslav artist called Gordana Stanišić, who had come to London for a holiday but had stayed on when war broke out in 1991. Stanišić's art work was simple: she planned to walk the *distance* between London and Belgrade. This may sound like a strange kind of exhibition, but it was a piece of 'performance art', that marginal but ever-present substrand of 20th-century art history stretching back to the Dadaists' nihilistic response to the First World War, in which the artwork is defined in part by the live presence of the artist. My own introduction to performance art had come a year or so before that bus ride through Yugoslavia, during our A-level art classes at Farnham Sixth Form College. My then teacher, a wonderful woman called Ann Weeks, had assembled the class and shown us a video of a film of a performance art work by a British artist called Stuart Brisley, called *Arbeit Macht Frei* – 'Work makes you free', the legend that was notoriously inscribed over the gates of Auschwitz. The film, perhaps five or ten minutes long and shot, as I now know, by the film director Ken McMullen, showed Brisley clad in black in some anonymous room, responding to Theodor Adorno's famous assertion that poetry, or art in general, was not possible after the Holocaust. The way that Stuart Brisley responded was simple, if not actually easy. He was vomiting, seemingly endlessly. It was the most abject thing I'd ever seen. It was as if he was saying, '*This* art is possible', or, more than that, that this was the only kind of art that was.

In this context, then, Stanišić's proposal to walk from London to Belgrade without traversing any actual distance, without leaving the gallery, let alone the country, sounded completely normal, if strangely fascinating.

But as well as being performance art, Stanišić's journey was one that couldn't be made in fact, for all kinds of reasons. For one thing, the country that she had left at the beginning of 1991 no longer existed.

Leaving the former Yugoslavia at that time was a matter of more extreme urgency for many men of military age, as a means of avoiding conscription. As at other times of political upheaval in the region's history, this meant that there was a significant former-Yugoslav population in London, but also in other cities across Europe and the rest of the world. For those who'd managed to get to London, or elsewhere in England, this put them in a kind of bureaucratic orbit around, of all places, Croydon in South London.

I'm not sure why the Home Office's drop-in centre for processing refugee claims should be located in Croydon, but it is. The two office buildings where the immigration service worked are called Lunar House and Quest House. There's a minor irony in this nomenclature, a word association: 'lunar' as in 'lunatic' (asylum); 'quest' as in search (seek).

The journey Stanišić was proposing was deliberately blank: walking to a country that no longer existed, but without actually travelling anywhere; walking on the spot. The plan, outlined to me one Sunday afternoon in the summer of 1993, was for the gallery to somehow buy a piece of gym equipment, a jogging machine, and to install it in the back half of the gallery building. This would be where she'd walk, every day, for as long as it took to cover the distance. We'd hang a large map of Europe in the gallery's front space where the route could be traced out, day by day, and hang a bouncer's rope across the adjoining doorway. There'd be no need for an actual bouncer: an undergraduate invigilator would be enough to stop people queuing up to have a go on the treadmill themselves. The thick coil of rope and two brass hooks would have the added benefit of becoming instant sculpture, a 'ready-made' work, in Marcel Duchamp's sense.

Unable, not surprisingly, to get sponsorship from any gym-equipment manufacturers for this project of Stanišić's, I ended up buying the tread-mill at John Lewis's on Oxford Street and manhandling the not so flat pack back to the gallery on the Tube. A late night was spent puzzling over the instruction sheet, working out which allen key fitted which bolt, tighten-ing the heavy rollers so the rubber mat ran straight, fitting the handrail, plugging in the control panel and – crucially – setting the clock, the milometer, to zero. At midnight on one evening towards the end of April 1994 Stanišić took the first step on her virtual walk to Belgrade and I took a photo for the gallery archive.

A couple of days later I opened the gallery doors to an as yet non-exis-tent public, while, cordoned off, the artist took a sip from the bottle of mineral water she'd brought along, then started walking, clocking up the miles. To save the gallery's budget I decided to invigilate some days myself, when I wasn't working. I needed something to read, something to take my mind off the metronome beat of the footsteps that were reverberating through the space under the old wooden floor. The gallery became a soundbox, an echo chamber, to the extent that the amplified impact of each footstep actually rippled the surface of my coffee, like an approaching tyrannosaurus in the *Jurassic Park* films.

I'd been mentioning the exhibition to anyone with a public stake in the wars that were at that time still going on in the former Yugoslavia. One of these people, the film-maker Pawel Pawlikowski, whose very necessary documentary about nationalism, *Serbian Epics,* had recently been screened on BBC2, suggested that Rebecca West's *Black Lamb and Grey Falcon* would be a good place to start reading. Curiously there wasn't much choice. There didn't seem to be many other books about the former Yugoslavia in print at the time, at least none that were readily available.

For alternative reading material one would have had to trawl the second-hand bookshops of Charing Cross Road for Edward Lear's travel journals, an edition of Lady Mary Wortley Montagu's writings, or a stained and yel-lowing copy of Jan and Cora Gordon's *Two Vagabonds in the Balkans*, a bizarre account of a bohemian year spent painting landscapes in Bosnia-Herzegovina in the 1920s. The Gordons' book reads like the archetype for what has since become the Provençal bestseller: begging eggs from uncom-prehending locals; gradually becoming members of the community;

tearful farewells when their stay was over. West herself may well have read this book. It's not included in *Black Lamb and Grey Falcon*'s bibliography, but there are what sound like tiny echoes of it in her text. In the space of a few pages both West and the Gordons discuss a then current problem with tuberculosis and overcrowded housing;[7] the locals' apparent inability to consider anything other than a waterfall as worthy of an artist's or writer's attention; and the little wooden turbine-driven flour-mills that stand on stilts above Bosnian mountain streams.

It is also intriguing that both West and the Gordons visit such mills in their respective travelogues and that both disturb a sleeping miller in his hut. The Gordons' book is full of comments on the backwardness of the peasants: 'Science teaches us all about the inertia of inanimate matter, but how can we learn to overcome the inertia of the animate?'[8] Visiting a mill where a man is 'squatting Turkishly on his haunches,'[9] the Gordons see a moment of primal idleness. The water is splashing 'against this primitive turbine and [causing] it to turn with a lazy reluctance, as if mill and miller were matched in lethargy'.[10] West allows that the principle of the turbine was actually invented here, above these dashing little mountain rivers and cascades, hundreds of years ago, but when her party approaches one of these mills and disturbs a sleeping youth she too loses heart.[11] Elsewhere, though, West is less charitable, seeing an idleness that she perceives amongst the inheritors of Ottoman traditions as a malignant and dangerous lack of interest, an apathy born of power, corruption and complacency.

This wasn't the Gordons' first book. They'd written several before. *Two Vagabonds in the Balkans* was the follow-up to their best-selling *Poor Folk in Spain* (the poor folk being them, one supposes) and its sequel *Misadventures with a Donkey in Spain.* They contributed to the invention of a new literary genre for the middle classes: getting away from it all and getting by. This was a world away from the kinds of privileged travel literature that preceded it, the grand expeditions with servants. Edward Lear might well have travelled light when he spent months trawling around Albania and Greece, but the Gordons and writers like them democratized travel writing and combined it with aspiration, generating a literature that would eventually fuel a real-estate boom in rural villages across Europe.

Rebecca West's travelogue, however, is a universe away from *Two Vagabonds in the Balkans*. It's a huge, encyclopaedic volume – *two* volumes in its first printing, in 1941 – which sees her travelling from city to city and from village to village, taking a guided tour across practically the whole of the former Yugoslavia during the course of two long visits that she and her husband made on the eve of the Second World War. On her return to Britain, West paints vivid and revealing character portraits of everyone she met and explains the history of the region in painstaking detail, but with the narrative urgency and breathlessness of an airport novel. I was immediately hooked. Invigilating the gallery became a pleasure that I looked forward to, and my enthusiasm for the book was initially fuelled by the very blankness of Stanišić's artwork. This month-long walk felt like a huge gap in my life, a gap that I needed to fill with information, as if this would give me some means of understanding why this artist would want to do something so apparently pointless. Arguably it was a mistake to see *Black Lamb and Grey Falcon* as primarily a source of information rather than a work of literature, but at the time I only knew that I couldn't wait to sit down and start reading every day. Soon even that wasn't enough and every waking moment saw me reading *Black Lamb and Grey Falcon*: at the bus stop or as I was walking along the street.

While Stanišić pounded away on the treadmill in the next room, I was following in Rebecca West's footsteps as surely as the thousands of others who had read her book in the intervening years. I followed her to Zagreb, to Sarajevo, to Belgrade, hanging upon her every word. It was and is an extraordinary book, though one that has provoked great debate. *Black Lamb and Grey Falcon* is seen variously as being an unqualified master-piece, a flawed (as in mildly pro-Serb, Serbocentric or anti-German) mas-terpiece, or by some of her detractors as a slab of rabid and right-wing Serbophilia. Occasionally in the contemporary literature about the wars in the former Yugoslavia you'll see the contention that British troops sta-tioned in Bosnia-Herzegovina were pro-Serb. Some of the evidence given to support this claim is that they, or the officers at least, were all reading *Black Lamb and Grey Falcon*. Brendan Simms, in his book *Unfinest Hour: Britain and the Destruction of Bosnia*, is one of the few to take the trouble to unpick this generalisation, and to catalogue the frequent British foreign policy disasters that might actually give credence to such allegations. With hindsight it's probably fairer to say that the reason some people in Britain were reading *Black Lamb and Grey Falcon* in the early 1990s was not that they wanted some pro-Serb bias confirmed, but out of genuine curiosity, combined with the fact that it was just about the only book on Yugoslavia that was generally available in high street bookshops.

That West should be seen as so extremely partisan in her depiction of the former Yugoslavia is a central and defining irony of how both she and *Black Lamb and Grey Falcon* are now perceived. Ironic, because this was a failing that she had identified in the succession of British writers and, to her mind, foolish do-gooders who had previously visited the region. She herself warns against a school of travel writers who 'all came back with a pet Balkan people established in their hearts as suffering and innocent, eternally the massacree and never the massacrer, which had all the force and blandness of pious fantasy'.[12]

Blandness could never be a description of *Black Lamb and Grey Falcon*, however. I'd have to put the book down reluctantly when people came to watch Stanišić walking; and people did come. They'd stand there for a few minutes, some of them unable to believe that this walk was an artwork, others enthusing about the walk being a metaphor for the impossibility of understanding the wars that were happening a short flight away. Sometimes I'd have to explain the work to journalists who'd come out to the East End of London in search of a story about Sarajevo (they thought) rather than Belgrade.

To the random pedestrian passing the gallery and casting a sideways glance into the gallery, it must have looked as if the Showroom had reinvented itself a fourth time: brush factory, furniture shop, art gallery, and now gym. Reinvention is, of course, the story of the East End, although back in 1994 there wasn't yet a gym on every street corner. It wasn't fashionable at that time to pay a fortune for a membership, to go to a gym on your way to work. Stanišić's treadmill in a loft space, her Walkman and her water bottle, made for a curious sight at that time, but became an unwitting premonition of a whole new regeneration trope, a lifestyle one-liner.

Her walk as artwork also echoed other journeys, some of which have been mythic or romantic, such as German film director Werner Herzog's walk from Munich to the bedside in Paris of his dying friend, the film critic Lotte Eisner, because of his superstition that she'd die if he caught the plane. It was as if the effort of walking could work some sympathetic magic, take the strain, slow down her cancer. Thinking of Herzog's legendary walk, I could imagine these two phantom journeys intersecting across time, the two pedestrians Herzog and Stanišić bumping into each other on an autobahn slip road, red car lights slipping past. The other journeys that Stanišić's walk echoed were more desperate: the columns of refugees that were streaming away from contested zones in the fragmenting Yugoslavia and landing up in safe areas, enclaves guarded by the UN in places like Srebrenica, in holiday camps on the Croatian Adriatic coast, or in refugee camps on the Greek-Macedonian border, where many still remain.

Stanišić's journey lasted for only a month or so. One and a half thousand kilometres paced out in the back room of the gallery, and incrementally drawn across the map of Europe at the end of each day, while I read a thousand or more pages of Rebecca West in the front of the gallery, the footsteps of the artist giving a metronome beat to my reading. I was hungry for information, but this was like eating food to music, keeping time with every mouthful. Those footsteps hammered home West's points of view, her readings of Balkan history, until they were ingrained in my mind. I suspect now that I was placing too much trust in Rebecca West's interpretations, but nevertheless I finished reading *Black Lamb and Grey Falcon* at roughly the same time that Stanišić finished her walk.

The end of this journey, even if Stanišić hadn't physically gone anywhere, seemed worth celebrating, so I coralled a few friends into turning up to witness its completion, the last few steps, just in case no one else did. At the appointed time the treadmill stopped, and Stanišić stepped off, walked across the gallery, unhooked the rope and filled in the last twenty kilometres on the map. The line had reached Belgrade and she had arrived right where she started.

We all stood around with our glasses of wine, and one or two people displayed an ignorance that was perhaps forgivable, given the level and quality of information available to them at the time, by asking, 'But isn't she a Serb? Aren't they the bad guys? What right does she have to make any kind of statement about the war?' Later, the film director Pawel Pawlikowski dropped in; he'd just arrived back in the UK from Belgrade. He told us that all official routes in and out of the city and the country were closed. He'd had to pool resources with a few other journalists and get a black market minibus from Croatia to Budapest in Hungary, then hang around for a day or two, until he could pick up another bus back in to Belgrade.

I mentioned that I'd taken him up on his recommendation to read *Black Lamb and Grey Falcon*. Pawlikowski smiled and said that I shouldn't believe everything I read.

Looking out of the window of the train one of my travelling companions, Borivoj Radaković, tells me that millions of years ago these Slavonian plains were the bed of the Pannonian Sea. The soil, thousands of feet deep, is the result of silting as the sea dried up. I see a man standing in the middle of one field and it takes a couple of seconds before I realise that it's a scarecrow; I see a pheasant taking flight and think again of Bentley in Hampshire. I imagine fossilized shells and sea urchins being regularly turned up by the plough and shoved in farmers' or dog walkers' pockets, as they are in the South of England, and lined up on people's porch windowsills.

Borivoj Radaković, known to his friends as Boro, is a novelist and play-wright from Zagreb. He speaks almost perfect English, with a slight cockney accent, has spent a lot of time in London over the years and is responsible for translating most of the literary fiction from the UK that's published in Croatia, from James Kelman to Julian Barnes. Boro is tall and slightly balding, with imposing features, and right now he's sporting shoulder-length white hair. He also has a way of speaking his carefully polite English that could easily be mistaken, by one who didn't know him, for pomposity. He's a natty dresser, too, in his trademark black suit. Boro is also the reason that I'm here on this train in September 2001.

I owe this trip, this train journey through Slavonia, to the fact that a short story collection[13] that I contributed to has been published in translation in Croatia. A couple of other contributors and the anthology's editors had already been over to promote the book in Zagreb, the capital of Croatia, and in Novi Sad in the Vojvodina region of Serbia. Now it is my turn.

Boro is one of the instigators of a group of writers called FAK, or 'Festival Alternative Književnost (literature). As the Yugoslav successor republics emerged from the shadow of war, FAK actively rejected the nationalist imperatives that had dominated the mainstream cultural lives of these countries since the late 1980s.

Authors such as Radaković, Edo Popović and Zoran Ferić from Croatia were creating a radical and alternative literature. The word 'alternative' is not being used lightly here, but to denote that these writers are not controlled by, or affiliated with, any nationalistic political project or official agency. Boro told me that they had also rejected a kind of ironic and academic postmodernism that had dominated the literary scene in the last days of Yugoslavia, and embraced humour. Our anthology had struck some sort of nerve with these writers for various reasons. For one thing, it

had been important for us all to set our stories in the present day. This perhaps had been the reason for the beginnings of a shared sympathy between
us: writers from Britain and writers from Croatia and Serbia. Yet it would
be fair to say that there was far more at stake for the writers who made up
FAK than there had been for the British writers. For the members of FAK,
who, after all, hail from countries where historical narratives had held sway
for more than a decade in both literary and political life, this was seen as
an act of political and social necessity; it was an act of resistance. Boro told
me that the writers who made up FAK also rejected the way that literature
had become politically instrumentalized in the former Yugoslavia during
the late 1980s and 1990s:

> When we started, we were alternative to the Association of
> Croatian Writers (who are right-wing conservatives and national-
> ists); to the writers of the Tudjman era who are now seen as liter-
> ary grandees; and also against the new 'official' writers who are
> now in the Social Democratic Party. We are also alternative from
> within – each of us writes in a different style. We are from differ-
> ent generations, but almost all of us opposed Tudjman's regime at
> a time when it was very dangerous to do so.

FAK had focused their activities around a series of festivals and readings,
new magazines, and the output of a growing number of independent and
anti-nationalist publishers, such as Celeber in Croatia and Rende, the publishing house co-founded in 2000 by the famous Belgrade novelist
Vladimir Arsenijević, who in 1994 had won the NIN literary award, the
Serbian equivalent of the Booker Prize, for his debut, the anti-war novel *U
Potpalublju* (*In the Hold*).

Boro tells me that, in Zagreb at least, the idea of audiences paying even a
nominal ticket price to hear writers reading is a new phenomenon, but it is
generally welcomed. Under Communism there were plenty of public readings, but they were generally by state-sponsored writers and, as you might
expect, free. As a consequence there is a suspicion of any free event, a ques-
tioning of the ideological motives behind it and an unwillingness to attend
something that is presented as being for the greater good. Eschewing ideas of
educating the masses, this emerging readings scene instead actively sought a
connection with the energy of such London events as Richard Thomas's Vox
'n' Roll series, the regular, rowdy literary evenings of music and live readings
by authors that still take place in Islington pubs and night clubs.

FAK have already held controversial festivals in the Croatian cities of Zagreb, Pula and Osijek, and even in Novi Sad, in the Vojvodina region of northern Serbia. This time – and this is the reason I'm on this train – they are breaking what, in Croatia, is the final taboo, and are travelling to Belgrade for a three-day literary festival, and have invited me to take part too, as the sole British writer on the bill. It is quite a privilege because here, for the first time in 12 years, writers and audiences from across the former Yugoslavia will be able to meet and read together in public. During the war this would have been suicidally dangerous, if it hadn't been impossible. Even now it is not without risk. In Zagreb, following my visit, a FAK event at which a documentary about the war was being screened was broken into and actively 'cancelled' by a gang of nationalist skinheads with baseball bats. The venue was smashed up. People were hurt.

Boro tells me that questions have been asked in the Croatian Parliament about the festival in Belgrade: how could the government possibly justify giving funding to Croatian writers so that they could travel to Serbia? Boro is indignant: 'We deliberately don't ask for government money! We are not instrumentalizing ourselves into anyone's political, nationalistic or militaristic project. Now you see why!'

As we talk we pass woods, more maize fields, an occasional road. Time is framed by the pylons carrying overhead power lines that swish past the window every half-second. Leon Trotsky took a train along this same line in the autumn of 1912, before the formation of Yugoslavia, on his way to cover the Balkan Wars. He recorded the following descripton:

> From the broad, clean window, there is a view out over the plain. Maize nearly everywhere, only interrupted by patches of hops. The maize stands broken and yellowing. In places it has all been cut and gathered into heaps. The Hungarian steppe looks dull now, under a wet, dirty sky. Hope remains that, farther south, sky and land will prove more welcoming – down there in Serbia and Bulgaria, where the plain begins to become 'Balkan'.[14]

About the only difference between his view from the train and mine is the name (rather than the location) of the country he was travelling through – which has changed several times since 1912 – and the weather, which today is bright and clear.

Today what may have been wheat, or beet, has already been harvested, the fields re-ploughed. Every now and then I catch a glimpse of an ornate church steeple, standing like an inverted Victorian table leg above the trees. Sometimes I notice hills in the far distance, but the overall impression is of flatness. It's strange and slightly chilling to think that this bucolic region has been fought over more times than can be counted. At this moment it all looks very peaceful.

What is now Slavonia may well have once been the bed of the Pannonian Sea, but over subsequent centuries the tides of peoples and empires have also overwhelmed this landscape. In 1899 Neanderthal remains were discovered in Croatia by Dragutin Gorjanović-Kramberger: 'Krapina Man,' of whom fragments of skulls and jawbones remain, along with assorted tibia and fibia. To this day, the world's largest single Neanderthal find. Gorjanović-Kramberger noticed that some of these bones had been burned and split open, and that the marrow had been scraped out. This was enough evidence for him to posthumously accuse these Neanderthals of cannibalism.

Then came the Bronze Age and the Iron Age. Celtic tribes settled here; then the Romans; then in the early 7th century, Slavic tribes. Others came in pursuit of farther goals: St Cyril and St Methodius, for instance, brought the Glagolitic or 'Old Church Slavic' alphabet north from Greece in the late ninth century to the already Christianized Slavs. Nations and empires rose, and were destroyed by the Ottoman Empire flooding north and west towards Vienna, or by the Hungarians, and later the Austro-Hungarian Empire, expanding south and east. Neither empire quite succeeded in its goals. For a start, each literally stood in the way of the other, so that for many years the Sava River, which currently meanders along somewhere off to the south of the railway line, formed part of the border between the two empires.

Old maps of the Balkan peninsula from the 17th and 18th centuries illustrate this well. They show none of the countries you'd expect to see in a contemporary atlas: Greece, Bulgaria, Albania, Yugoslavia (if it was published before 1991), let alone Slovenia, Croatia, Serbia, Montenegro, Macedonia, Bosnia-Herzegovina. Sometimes all that's shown at that end of the Mediterranean is a vast 'Austria' or 'Hungary' and below it an even vaster 'Turkey'. Until the early 20th century this railway line would have been at the southern edge of the Austro-Hungarian Empire, since it's on the northern side of the Sava River, which, roughly, defined the border as far as Belgrade, where it joins the Danube, and that river took over border duties almost as far as the Black Sea. The Ottomans never managed to occupy Vienna, although they came close enough to besiege it twice, and the Austro-Hungarian Empire never really made it further south than this, give or take a bit of post-Treaty of Berlin jiggery-pokery that saw Bosnia-Herzegovina annexed by Vienna in an attempt to stifle the newly independent Serbia.

The stand-off did last a few centuries, so, as you'd expect, the two empires each left their traces in the languages, the food and the culture of these places, like the flotsam from some flood tide stranded high on the beach: Turkish coffee and strudel, the Muslim and the Catholic. Additional and significant legacies of these empires are the divisions that they created among the peoples of this peninsula, which are in part a derivation from this Ottoman and Austro-Hungarian rift, but also from the Ottoman form of administration, which through time set up administrative, political and social structures, the *millets*, that were defined by the religions of the populace.

I'd arrived in Zagreb, capital of Croatia, the day before setting out on this train journey to Belgrade, the capital of Serbia. I'd been told that I was being met by a journalist called Danijela Stanojevic, who would then be interviewing me for one of the local daily newspapers. Once I got through passport control, however, there seemed to be quite a few people waiting, but none of them showed any sign of searching for me. It took about ten or fifteen minutes before the crowds dispersed. By this time the arrivals hall was empty, apart, that is, from myself and a young, dark-haired woman who had previously looked straight through me. I looked over and raised my eyebrows in tentative greeting.

Zagreb lies on a flat plain at the foot of one quite large mountain, which is officially named Medvednica ('Bear Mountain'), but which everybody refers to simply as Sljeme, although the old town itself is built on two modestly sized hills. In fact the two old towns that made up Zagreb are built on these two small hills, Kaptol, the area around the cathedral, which was ruled by the bishops, and Gradec. They were once divided by a small river, which is now long built over, and the bridge between the two had served as a battlefield more than once. A river runs through Zagreb: the Sava. As Danijela and I approach the city from the airport, we pass farmland that is soon replaced by glass and concrete. We drive past several generic-modernist civic buildings that might be national libraries, concert halls, uni-

versities or combinations of all three, and it feels as if we could be anywhere in the world, from Coventry to Buenos Aires. But then, after crossing a couple of wide boulevards, the road sweeps down beneath a railway
bridge and as we emerge out the other side it's as if we've gone back a century or more in time.

We're dropped off outside the broad stone frontage of the railway station. We dodge cars and blue-and-white trams to cross the main road, and
find ourselves in a huge square, among meticulously kept gardens. There
are stone pavilions and statues set among the grass and flowers. The architecture in this part of town is in the decorative Viennese style. That's
inevitable, perhaps, since Croatia was part of the Austro-Hungarian
Empire until the end of the First World War. The city is beautiful in the
afternoon sun, its buildings sharply lit against a clear blue September sky.
There are tall stone apartment buildings whose balcony windows are open
to the warm breeze. People mill around, some shopping, others sitting in
the sun. Young men and women walk around in groups, eyeing each other
up and laughing. Perhaps it's the weather, but everyone seems to be in a
good mood.

We walk across the city's main square. Over to the left is the statue of a
Croatian hero called Ban Jelačić, astride his sturdy horse. We walk up a
winding cobbled street to the old town, where, beneath the twin spires of
Zagreb's handsome Gothic cathedral, we find a pleasant bar. There are
wooden benches and tables outside, so we buy beers and find a seat in the
sun. Danijela makes numerous phone calls and within minutes a photographer turns up to take some pictures, while she retrieves her notebook
from her bag and starts interviewing me. It's all very painless; nice to sit
and chat outside. A few more phone calls and Danijela's sister Valentina
arrives. The plan is for us to go to some sort of 'millennium festival' – there
will be food and drink, and dancing. The pay-off is that I may have to do
an interview there too, but on stage this time, a fact that is presented to me
as if I still have some choice in the matter.

Valentina is a civil engineer, and is in charge of building a new business
and shopping development on the outskirts of the city. The festival itself is
in a huge semi-permanent marquee-type structure alongside the new
buildings; inside there are a stage, a dance-floor, and rows of benches and
tables. I'm introduced to some people who work for the local authority and
to Valentina's colleagues on the project. Danijela was right: They want me

to be interviewed by her on stage, but first I'm offered food and beer. My plate is filled with meat – big red sausages and pork fillets in a thick, orange gravy – and hunks of bread. I'm handed a plastic pint glass of lager. I hurriedly eat what I can before, a few minutes later, I'm informed that we're next on the bill.

The festival is busy, a couple of hundred people are gathered for an evening's entertainment. The audience looks as if it's mainly made up of local workers and their families, with beer and sausages uppermost in their minds as well as on the tables before them. After the winners of a children's raffle are announced, and prizes are handed out, we duly step onto the stage to discuss literature, ideas and the hospitality of the Zagrepčani (the people of Zagreb). Some people are listening, but most are chatting with their friends.

Perhaps someone should have warned me or I should have figured out for myself that there are certain subjects that might not be appropriate for this discussion here at the Millennium Festival. Or I'm just too tired to think straight, but when Danijela innocently asks how I plan to spend my weekend in Zagreb I don't discuss the many attractions of my host city, nor do I say, quite truthfully, how beautiful the architecture is and how friendly the people are. Instead, I blithely admit that the next day I'm going to Belgrade.

There is a sudden, stunned silence.

I look up and see several hundred people staring at me open-mouthed, their forkfuls of sausage or paprika pork frozen in mid-journey. It's like a Bateman cartoon: 'The man who mentioned Belgrade to a marquee full of Croatian ex-servicemen'.

The silence stretches out in front of us until there's a small flurry of activity in the audience and the festival director hurries towards the stage waving a piece of paper which he passes to Danijela. She reads it and then translates it for me away from the microphone: 'Thank the sponsor and wrap it up. Now.' We cut the interview short, but make it seem as if we'd been due to finish anyway. Roadies come on to the stage and clear away our chairs almost before we've stood up, then they begin to do a sound-check for the band that's coming on next.

Once we've jumped off the stage I apologise to Danijela and everyone else I'm introduced to. A few minutes later the festival director gestures me towards a table, where another plateful of sausage and pork, and more beer, await. At first I wonder what he's doing – I've just eaten after all – but then

I realize that his action is doubly hospitable. I have been supplied not only with a good meal but also with a means of demonstrating to anyone who's interested that I am indeed a grateful and worthy guest, and one who knows good Croatian food when he sees it.

By the time I finish eating the band has taken the stage – which is surely what most of the audience had been waiting for. Valentina, the civil engineer, asks me to dance and I gratefully accept. Now I really can be the tourist again and forget about my embarrassing *faux pas*. Actually I don't have to pretend to be enjoying myself – it is fun. Some press photographers gather around to get a picture of us dancing.

The next morning I find myself at Zagreb's main railway station. There's a large crowd of people waiting in the ticket hall. All are writers, and more will join us in Belgrade.

The train we're going to catch is in fact a 'sleeper' from Venice, and once we've hefted our bags across to the platform it's waiting for us. It is pretty comfortable inside; the carriages are divided into large compartments with sliding doors and big plate glass windows. Boro, Danijela and I spread out in one compartment, and settle in for the journey to Belgrade. Boro tells me that this journey is part of the route of the old Orient Express. There were several Orient Expresses in fact, but this route was known as the 'Simplon'. It travelled from Paris through northern Italy to Trieste, then on to Ljubljana and Zagreb, before splitting off to Bucharest or carrying on a bit further through Belgrade to Niš and then to Athens or Istanbul. The carriages that pulled out of Zagreb Station might not have been the kind of luxurious Pullman coaches that the words 'Orient Express' bring to mind, but they were still in far better shape than any running in Britain. Possibly the privatization of formerly public utilities and state industries hasn't yet reached the railway system here. Presumably it's only a matter of time.

The stretch of line that we're travelling on between Zagreb and Belgrade was heavily damaged during the war, Boro tells me, and I'm now becoming used to the fact that 'during the war' doesn't mean – as it does to anyone British of my generation or thereabouts – some time between 1939 and 1945, but refers to the 1990s. In fact it's only very recently that the line has been reinstated – so recently in fact that at journey's end, when people in both Zagreb and Belgrade ask how I made the trip, and I tell them that I went by train, they look at me in disbelief. The journey from

Zagreb to Belgrade takes much longer than it did before the recent wars. Because stretches of the track had only just been repaired the train had to go quite slowly. At one point I went to sleep, and when I woke up the train had stopped and I could hear voices coming down the corridor. Croatian police or border guards were on the train. We could hear them working their way down the carriage, and it wasn't long before they came in to check the passports and visas of everyone in our compartment. Outside the windows, across the platform, there were a number of two-storey buildings with metal grilles on the windows. Twenty minutes or so after the border guards had gone, the train shunted forward a few yards, and the Serbian border guards boarded the train and repeated the process of checking everybody's passports. Looking out of the window, I could see that the red checkerboard of Croatia's coat of arms – the Šahovnica – had disappeared from the side of the car number plates, as well as from police badges; we were now in Serbia.

When we were on the move again, a small, dark-haired man who had also got on at Zagreb but had slept for the entire journey thus far showed us all his passports, laughing. He explained that he'd been trying to work out whether to use his Croatian, Bosnian or Italian papers, and had finally decided on the Italian ones. They were not questioned. I wondered if he was a spy or a black marketer, or whether this level of intrigue was a prosaic necessity.

From the window, as the train gathered pace, the only noticeable difference in the landscape to tell us that we're in Serbia is the sudden proliferation of domed Orthodox churches, and the disappearance of the elaborately ornate Austro-Hungarian steeples of Catholic Croatia. The first sign of the war on this side of the border comes about 20 minutes later, when we pass a train depot next to the railway line. Five or six relatively modern metro-style trains are standing outside an engine shed. At first sight I can't work out what is amiss, then I realize that there are no visible tracks. The trains are stranded in what might as well be the middle of a field. The grass is higher than the buffers. They can't have moved for years.

As we near Belgrade, the grassland becomes littered with the shells of empty houses and other buildings, mile after mile of them. Like those trains a few miles back they are stranded in the grass, and there are no paved roads that I can see. People are obviously living in some of these buildings – I can see that they're camping in the very few that are nearest to being completed – but most stand roofless and empty. These aren't the burned-out houses that were shown on the news during the early 1990s. They're apparently the result of a vast rehousing scheme that sought to build thousands of homes for the Serb refugees who had been the victims of 'ethnic cleansing' in Croatia. But there is little sign of urban planning and certainly no station stop: the 'Orient Express' just carries on past.

I'm told that with the endemic corruption legitimized and practised under the Milošević regime – which, indeed, for some people, character-ized it – the project collapsed. No building licences had been obtained and the infrastructure was never considered, much less built. There is no run-ning water or electricity, and many of the houses remain unfinished. In spite of this, refugee communities have been living in some of them for the last six or seven years.

The late Italo Calvino might have imagined this terrain of half-built houses. It could have come from his novel *Invisible Cities*. A town without a centre and lacking any civil infrastructure stands here – perhaps symbol-ic of other displacements – waiting to be fully occupied and, more impor-tantly, waiting to be connected to the rest of society, but without even the means of arrival or departure. It remains a black market city. There seems to be no immediate prospect of the settlements even being retrospectively legalized in order to ease the burden of the refugees who live here, because this whole area is still designated as farmland,[15] but the path of least resist-ance is probably to leave them standing. It's easier than demolishing them, or re-zoning this part of Zemun Municipality.

A much-reported scam operated in recent years, since sugar was added to the small list of things that Serbia was now allowed to export. This move to support the Serbian agricultural industry was, however, undermined by the sanction-busting smuggling networks that operated during the war to bring petrol and arms into the country, and to take out money, but which now swung into operation to import vast amounts of cheap sugar from other countries, Romania perhaps, to be then repackaged as 'product of Serbia' and sold on to EU markets at the official price. It would appear that fictional crops are all that can be grown when a country's infrastruc-ture has been devastated by a decade of war. A few enterprising people, unfortunately none of them farmers, made millions from this deception, until someone (at whichever transnational organization monitors these things) realized that there wasn't the capacity in the country's remaining undamaged sugar refineries to have manufactured so much. Sugar was placed once again on the list of banned goods.[16]

Nearer still to Belgrade, and without warning we are plunged into total darkness. It's a tunnel, and the train's lights are all switched off, which seems odd, since there's obviously enough electricity to keep the train running. It crosses my mind that they've been switched off for dramatic effect; this is the Orient Express, after all. It's a very long tunnel and we sit in the dark for several minutes, joking nervously. The only thing we can see is the glowing ember of Danijela's cigarette. 'Is very funny,' she says. 'Like a spy movie. By the time the train gets out of the tunnel, one of us will have disappeared.'

Chapter Two
Zemun railway tunnel (2001)

The cover of darkness gives me a chance to think about what I'm undertaking. Writing a travel book seems to be the least of my worries next to the daunting prospect of following in Rebecca West's footsteps, but even the former is not without its difficulties. Dubravka Ugrešić, a writer and essayist who has been exiled from her home in Zagreb since the wars in the former Yugoslavia, says something pertinent:

> I have always believed … that a writer with any self-respect should avoid three things: (a) autobiography, (b) writing about other countries, (c) diaries. All three smack of narcissism, which is undoubtedly the basic premise of any literary act, but ought not also to be its outcome. And in all three genres this outcome is hard to avoid.[1]

True, although narcissism is not the greatest concern for anyone who's writing about the former Yugoslavia, or the region generally, particularly somebody from outside the region. Much current thinking on the subject of travel writing about the Balkans is informed by post-colonial studies, particularly the late Edward W. Saïd's *Orientalism*. This should come as little surprise, even though the (possibly narcissistic) tendency in Britain might be to think of post-colonial studies (if they're thought of at all) as pertaining to the repercussions of the decline and fall of the British and other European empires and independence movements in faraway places during the 20th century, rather than as concerning the impact and legacy of imperial domination and independence movements across parts of mainland Europe between the 15th and the 19th centuries.

'Balkanism', as this field of study is known, suggests, or manifests, that the collective self-image of 'civilized' or 'western' cultures (the two terms being used synonymously by those cultures, it is suggested, to maintain a justification for their position of power) is in part actually defined against a necessarily barbaric or at the very least exotic Other; that a barbaric 'Other', against which western Europe can claim to measure its own progress, continues to be a necessary ingredient in the formation of western Europe's sense of itself as a civilized region. For many, the Balkans have provided, and continue to provide, this prop. Arguably, this can be seen in NATO justifying its bombing campaign against civilian targets in Serbia and Kosovo in 1999. It's echoed in the way that some elements of the British press generated hysteria in early 2004 about economic migrants from the countries that were then just about to join the European Union. It's what informed the casual racism of Harry Pots and Pans, the German writer-manqué whom I met in Corfu in 1982.

The acclaimed novelist Miljenko Jergović, who was born in Sarajevo in 1966, but now lives and writes in Zagreb, frames this Balkanist dynamic even more pointedly: 'The beauty of Paris or London is only an alibi for the criminals who have allowed ... Vukovar and Sarajevo to disappear.'[2]

George Orwell, in a letter to the Duchess of Atholl, displayed a refreshingly prescient and nuanced understanding of something like Balkanism in 1945, long before this field of study existed. In response to an invitation to speak for the League of European Freedom about 'crimes' in immediate post-Second World War Yugoslavia he writes:

> I am afraid I cannot ... I could easily get out of it by saying that the date is impossible or – what is quite true – that I know nothing about Jugoslavia [*sic*], but I prefer to tell you plainly ... It seems to me that one can only denounce the crimes now being committed in ... Jugoslavia, etc. if one is equally insistent on ending Britain's unwanted rule in India.[3]

Balkanist studies have suggested that, by using travel and other literatures to write (in other words to 'create') an inherent exoticism and backwardness in the Balkan cultures, western culture was not only enabled to see itself as civilized, but was, and is, also able to gloss over its own shortcomings: to ignore its own genocides, for example. Maria Todorova's seminal book *Imagining the Balkans* contains a comment by one Count Hermann Keyserling that is now seen as paradigmatic within this field of scholarship: '*Si les Balcans n'existaient pas, il faudrait les inventer.*'[4]

In 1999 Tony Blair said that the Balkans are 'on the doorstep of Europe'.[5] Some took this to mean that he was recognizing the region as a part of Europe (a doorstep is, after all, part of the house), but others heard it as a statement that the region was outside the Europe shared by the more 'civilized' countries to the north and west. The ambiguity itself spoke volumes.

'Turkey in Europe', 'the Balkans', 'Southeastern Europe': none of these historical terms is neutral. 'Southeastern Europe', which might sound relatively progressive and modern to the contemporary ear, descriptive rather than loaded with pejorative meaning, originally came into favour and use among the Nazis. Even the term 'the former Yugoslavia' wasn't invented, as one might think, in the early 1990s, as a politically correct means to describe the group of new republics and federations that emerged when war broke out. Rather, it was a crowing term that was used during the Second World War, not only by the occupying Nazis and the Italians who'd carved up the country between themselves, but also by the fledgling Communist resistance, who identified Yugoslavia with the pre-war royal dictatorships of King Aleksandar and Prince Regent Pavle.[6] There's another designation in use at the moment, which has been adopted in order to differentiate the parts of the Balkans that are not among the ten countries that joined the EU in May 2004: 'the western Balkans (which is diplomatic speak for the former Yugoslavia minus Slovenia plus Albania)'.[7]

In order to begin to explore, through the course of this book, where Rebecca West fits within all this, I need to do more than simply list her itinerary, but look at how she represented her experiences to herself and others, both in *Black Lamb and Grey Falcon* itself, and in other documents. According to her own account, in the introduction to *Black Lamb and Grey Falcon*, her interest in Yugoslavia was sparked by hearing of the assassination of King Aleksandar of Yugoslavia on the radio on 9 October 1934, while she was in hospital in London recovering from an operation. Aleksandar had been killed in Marseilles with the connivance of an organization of Croatian separatists called the Ustaše, the Macedonian terrorists VMRO (Internal Macedonian Revolutionary Organization), and, supporting both organizations, the Italian dictator Mussolini. West sensed that Aleksandar's murder was important, but couldn't get anyone to take her interest seriously. Realising, as we may, that she knew nothing of the Balkans but violence,[8] she had the intuition that she would have to travel there and see for herself. Her opportunity came in the spring of 1936, when she was invited to visit the region on a British Council lecture tour, a visit that crystallized her thoughts about the importance of the Balkans, and Yugoslavia in particular, to an understanding of contemporary Europe, and forced her to abandon a planned book on Finland, the country she'd previously thought might provide the crucible for her political, cultural and spiritual theses.

To write *Black Lamb and Grey Falcon* Rebecca West made two further lengthy trips across the length and breadth of the former Yugoslavia in the springs of 1937 and 1938, and also incorporated her experiences on the British Council lecture tour. She did, however, weave these three journeys into one continuous travelogue. So successfully was this interweaving achieved, in fact, that a review of a recently published book of travels in Serbia is characterized as being different from Rebecca West's *Black Lamb and Grey Falcon* in that it was not based on 'one visit', but was written by somebody who 'returned twice'.[9]

At the time of West's visits Yugoslavia hadn't actually been 'Yugoslavia' for very long. Until 6 January 1929, less than ten years before she arrived, the new entity that had been wrested from the wreckage of the Austro-Hungarian and Ottoman empires and the First World War in order to unite the southern Slavs had been called the Kingdom of Serbs, Croats and Slovenes.

When one is young it's easy to think that all kinds of things about the world are fixed, that they have always been there. With adulthood, though, comes the realization that very little is fixed, that things change all the time, that what we think of as constants are stories, albeit ones that might be temporarily manifested in bricks and mortar, or by borders. Countries, nation states or peoples may well generate myths (as all countries do) around their own antiquity in support of their claims to existence, but they can be fairly fly-by-night entities. They may even come and go, as Yugoslavia has, in a matter of a few generations. This realization is salutary: the realization, that is, that sometimes we have both agency and responsibility, and that we can create our own societies. Of course, in talking of such things as 'agency' and 'responsibility' we need to remember that most people are oppressed and because of that have no ability to effect change. This kind of talk sounds insufferably pompous to the contemporary ear, and reading West can sometimes feel like being lectured by an opinionated parent. It was, though, precisely this kind of responsibility that Rebecca West was trying to awaken in her readers.

Strong opinions may seem like quite old-fashioned things to have these days, but Rebecca West's journeys to Yugoslavia were themselves of a peculiarly old-fashioned variety. She and her husband, Henry Andrews, were chauffeur-driven with a series of guides, most notably 'Constantin', a thinly disguised portrait of Stanislav Vinaver, who was a noted poet of the day, but also happened to be the Press Bureau Chief[10] for the government of the then Prime Minister Milan Stojadinović, who served under the regency of Prince Pavle that succeeded the assassinated Aleksandar until his heir, King Petar, came of age.

The sheer scale of the task dogged Rebecca West when she was writing *Black Lamb and Grey Falcon*. Initially she had thought that her journeys through Yugoslavia would produce a long essay, but it quickly grew beyond all measure. Thanks to Bonnie Kime Scott's wonderful edited selection of West's letters we are able to catch glimpses of her pride and horror at this process. In a letter to her husband written in May 1938, during her third visit, she laments that her essay can't exceed 25,000 words, but that she's already written 50,000.[11] At the end of the same year she describes *Black Lamb and Grey Falcon* as an incubus,[12] which is taking up all her time and money to complete. By 1941 she is recording her astonishment at having embarked, five years previously, on a book that flew against normal artistic or commercial sense, but which proved so uncannily prescient.[13] By this time the book has grown to 350,000 words.[14]

In *Black Lamb and Grey Falcon* itself West wrote about both the futility of her attempt to communicate the history of Yugoslavia, and its absolute relevance to an understanding of what was at stake in the impending war with Germany, to what she saw as a then dominant pacifist and appeasing tendency in Britain. It was an undertaking that was dependent on her ability to unpick and to explain the complexity, there, behind almost anything you care to name – a complexity that in fact burdens even the simple act of naming something. The example she cites is a Macedonian mountain, the Kajmakčalan (which may be roughly translated as 'butter churn'), which, at the time of her visit, was in southern Serbia.

Kajmakčalan had been the site of a great battle during the First World War in the late summer of 1916 in which French, British and Serbian troops defeated the Germans and Bulgarians (who themselves had huge claims on Macedonia) on their way to take back Serbia after a German, Bulgarian and Albanian rout had forced a famous midwinter retreat – of the entire surviving Serbian army, royal family and government – across the mountains of Albania to Corfu. West pointed out that if anyone wanted to know what it was that this mountain represented and why, even to begin to explain was a near impossible task:

> The answer is too long, as long indeed, as this book, which hardly anybody will read by reason of its length. Here is the calamity of our modern life, we cannot know all the things which it is necessary for our survival that we should know.[15]

The answer, of course, is far *longer* than her book, even if that does fill 1,200 pages. *Black Lamb and Grey Falcon* was written in the late 1930s. Plenty more complexity has accreted around even an obscure mountain like Kajmakčalan.

Hunting for more information on Kajmakčalan, I found a military history website[16] run by a Scottish 'wargames' enthusiast called Dave Watson, also known as 'Balkan Dave'. This is a fascinating and useful website. It gives detailed descriptions of numerous battles from the region, and a huge number of thorough and knowledgeable book reviews, even if these are primarily aimed at other 'wargamers'. I send him some questions, and a few days later I receive a response:

> I am often asked what sparked my interest, but to be honest I can't remember. I have always been a history buff and I just got interested in various Balkan conflicts. The need to see how each one fitted in led to a substantial collection of books then the website and so on. I wrote a few articles for several journals on some of the more obscure conflicts and that led to further discussion and a couple of invitations to lecture abroad. I wouldn't say there was a big wargame community in the UK interested in the Balkans, [but a] number of my regular opponents are happy to humour me, particularly when [I'm researching] a new period.[17]

I'm curious about where the enjoyment lies in historically accurate wargaming like this. There are obvious pleasures to be had in the travel and the research, and there are less obvious, but understandable, pleasures in the sourcing and adapting of figures, the building of detailed model terrains in attics, and, of course, the playing of the game itself. However, I wonder if part of the interest is to set up one's armies accurately enough, with the correct handicaps, strengths and weaknesses, range of weapons, weather conditions etc, that the outcome of the original battle is replicated in the game. I can well imagine that if one has been playing this game of chance and strategy for a few days, or weeks, and actually arrived at something approaching the historical result, it could be considered to have been a great game.

I wonder, though, whether it would be conceivable or desirable in a wargaming situation for, say, the Serbs to defeat the Ottomans at Kosovo Polje, to reverse the outcome of the battle of 1389 that is both a matter of historical fact and a cornerstone of Serbian nationalist mythology, or whether wargames just naturally tend to replicate the historical results anyway. I e-mail Dave back to ask him about this. 'Very much so,' he says. 'Of course, many still argue that the Serbs *did* win ...'

Dave is referring to the way that the battle of Kosovo Polje is represented in medieval Serbian epic poetry. During the centuries of Ottoman rule over the Balkans these poems formed an oral folk tradition that, alongside the persistence of the Serbian Orthodox Church, was one of the main storehouses of Serb culture and tradition.

According to the poems, Tsar Lazar, who led the Serb forces at Kosovo Polje, was visited on the eve of battle by the prophet Elijah in the form of a grey falcon – hence the second half of the title of West's book – who offered him the choice between winning the battle against the Ottoman forces and having an earthly kingdom, or losing the battle and creating a heavenly kingdom. He is said to have chosen the latter.

Then Dave reminds me that:

> It's primarily a game. You can never accurately replicate any conflict on a tabletop. Even for battles that we have a lot of detail on. But you can learn more about the tactics or try alternative 'what ifs' in addition to a straight re-fight. Historical hindsight is also a problem for well-known battles. Most rules reward the commander that uses historical tactics for his/her army. In the end it all comes down to the skill of the individual player.

Dave Watson, too, followed in Rebecca West's footsteps and visited Kajmakčalan. The mountain is currently situated on the border between Greece and what the international community now calls the Former Yugoslav Republic of Macedonia. (This is another bone of contention, as most people in the Former Yugoslav Republic of Macedonia, also known as FYROM, want it to be called, simply, Macedonia, but Greece insists upon its prior right to the name, seeing the adoption of this simpler designation as a prelude to expansionist claims on northern parts of its own territory.)

As for Kajmakčalan, so it is for the whole of the former Yugoslavia and arguably the entire Balkan region. If one was so minded, it would be possible to base a lifetime of research and several huge volumes on pretty much any location, period or artefact. But even then there still wouldn't be the necessary scope to adequately explain even a single, central document such as, for example, the Yugoslav Constitution of 1974, which underpinned the terminal phase of Titoist Yugoslavia. This constitution, years in the planning, set out a bafflingly complex system of delegates, workers, citizens and processes of self-management, not to mention Socialist Republics, Socialist Autonomous Provinces, a Federal Parliament comprising a Chamber of Republics and Provinces and a Federal Chamber whose delegates were elected by the Socialist Alliance of the Working People, and which were overseen by a Presidency that was distinct from the President of the Federal Socialist Republic (Tito, although he did also happen to be President of the Presidency). The Presidency was not, then, a single person or office, but an entity representing each of the Socialist Republics whose chair rotated annually in alphabetical order by Republic, and which was further complicated by the fact that written into the 1974 Constitution was the means by which the delegates of Serbia's Autonomous Provinces (Vojvodina and Kosovo) outnumbered and could (and did) outvote Serbia itself. This would in some respects be comparable, for example, to Yorkshire having a power of veto over the UK Parliament.

It's mind-bogglingly complicated. Vojin Dimitrijević, who has examined it in some detail, suggests that this constitution set in motion, or accelerated, even exacerbated, some of the irreconcilable processes that led fairly inexorably towards the collapse of Yugoslavia in the early 1990s.[18]

George Orwell once reminded us that 'a story always sounds clear enough at a distance, but the nearer you get to the scene of events the vaguer it becomes'.[19] He's correct, and there is what we'd now call a 'fractal' quality to the history of the Balkans and the former Yugoslavia that is initially intimidating. As with the computer-generated fern-like images generated from simple, mathematical equations by the scientist and visionary Benoit B. Mandlebrot in the early 1980s, one can keep on zooming in as far and for as long as one wants, and yet those complex patterns keep appearing, keep imploding in on themselves, in an endless, vertiginous complexity. There is too much, rather than too little, information. This is not, of course, a specific attribute of the former Yugoslavia, it's a basic fact of life, but it does call into question any single attempt at an authoritative or comprehensive account. The problem, as 'Balkanism' teaches us, is that the Balkans and the former Yugoslavia are ridiculously overburdened with such accounts, each wilfully denying their own partiality, and each, knowingly or not, confusing opinion with fact.

Superficially, things have changed since Rebecca West heard about King Aleksandar's assassination on the radio in October 1934. There's now so much that we all know or think we know – things that we've read or have seen on television – to the degree where everyone believes that they 'know' about the Balkans. Everyone's an expert. We know the names of towns such as Banja Luka, Tuzla, Vukovar and Osijek, and have heard of the Krajina or 'the Bihać pocket', even though we may not be able to pronounce them properly, to fully understand what they all mean, or even to know the difference, in 'policy speak', between a 'safe area' and a 'safe haven'. Pictures of shelled villages, bombed bridges and burning houses are familiar to anyone who watched the television news or opened a newspaper in the early 1990s, as are the sights of BBC correspondents crouching for shelter from snipers or rockets, and the knowledge of rapes. We've seen the blue helmets and white vehicles of UN peacekeepers, seen the video footage of emaciated men behind barbed wire and the still utterly shocking images of rotting bodies in mass graves.

Writer and academic Vesna Kesić tells of 'a popular saying that the news from the Balkans has to be checked not twice, but three times'.[20] This is probably not so much about verification as an acknowledgement that the reader should probably make an effort to see whatever story it is from more than one perspective. The problem with this sound advice is that the news coverage of the region, in the UK press certainly, is now so scant that you'd be hardpressed to check it once. Those images from war-torn Bosnia-Herzegovina, Serbia and Croatia have largely vanished from our screens now that the wars are over. News coverage of the region has become increasingly scarce and the media's attention has, understandably, moved elsewhere.

The author and Balkan expert Misha Glenny, speaking from the World Economic Forum at Davos, Switzerland on BBC Radio 4's programme *From Our Own Correspondent* in early 2004, said that there was a time when he would regularly be invited to the forum to speak about the Balkans during the wars of the early 1990s:

> This was of course at a time when the agglomerated power of the global movers and shakers attending the forum could do nothing about restoring equilibrium to the battered Balkans. Now, when these people really could contribute to the redevelopment of the region, the organisers no longer deem the subject sexy enough to warrant issuing me with an invitation.[21]

So it seems to be with press coverage currently, in the UK at least: the Balkans are not 'sexy enough'.

Serbian and Croatian friends have taken comfort from this lessening of media coverage, however, and understandably so. 'Thank God, then,' one said to me, 'if we are not in the papers all the time. Because if we were you know it would mean that things had got really bad again.'

Yet in recent years the number of books on the subject that are available has increased tremendously. Reading this ever expanding body of literature, I stopped underlining and started fretting when I realised that many of the newer books still contained, still expounded, a variation on '...this amazing peninsula, so kindly favoured by nature and so cruelly mutilated by history...'[22] That phrase was written by Leon Trotsky, in fact, though it could have been by anyone. Just because it's the Ur-cliché of Balkan travel writing doesn't mean that it's incorrect, just that the sentiment doesn't bear repeating too often.

One Croatian writer, Slavenka Drakulić, suggests that part of the reason for the wars of the 1990s was precisely that her parents' generation never discussed what had happened during the Second World War; never discussed the fact that war crimes were not just something visited upon Yugoslavs by Hitler and the Nazis, but a matter of historical fact between the Serbs and the Croats, between the royalist Četniks and the Partisans, between the Partisans and the various 'Home Guards', etc. Drakulić describes how these truths, these great scarring traumas, massacres, concentration camps, were obscured by the triumphalist but partial narrative of Tito and the Partisans' road to victory in 1945, and how after the war, during her childhood, they were never spoken of. She tells how she'd once seen this 'as a sign of sanity and self-preservation',[23] this willingness or determination to forget about such mass trauma.

Certainly Drakulić's fear is that not talking about what happened during the early 1990s, in the then rapidly fragmenting Yugoslavia, will lead to a repeat of the same thing. It's precisely to address this, in fact, that she's written her latest book. But even if, as she maintains, there are still towns in Croatia where a deliberate policy of silence is practically enforced, where someone who speaks out about war crimes or gives evidence is still likely to be killed, there is at least a growing body of literature where such traumas are actively discussed, in the present, rather than being ignored, only to blow up when we're not expecting it, again.

Gustav Metzger, the revered artist who came to London as part of the Kindertransport in 1939 after an early childhood spent in Nuremberg, where he had witnessed the gradual rise to power of the Nazis, talks on film about the fact that he can't open a German newspaper, still, without finding some discussion of the Nazis, some article, book review or commentary. Metzger suggests that this is constructive.[24] How else can you hope to understand what happened? Similarly with the former Yugoslavia: it's better that there are a hundred books than just one on the shelf; better that there are books coming out every month. Whether these are war correspondents' memoirs, political theory or popular history, it doesn't matter, as long as it is still being discussed rather than swept under the carpet.

But it's not just books. Click on 'connect' and that's when the amount of material about the former Yugoslavia becomes overwhelming, with weblists, e-mails, war veterans' websites, accessible archives and late-night dialogues in the staccato, two-steps-forward, three-steps-back time-lag of the chat room.

Every day my e-mail inbox is full of news items on human rights and the return to civil society in the Balkans. I used to open of all these and read them as soon as they appeared, but most of them have to go unopened now. The sheer volume of material means that I just don't have time to read them. There are daily bulletins and digests of announcements on transition, reconstruction, higher education, culture. There are press releases from every non-governmental organization (NGO) in the region. The important thing is that information is starting to flow freely again, and it's beyond the control of the state powers.

There's even a website for the International Criminal Tribunal for the Prosecution of Persons Responsible for Serious Violations of International Humanitarian Law Committed in the Territory of the Former Yugoslavia since 1991, which is known, for short, of course, as the International Criminal Tribunal for the Former Yugoslavia or ICTY, but known generally as 'The Hague'. Or as a BBC Radio 4 newsreader once spoonerishly put it, the 'war trimes cry-bunal' [*sic*].[25]

The transcripts of the proceedings at the Milošević trial at The Hague alone amount to thousands upon thousands of pages. Reading those transcripts, one feels for the teams of people whose job it is to write them up, to read them, to translate them. After I had read only a hundred or so pages the things that started to catch my attention were the asides. I found myself clinging to these small and fleeting human interludes as if they were life rafts. At one point Milošević complains that the lead on his headphones, through which he listens to the simultaneous translations of what everyone else is saying in the courtroom, is too short, before realising that it's tangled on something. Among the unending detail, these occasional asides become so conspicuous precisely because they're nothing more than simple, truthful human communication, uncontested, irrelevant.

At a sound-bite, photo-opportunity level there have recently been widely publicized mutual apologies for past hostilities from the heads of state of Croatia and Serbia, while symbolically constructive gestures counter symbolically destructive ones: the beautiful, delicate Ottoman arch of Mostar's bridge, which was destroyed by Bosnian Croat infantry, has been rebuilt, for instance, and was reopened in July 2004. During early 2005 a sudden flurry of activity saw indictees from Serbia and Montenegro, Bosnia-Herzegovina and Albania voluntarily surrendering to The Hague, while Croatia's accession talks with the EU were postponed for most of 2005 because of the Croatian government's inability to arrest General Ante Gotovina, the most notorious of the Croatians who have been charged with war crimes (until his dramatic arrest on camera in Spain early in December 2005). Even though Radovan Karadžić and Ratko Mladić were still at large at the time of writing, the proceedings at The Hague are televised live, at least in Serbia, now that the former dissident student radio station B92 has become a mainstream TV channel as well. The media have to a certain extent been wrested from the hands of the politicians.

Opportunistic politicians across the region from Macedonia to Vojvodina still, however, regularly denounce journalists and newspaper editors, calling them spies or traitors. It's as if these politicians were actively chasing column inches on the *Helsinki Monitor*. It's not so long ago that a politician branding someone a traitor in print would have served as advance notice that they'd get a knock on the door at three in the morning and be 'disappeared'.

Slavko Ćuruvija, a journalist and newspaper editor, and one-time friend of Mira Marković, Slobodan Milošević's wife, wrote a number of articles critical of the regime when Milošević was still in power, and voiced the opinion that 'Serbia...was becoming a fascist country'.[26] He was denounced on state TV.[27] It wasn't too long – just four days – before he was assassinated outside his apartment building. Nowadays, across most of the 'Western Balkans', journalists who offend politicians or powerful businessmen in print are more likely to be hit with a libel action that, however spurious, can result in their being sacked or receiving a suspended sentence. However, in Kosovo as recently as June 2005, there was an attempted assassination of a journalist, Bardhyl Ajeti, who writes for one of the province's Albanian-language daily newspapers. At the time of writing Ajeti is in a coma and the New York-based Committee to Protect Journalists is investigating whether the shooting was related to his journalism, which was often critical of opposition political parties.

Apart from major developments, newspaper coverage in the UK largely ignores these 'transition' issues, and often comprises little but comic one-liners about such things as 'blonde jokes' being banned in Bosnia-Herzegovina[28], but at least the presence, as throughout much of the last century, of large ex-Yugoslav communities in London means that I can buy international editions of Serbian, Croatian or Bosnian newspapers once a week from the newsagents at the Tube station. That's not how often they come in, just how long it takes me to read them. I usually buy *Vesti*, a Serbian-language paper that is edited in Belgrade by the offices of *Borba* ('The Struggle', the paper that Tito's Partisans started as a twice-weekly samizdat during the Second World War) and printed in Frankfurt for *Gastarbeiter* ('guest workers').

One of Rebecca West's two official biographers, Carl Rollyson, writes that she attempted to get to grips with what was then called Serbo-Croat, but which has now been officially fragmented into the increasingly distinct languages of Serbian, Croatian and Bosnian. Rollyson tells us that West's notebooks were full of language exercises,[29] but that, in spite of these efforts, she never achieved fluency. Failing to become fluent is far from a disgrace, however, and she did persist in grasping the complex historical backgrounds and the personal stories relating to all the places that her punishing schedule took her to, which is no less challenging a task. She doggedly untangles the complexities of her day, and of history, for the invaluable lessons that they might hold. But it's arguably no surprise that her writing is seen as so partisan when in the middle of all this she can also baldly declare, for example, that 'the Croat is weakened by Austrian influence as by a profound malady'.[30] A generalisation which is grossly unfair.

West herself, in her letters, acknowledges that *Black Lamb and Grey Falcon* is broadly pro-Serb,[31] but goes to some lengths to dispel any idea that she was used as a propaganda 'puppet' by Prime Minister Stojadinović's regime. She stresses that the government bureau had not influenced her view of Yugoslavian politics, and that she had only contacted them after deciding more or less the kind of book she was going to write.[32]

She also writes, very perceptively, of the exhaustive research that she undertook before writing,[33] and that she wrote *Black Lamb and Grey Falcon* partly to defend Yugoslavia against the propaganda of those who would wish it to be occupied, or partitioned.[34] Again, here, West is reiterating what was a common perception for much of the late 19th and early 20th centuries, voiced by commentators including the young war reporter Leon Trotsky, that Southern Slavs would be better off united than endlessly being exploited and divided by their Great Power neighbours.

It's held by some that Rebecca West duplicated and perhaps privileged the anti-Ottoman rhetoric of the 19th-century Serbian independence movement, and the anti-Croat atmosphere that existed in the pre-war Belgrade government in response to party political flickerings of Croatian nationalism and resistance to the Belgrade-driven centralism of the time. West wasn't coming to these issues lightly. It was her stated intention to 'show the past side by side with the present it created,'[35] but also to 'put on paper what a typical Englishwoman felt and thought in the late 1930s when, already convinced of the inevitability of the second Anglo-German war, she had been able to follow the dark waters of that event back to its source'.[36]

West was convinced that in Yugoslavia she'd learned not only how dishonourable history could be, but also how others had fared in the face of similar dangers, what the true scale of the danger that the world faced from Nazism really was and how it represented the contemporary historical aspect of a universal tendency towards destruction, a worship of death rather than of life.

In the persistence under extreme duress of Serbian culture under Ottoman rule, in the Serbian struggle for independence and the Serbs' leading role in the then very necessary union of southern Slavs, and (by the time she came to finish the book) in the then current Yugoslav resistance to Nazism, West heard a rallying cry for a Britain that risked being wiped out in the coming war if the appeasers failed to appreciate what was at stake.

It may be quite hard for some of us to understand appeasement from this vantage point, when general knowledge about the Second World War is dominated, or defined for us, by heroics such as D-Day, the Battle of Britain or 'the Blitz spirit'. But by reading other contemporary accounts it's still possible to encounter references to what West considered herself to be up against, not only from such politicians as Neville Chamberlain, or what she viewed as a terminally weak and foolish British ruling class, but also from the broader cultural and political communities.

An interesting glimpse into this backdrop of appeasement, against which (in both senses) she was writing *Black Lamb and Grey Falcon*, can be seen as late as 1942, a year after the book's first publication (in the USA, it was published in the UK in 1942), in a flurry of letters responding to an article by George Orwell in the *Partisan Review* in which he had outlined a phenomenon whereby the 'out-and-out, turn-the-other-cheek pacifists ... started by renouncing violence, [and ended] by championing Hitler'.[37] One of his correspondents wrote:

> Who is to say that a British victory will be less disastrous than a German one? ... the 'intellectuals' among us would scorn to mentally compromise themselves with the Government. ... The pacifists' 'championing' of Hitler referred to by Orwell is simply a recognition by us that Hitler and Germany contain a real historical dynamic, whereas we do not ...[T]here would be a profound justice, I feel, ... in a German victory.'[38]

This kind of idiocy was no less shocking for West than it may be for us, coming across it more than 60 years later.

For West, though, it represented something like a doomsday scenario, which was brought into focus on her travels by the Serbian Orthodox monasteries she visited. They were scattered across devastated Kosovo and southern Serbia, and were all that remained of a powerful and cultured medieval civilization. It was, she wrote,

...as if Chartres Cathedral should stand alone on a land that has been shorn of all that was France when it was built and has been France since then; with no Paris, no Sorbonne, no Academie française...[39]

By extension, she implies, monuments such as St Paul's Cathedral could be all that remained of a Britain wiped out by the violence and stupidity of the Nazis, standing alone on some metaphorical windswept plain. She writes:

Such spectacles are commonplace in Africa or Asia or America, which have their Pyramids and Angkor Vat [sic], and Inca Memorials, but in Europe we are not accustomed to them. Our forms of historic tragedy have blotted a paragraph here and there, but they have rarely torn out the leaves of an entire volume, letting only a coloured frontispiece remain to tease us.[40]

With hindsight we can see that West's doomsday vision was not exaggerated. After all, the Nazis almost succeeded in doing exactly this to European Jewry.

Rebecca West was hugely interested in, and inspired by, a kind of virility that she saw in the then Yugoslavia, in people who had never not defended themselves when necessary,[41] and that she understood as an exemplary response to imperial domination and continuous struggle that Britain was in sore need of if it too were not to be dominated and destroyed. This understanding of the effects that a continual need to fight can have on a people emerges elsewhere in her writings, sometimes in the most unlikely places, for example in her 1957 novel *The Fountain Overflows*, where she writes:

But the farm cats spat at us, and we had to draw back our hands, brave or not, while they glared at us, coarse as burglars... not like cats at all. 'Remember,' cried Mamma, 'the poor things have to fight rats, they could not do it if they let themselves be gentle. It would be a luxury they cannot have.'[42]

Such is West's continuing influence that several writers on Yugoslavia have actively attempted to take a lead from her. Perhaps the best-known is the American travel writer Robert D. Kaplan, who tried to 'aim [his] star'[43] in West's direction in his well-researched travel book *Balkan Ghosts*, which was written before the break-up of the former Yugoslavia, and is most notable for some excellent and extensive interviews with the leading ex-Communist Yugoslav dissident Milovan Djilas, who foresaw the inevitability of the country's destruction in war. Kaplan and others suggest that when Bill and Hilary Clinton read *Balkan Ghosts* in 1993 it informed 'a shift of US foreign policy ... convincing [Clinton] that the inhabitants of the Balkans were doomed to violence'.[44]

In a new introduction to a more recent reprint of this book Kaplan also makes an astonishingly 'Balkanist' declaration when he suggests that 'Nazism, for instance, can claim Balkan origins. Among the flophouses of Vienna, a breeding ground of ethnic resentments close to the southern Slavic world, Hitler learned how to hate so infectiously.'[45] This assertion would have surely infuriated Rebecca West so absolutely contrary is it to her own hard-won knowledge.

In a very real sense, any writer visiting the former Yugoslavia is following in the footsteps of Rebecca West. However, *Another Fool in the Balkans* does not aim to shadow Rebecca West's ghost on its travels. I shan't be setting out on highly resourced official visits in order to compare notes with her on every village, hamlet or hill that I come to, giving my own historical glosses of her versions of events and comparing the two with what's happening in each of those locations now. Such a huge and exhaustive trip would be impossible today, even if the country she visited still existed. Anyway, the result could never do West justice. It would also be to monumentally miss the point, which is to describe, through travelogue and through interviews with anyone but politicians and official spokespeople, some of the things that are happening in a cluster of relatively young republics that are emerging from a collective nightmare.

So what kind of journey will this be? In 1993 the British artists Tracey Emin and Sarah Lucas had a little shop at the Bishopsgate end of Bethnal Green Road, near the top of Brick Lane in the East End of London. It was a real shop, in that you could buy things there, though what was for sale was an array of junky and slap-dash art they'd made: mugs with photos sellotaped to them, T-shirts with crudely painted slogans. They also had some collages on the wall, each one actually just a picture cut out of a magazine and stuck on to piece of paper, called 'Great British Journeys Across the Road', which I was really struck by. I mention them now because this journey, my journey, is more like that: a short hop or two to a part of mainland Europe that's as close to London as, say, Rome, but about which most of us remain almost wilfully ignorant. When Croatia, Serbia and Montenegro, Bosnia-Herzegovina and Macedonia eventually follow Slovenia into EU membership that continued ignorance may well prove to have been a mistake. There's surely no excuse, any longer, for considering the Balkans exotic, much less for assuming that they are 'doomed to violence'.

So what I will do is visit places of particular interest today. I will visit the Serbian (and former Yugoslav) capital Belgrade, and Zagreb, the capital of Croatia. I will also travel to the Dalmatian coast and to Istria, a region of Croatia that did not become part of Yugoslavia until after the Second World War, and therefore was not part of Rebecca West's itinerary at all. I will meet a lot of people en route, but in place of the chauffeur-driven limousine I'll take the ubiquitous and reliable Yugo taxi. Like Lucas and Emin's collages, this is a journey across the road, not a grand expedition. Learning from all the previous accounts of visits to the former Yugoslavia, I'll do what I can to avoid the ill-founded opinion, the baseless generalization and the cheap gag, but all the while I'll be aware that I may well be yet another fool in the Balkans. Rebecca West will inevitably be a continual presence, and there's no doubt that I'll encounter places, events or people that will have me flicking back through her 1,200 pages in search of some remembered passage that still rings out across the 60-odd years that separate her epic journey and my own series of visits, which will recommence once we get out of this interminable tunnel.

Chapter Three
Belgrade (2001)

It doesn't take quite that long to get through the Zemun railway tunnel, but it certainly seems to take about five minutes before we all emerge, blinking, into the suburbs of Belgrade. None of us has disappeared. There was no murder on this Orient Express!

We pass through Zemun itself then, before I know it, we're above the streets of Novi Beograd (New Belgrade). The contrast couldn't be greater between the leafy kitchen gardens and chicken coops of Zemun and the vast, Brasilia-like terrain of low-, high- and very high-rise blocks of flats that make up Novi Beograd. Some of the blocks look so vast and squat that one wonders if there might be flats without windows set deep inside the structure, like the cabins down below the waterline in the middle of a cruise ship. The heavily built-up areas are punctuated only by huge expanses of overgrown concrete terracing, unkempt parkland and long straight boulevards.

Belgrade itself was built on the tall, rocky promontory that stands above the confluence of the Sava and the Danube rivers, while Novi Beograd occupies a large area of reclaimed marshland on the opposite bank of the Sava and didn't exist 50 years ago. When Rebecca West visited, the whole area was under water.[1] The area took its name from what had been one of the few buildings on that side of the river, the Novi Beograd coffee shop, which was opened in 1924 by one Petar Kokotović to catch passing trade on the road to Zemun. A newspaper called *Novi Beograd* was published in Zemun from about 1939, but it wasn't until 11 April 1948 that workers actually started fulfilling the prophecy by draining the marshlands and building the place.[2] The official line is that Tito's Youth Work Brigades built Novi Beograd, though the economist and exiled Slovenian dissident

Ljubo Sirc, who was imprisoned in one of the early Tito-era show trials, suggests that the core of the workforce was 'forced labour', comprising some 30,000 political and other prisoners.[3]

My travelling companion, Boro Radaković, points out a huge skyscraper that dominates the skyline. Two enormous concrete towers rise side by side and are linked at the very top by a slender arched bridge, atop which, set asymmetrically, is a circular control-tower-type structure. It looks like something from one of the nightmares of the modernist architect Ernö Goldfinger, but is close enough to the style of his buildings to be somewhere between a parody and an homage. It's as if Goldfinger's most famous building, Trellick Tower in Notting Hill, London, has hauled itself over to Canning Town in East London to stand side by side with its less-well appointed sister building, Balfron House. 'It is called Western Gate, this building,' says Boro. 'You know motorway goes through the middle, right through the arch. Another time, maybe, we can drive to Belgrade this way.'

The train tracks run alongside a broad boulevard. I see a chicken restaurant, some shops, grassy wastelands. People are standing on tram platforms in the middle of the road, waiting to travel into the city centre. It must be freezing standing there in the winter, with nothing to shield you from the bitterly cold wind that blows in from Siberia. Behind the tower blocks is a bomb-damaged skyscraper, smoke-blackened, the TV mast crumpled on its roof.

As we cross the Sava River, the man with the many passports who is sharing our compartment points out a huge and busy road bridge, the Gazela, which links Novi Beograd and Belgrade itself, telling us that the Americans wanted to bomb it in 1999, but the French vetoed this one target.

We pull into Belgrade Station and bundle out of the train. We're all loudly excited to be in Belgrade, and walk past a clamour of beggars and taxi touts on the platform, and out through the large booking hall and into the sunshine. Vladimir Arsenijević, the Belgrade-based novelist and publisher, has come to meet us and leads the way, greeting and laughing with us all in turn. A line of cabs that is waiting by the flowerbeds outside the yellow-painted station building will take us to our hotel. There is not much room in a Yugo, that austere product of the former Yugoslav Fiat franchise, but four of us manage to somehow cram ourselves into each one, and we set off up the hill to the centre of town. 'It is splendid hotel,' says Vladimir, who is squeezed into the back of a cab with Boro and me.

On the way to the hotel we pass more bomb-damaged buildings, includ-ing the former headquarters of the former Yugoslav Army, two huge, mod-ernist buildings on either side of a main road. There are big round holes punched through the walls of each where Cruise missiles found their tar-get during the NATO bombing campaign of 1999. The holes made by the missiles remind me of the work of Gordon Matta-Clark, a US artist who, in the 1970s, made a series of incredibly precise and geometric architec-tural 'interventions' in abandoned buildings by cutting cylindrical or conical sections through them. NATO may not have been quite as precise as Matta-Clark, although the result, as we drive past, craning our necks to see out of the back window of the taxi, is still a sense of disbelief that such a huge building can remain standing when so much of its structure has been removed. Through the holes iron girders and huge slabs of reinforced concrete are visible, but they are twisted and smashed with the force of the explosions. Bizarrely, some doorways at street level are still intact and soldiers stand on sentry duty, just as they probably did when the buildings were occupied, in a gesture that seems simultaneously futile and defiant.

The writer Srdjan Jovanović Weiss, who is a member of an architecture practice called Normal Group, wrote a satirical article that recasts NATO's bombing as the actions of an architecture critic. He describes the paradox whereby buildings that had been designed, in the immediate aftermath of the Second World War, specifically to symbolize the resistance to fascism, had now become reclassified as the architecture of a fascist state and as such needed to be destroyed. He acknowledges, though, that 'NATO faced a problem of identification: how to read architecture that neither looked Stalinist nor had the classical aspirations of the Third Reich'.[4] The exam-ple he uses is precisely this army headquarters, which was apparently mod-elled by its architect, Nikola Dobrović, on Sutjeska Canyon, the site of a decisive battle during the Partisan liberation of Yugoslavia in the Second World War. At the time of the NATO bombing the buildings were unoc-cupied, since the army's headquarters functions had been moved elsewhere long before, so NATO's bombing of it, he argues, was itself entirely sym-bolic. It's an academic discussion, but interesting in that the main symbol-ic feature of the building's design was not these two actual buildings at all, but the space between them, which was designed to represent the canyon itself. Jovanović Weiss waggishly suggests that if NATO had intended to bomb something symbolic here they should perhaps have bombed this void rather than the buildings on either side.[5]

There were well-documented and fatal blunders during the NATO bombing of targets in Serbia and Kosovo, however. These included the bombing of civilians, of refugee convoys and commuter trains, and, most infamously, the accidental bombing of the Chinese Embassy in Novi Beograd.

During the NATO bombings of Serbia and Kosovo the international postal service was suspended, and e-mail or telephone were the only ways for many people both in and outside the war zone to communicate. It may be quite hard to believe, given the contemporary ubiquity of the internet and e-mail services, but at the beginning of the war in 1991 there was no internet service at all in Serbia. When international sanctions were imposed against what was still called Yugoslavia, even the European Research Networks, the academic internet that links university research departments around the world, complied and severed links with universities in the then Yugoslavia. This was unfortunate because such links as existed were largely being used to coordinate anti-war and anti-Milošević protests within Yugoslavia itself. The radio station B92 was the single voice of dissent in a media landscape that was completely dominated by the Milošević regime, as is well-documented by Matthew Collin's remarkable book *This is Serbia Calling*.

Dražen Pantić, who was at the time a professor of mathematics at the University of Belgrade, specializing in, of all things, probability and randomness, worked with B92 to establish Serbia's first internet service provider, Opennet. This internet service initially ran from just one very slow phone line to a service provider in Amsterdam. What this meant, as well as allowing people aligned with the anti-Milošević movement to once again communicate with the rest of the world, was that whenever B92 was shut down it was able to reroute banned broadcasts to radio stations outside Serbia via the internet, from where they could then be broadcast back into the country. Pantić also set up 'mirror' sites on internet servers outside the country that circumvented government attempts to block access to the station's website.

There is footage from one period when B92's transmitters had been shut down that shows the station reduced to 'broadcasting' to protesters on the street outside the building via two loudspeakers set up in the windows. When the government was forced to lift the ban a few days later, it blamed the shutdown on a technical fault, saying that water had got into the transmitter. Government attempts to shut down B92 continued even as recently as 1999. Indeed, the night before the NATO bombing campaign started the station was shut down and the director of the station was arrested. Pantić was abroad at the time, but someone in the studio managed to send him an e-mail, which he then was able to forward to lists of international journalists. Almost incredibly, this meant that news of the arrests and the shutdown of B92 was in the public domain around the world within half an hour of the police arriving at the radio station's door. As the US-based non-governmental organization (NGO) the Electronic Frontier Foundation put it, when they presented Pantić with a 'Pioneers' award only a few days after the bombing started, Pantić's work had made it 'much more difficult for the Milošević government to censor independent sources of news and information. [This was] a brilliant example of how activists and journalists can leverage both traditional media and the Internet to increase diversity of opinion and to counter efforts at censorship.'[6]

Thanks to the work of Pantić and B92, then, the Opennet service meant that people were able to communicate with friends outside the country to let them know what was occurring literally while it happened. One e-mail I received from a friend said simply:

> We are fine but going bonkers. I can hear the planes as I write this. We are all becoming sound experts. I am not allowed to carry my camera. Each night we drunk [*sic*] ourselves to sleep. Do a bit of bomb watch. Cheer when a rocket goes down. Crazy but true, everyone is on the street or on the roof.

The Serbian comic artist Aleksandar Zograf's book, *Bulletins from Serbia*, is a collected e-mail diary of the bombing as seen from the vantage point of Zograf's flat in the heavily industrial town of Pančevo, which was bombed more than most. Zograf was a member of an informal network of comic artists around the world, and it was to these friends and peers that he sent out his bulletins and cartoons of 'friendly' bombs falling on Belgrade. This book was subsequently published around the world in various translations, formalizing the thousands of e-mails that had been whizzing out of Serbia via Opennet, just as the NATO Cruise missiles had been whizzing in, and creating what is now practically a publishing genre:

e-mails from war zones. If the current convention had applied then, he might have been called the 'Belgrade Blogger'.

Our convoy of taxis swings around a corner and onto a broad tree-lined boulevard, the Bulevar Revolucije. Vladimir Arsenijević points out the Parliament building. I recognise it from television coverage of the fall of Milošević from one year before. The taxis come to a halt outside what is obviously our hotel. It is called, of course, the Splendid. It's a tall narrow-fronted building with a fluted awning over the door. We check in and hand over our passports – the police will check them. I have a room on the third floor. The bed was built with someone much shorter than six foot two in mind, but the room is simple and comfortable. It looks out over a small park. To the left I have a clear view of the Bulevar Revolucije and the Parliament building, while over the road to the right, facing onto the park, is another imposing civic building.

Finally I'm in Belgrade. I'd been wanting to come here ever since I'd commissioned Gordana Stanišić to undertake her quixotic gallery-bound walk in 1994.

In the opening line of the large section about Belgrade in *Black Lamb and Grey Falcon* Rebecca West writes: 'We ate too large a lunch, as is apt to be one's habit in Belgrade.'[7] I'd soon find out that not much had changed in that regard. Apart from the expectation of good food, all I did know was gleaned from conversations with Stanišić, who had finally returned to Belgrade in the late 1990s.

I had been told that the city is built on seven hills, as indeed are Rome and Sheffield. I'd also heard that where the Sava and the Danube rivers meet the water from each river is a different colour, and that the waters don't mix for several miles. But nothing has prepared me for the scale and the energy of the city. Its huge roads and broad boulevards stretch away down the hills, into the hazy distance. Pavements and streets are teeming with traffic and pedestrians. Everywhere there are taxis, trams and dilapi-dated trolley buses. The energy of the place is palpable, epitomized in the chaotic choreography of the roads. It's hardly surprising that I don't see a single cyclist on the roads; they wouldn't survive. Drivers switch lanes in microseconds through gaps in the traffic flow that are imperceptible to the untrained eye. It takes a while to get used to a style of driving that makes cars seem to flex and pounce, and become muscular. This is as true now as it was in the 1930s, evidently: in *Black Lamb and Grey Falcon* West describes a car lifting itself out of a rut, 'with a movement not to be expected from a machine, credible only in a tiger leaping out of a pit'.[8] There are corners where there shouldn't be corners, contraflows, merges, fractal junctions. It's as if the Staples Corner interchange, where the M1 motorway meets the grimmest section of London's North Circular, were spread across the whole city. But it's not just the roads that are full of cars. They're parked neatly, cross ways, on most of the pavements too. There's no room to push a pram or a wheelchair.

The buildings in the centre of the city are built on a grand scale. There's a lot of concrete, stone and neon, but there are few of the post-1960s curtain-glass-walled buildings that one might see in the City of London. This is the architecture of the period immediately after 1945, an architecture of necessity, since Belgrade too was blitzed mercilessly by the Luftwaffe in 1941. A design historian could probably date these periods of investment and building, and the moments when the investment stopped, to within a month or two.

The legacy of Milošević's rule is also evident in a rash of new building that has been called 'turbo-architecture', after turbo-folk, the nationalistic techno-pop – folk music to an electronic beat – that Milošević's state radio championed during the wars of the 1990s. It's not that the architecture itself is necessarily mindless, but a mood of official self-aggrandisement coupled with the conditions of a country at war, and subject to sanctions immediately following the economic crisis of the 1980s, saw the creation of an urban environment that has been described as 'banks without savings, gas stations without gas, subway stations without subway system [*sic*], housing without population, monuments without memory'.[9] Not to mention 'hotels without tourists'.[10]

Not so the Splendid Hotel, however! We all convene in the foyer. The plan is for us to stroll to the festival site for a look around, but first we take a quick detour to a famous *pekara* (bakery) nearby, which is called Aca and is packed with customers queuing the whole length of its brightly lit display cabinets. There are some delicious-looking ham and gherkin sandwiches, and all manner of cakes, tarts, and savouries. I'm bowled over by the choice and ask for advice. Vlada suggests that I try *gibanica*, a dense slab of cheese and egg pie, comprising layer upon layer of flaky pastry, and that I wash it down, as is the custom, with a carton of drinking yoghurt. This is a traditional breakfast here in Belgrade, he tells me, and since I didn't have breakfast in Zagreb I might as well have it now, even if it is late afternoon.

The route takes us past the Student Cultural Centre (SKC) and through Belgrade's thriving pirate CD market, a series of wooden kiosks that look like fancy garden sheds, spread out along 50 yards of pavement. Here almost every record ever released is available on a bootleg CD for about ten deutschmarks, or one pound sterling. Walking down the pavement one passes rack after rack of CD boxes with colour-photocopied covers. Every style of music you could think of is represented, although there's probably not as much 'turbo-folk' as there would have been a couple of years ago. Every now and then the police clamp down on this illegal trade in music and close down the market, but half a day later it's as if nothing has happened. All the kiosks are open again. Life goes on.

Later I hear a story about the teenagers of Belgrade ordering 'the things that teenagers need' – records, clothes, videos and computer games – through the internet, using hacked credit card numbers. I don't know if this was an exaggeration, but I was told that these enterprising young consumers figured out that no company based in western Europe would knowingly send goods to Serbia, so the teenagers would give a delivery address in Belgrade, in Cyrillic letters, then write 'Hungary' at the bottom. The famously efficient Hungarian postal service, Magyar Postar, would then redirect these culture-packed Jiffy bags to Belgrade. It's obvious that this CD market is what the music industry would describe as 'piracy', but there's very little money here, so if legal CDs were imported – and for most of the 1990s cultural products were subject to the sanctions imposed on the then 'rump Yugoslavia' of Serbia and Montenegro – few would have been able to afford them at full price. The black market in CDs was one of the only viable routes into the contemporary culture of the rest of the world.

The literature festival, the reason we're all here, is to be held in an arts centre called the Centar za Kulturnu Dekontaminaciju (CZKD, the Centre for Cultural Decontamination), which is a brisk ten-minute walk from the Splendid Hotel. It doesn't take long, of course, before 'Splendid!', said in a cod-English accent, becomes a phrase of common currency among all the authors present. The CZKD is a collection of buildings clustered around a cobbled and pleasantly ivy-clad courtyard off Birčaninova Street. The signs on the gate and the exterior of the buildings are brand new, but you get the impression that this place might not have wanted to advertise its existence too much prior to the downfall of Milošević. It is a lovely afternoon, and there are tables and chairs set up in the courtyard along with lamps and big tubs of geraniums. Through the trees we can see apartment buildings that overlook the courtyard.

As, I suppose, in any arts centre, there is a bar; here it's in a small chaotic room, with crates of empty bottles stacked up in one corner. A radio is balanced on top of a TV set in the corner. There are posters for previous exhibitions and plays on the wall, and a large OTPOR banner showing a clenched fist. OTPOR was the name of the resistance movement during the 1990s, which was anti-war and anti-Milošević. It was anti-NATO too by the time the bombing had finished. There are artworks hanging on the wall, including a painting of the International Red Cross's symbol dripping red paint. Shelves in an alcove are stacked with books, magazines, bottles, ashtrays and glass jars. There's a decrepit wood-burning stove in the corner, and various unmatching chairs and benches are grouped around some tables. The bar has entirely what Rebecca West called, whether with justification or not, 'the Balkan touch', by which she meant that everything 'in the place looked as if it had been brought from somewhere else and adapted to its present purposes by a preoccupied intellectual'.[11] By this reckoning, though, the homes of just about everybody I know display this 'Balkan touch'.

The opening Friday night of the literary festival is astonishing. We are all well-aware that this is an historic moment, the first time that a literature festival in Belgrade has presented public readings by writers from across the former Yugoslavia since before the wars of the 1990s, but none of us is prepared for the reception that awaits: one minute the courtyard is empty, the next it's jam-packed with four or five hundred people. Television crews jostle to interview everyone. The readings start at seven and go on until the early hours. They are punctuated with hour-long intervals – the cue for innumerable intense discussions to start up in the courtyard. I weave through the crowd, leaving unfinished conversations everywhere I go. A man comes over and tells me that there's someone he'd love me to meet, a friend of his, a Serb from Belgrade, who is one of only a handful of people in the world who writes fiction in the Cornish language, but before I can be introduced I'm whisked off to meet someone else. I just have to go with the flow, at least until much later when the pace has slowed a bit and people have started congregating in smaller groups, huddled around tables, sitting on benches or standing by the door to the bar. Each conversation takes place around a litre bottle of imported 'Tikveš' brand Macedonian red wine. Our small deutschmark-denominated *per diems* go a long way and in Belgrade at this time any hard currency is semi-legal tender – especially deutschmarks. Exchange rates are instantly calculated. Any combination of currency will work as tender. The audience file in and out, and occasionally I poke my head around the door to see what's going on in the *paviljon*, to try and gauge the atmosphere. Each time I do this I see that the audience are rapt and that people are standing because there aren't enough seats.

Later we all tramp around the city centre trying to find somewhere that will serve food at four in the morning. We succeed, eventually, and are ushered downstairs to the basement of a pizza restaurant called Orao (Eagle). I order a dish called *karadjordjeva šnicla* with fries and salad. This dish, a pork fillet cooked in *kajmak* and breadcrumbs, is named after Djordje Petrović, who was better known as Karadjordje ('Black George'). He was the military commander of the First Serbian Uprising of 1804 and the founder of the Karadjordjević dynasty, which then flip-flopped in and out of power with another royal family, the Obrenović, until the outbreak of the Second World War. After serving in the volunteer forces of the then Austrian Empire Karadjordje had become a pig farmer, hence the pork in the dish that bears his name. In 19th-century Serbia being a pig farmer wasn't quite such a humble occupation as it might seem, since the region was locked in to trade agreements to supply half the pork needed by the Austrian Empire, so the men who controlled and supplied this trade could become incredibly wealthy. The eponymous dish is pretty good with fries and a good spicy salad to sharpen the palate, but *kajmak* is certainly an acquired taste. It's a kind of butter, I'm told, that's made from the creamy skin on warmed milk, and it definitely has a strong 'off milk' taste which is curious if you're not accustomed to it, and which crops up in all kinds of food in Belgrade.

I'd heard about *kajmak* before, in connection with the 20th-century British author Lawrence Durrell, who worked at the British Embassy in Belgrade in the period after the Second World War, acquiring experiences that he satirized in some of his Antrobus stories, the bitterly satirical comic pieces he wrote about life in the Diplomatic Service, in which Durrell barely manages to conceal his distaste for post-war Yugoslavia.

I chanced upon somebody who had worked at the British Embassy in

Belgrade at the same time as Lawrence Durrell. She used to type out the notes generated by the media monitor in the attic, who spent the night transcribing and translating, and then would stick the sheets of paper together end on end to create huge rolls that would be waiting on her desk for typing when she arrived in the morning.

It seems to be common knowledge that Durrell hated Belgrade, although I've never actually read this sentiment in his own writing. Similarly, everyone seems to have an opinion on Durrell, even if their knowledge of him is drawn from the character of the pretentious older brother in his sibling Gerald's *My Family and Other Animals*. Someone else told me that the thing Lawrence Durrell hated most about Belgrade was the slightly off-milk smell of *kajmak*. He couldn't get it out of his nostrils, off his clothes. 'Bloody *kajmak*!' he'd say, apparently. In *White Eagles Over Serbia*, his ripping yarn about a spy who infiltrates a network of anti-Tito royalist guerrillas in the aftermath of the Second World War, the main character, a career diplomat-cum-spy called 'Methuen', laments 'the curious stale smell that the Yugoslav public seemed to carry everywhere with them: … rancid *kaimak* [*sic*]'.[12]

Durrell's post in Belgrade was only one of his Eastern Med diplomatic positions. It was also his last. He retired afterwards when given a choice between Turkey and the Soviet Union: he couldn't face either. Bureacrat in Corfu, Press Officer in Cyprus, he was always just catching the end of empire. His books on these two islands have a great undertow of bemusement and inertia, an inability to understand what the natives want or why they're so ungrateful, a continuous puzzlement at schoolboy terrorists. There's a setting sun feel about them. That simple English life – reading books and sailing, renovating some old house and having late-night discussions with local-historian neighbours, dignitaries and whichever writer was passing through town – proving to be an act of will, to be taking place in defiance of conspiracy, espionage and nationalisms, bombs in Nicosia. It seems that he was always there as things turned sour. No wonder he couldn't stand *kajmak*.

In Belgrade the late nights are par for the course, but at least we have the days to ourselves, so I arrange to meet Gordana Stanišić the following morning. Who better to show me around Belgrade, on foot, than the artist who (virtually, at least) walked all the way here?

We start by getting a bus out to Topčider, the forested suburbs to the southwest of the city centre. 'That was Milošević's house,' Gordana says, pointing through the trees. I'm not sure if I can see it or not. This is where he barricaded himself in after finally being forced to admit that he'd lost the election in 2000. It was here too that he was arrested and taken to jail before being extradited to The Hague.

At one point we take a short cut through some woods behind some newly built pink stuccoed apartment blocks. There's a well-worn path through the trees, up dusty, brambly banks. Emerging into a clearing, we come across a settlement of Bosnian Serb refugees, who are living in trucks and huts around a semi-derelict gravel depot. The huge machinery and massive old conveyor belts are long out of use, rusted and ignored, but there are curtains hanging in the windows of the old machine buildings. No one pays us any attention at all as we pass through. Next to a big wooden hut a group of elderly people are clustered around a vast barbecue the size of a pool table. They're burning the skins from sackfuls of fresh paprika. The smell is delicious. The paprika will then be roasted in oil and salt and bottled for the winter. Some will be chopped and made into *ajvar* (pronounced 'eye-var'), a sharp-tasting paprika paste that can be eaten straight from the jar as a kind of relish or used in cooking. *Ajvar* is a traditional winter food, providing vitamin C for the months when no fresh produce is available here. It's sold in the shops as well. It's even available in London, if you look hard enough in the Turkish supermarkets that are scattered around the East End, although there it tends to be the slightly bitter, plummier-tasting variety, with added aubergine.

Over the next few days this is a sight I see repeated all over Belgrade. Everywhere I go people have set up enormous barbecues: in their gardens, in the back yards of cafés, in alleyways or in the streets next to kiosks. People are walking down the street with enormous sacks of paprika on their shoulders, a sight that gives the city an almost rural atmosphere. It's as unlikely as seeing a tractor in Oxford Street. This rural/urban incongruity is something Rebecca West writes about when she describes her surprise at seeing a young man standing in the smart bar of her hotel holding a little wriggling black lamb.[13] This is not the black lamb of her book title, though – that refers to a traditional pagan sacrifice that she witnesses later during her travels in Macedonia, an experience that proved pivotal to her understanding of what she saw as the destructive impulse in human culture and society.

We leave the elderly Bosnian Serbs to their paprika and, after finding our way along a few more tracks, through yet more trees, we reach the main road once again, and the bus stop. For the entire journey back into the city centre we are serenaded by a young Roma ('Gypsy') accordion player who can't be more than ten years old. He's playing a complex, jaunty piece of music that slides up the scales in half-tones and flats.

Belgrade is crowded and the sun is beating down. A hot weekend at the beginning of October is not so unusual, but it's welcome enough that it brings half the population out onto the streets. There is graffiti everywhere, on the walls, on the kerbstones. There's the usual macho posturing of gangs from this or that area ('Psycho Boys are everywhere'), as well as sloganistic dialogues between the rival fans of the two local football teams, FC Partizan ('We are strong!') and Red Star Belgrade ('We are stronger!'). Some of the graffiti is more serious, however, and serves as a reminder that during the protest era this might at times have been the only reliable 'media' in the city; uncensored and therefore able to say things that the state media couldn't, a means to distribute information that even the dissident B92 Radio might not have had access to. As if to illustrate this, a famous graffito in Zemun says '*Nemamo novine, imamo zidove*' ('We don't have newspapers. We have walls.'), while in Belgrade, one chilling graffito says simply 'Bombing Thursday'.

Belgrade's fortress dates in part from the Roman occupation of the great rocky promontory. The park surrounding it is called Kalemegdan and is teeming with people. From these ramparts you can gaze down on the confluence of the city's two great rivers, the Sava and the Danube. Sure enough, as I'd been told, the water of the Sava is brown, while the Danube is black, and at the point where the rivers meet their waters don't mix. Elsewhere the windows of the American Cultural Centre have been repaired. The building had been closed since the bombing in 1999, though the only indicator of business as usual is a photocopied sign taped to the glass, which announces that an entrance examination for new staff will take place the following week.

On Knez Mihailova Street, the main pedestrianized shopping street that leads to Kalemegdan park, people are grilling sweetcorn at street stalls or selling war memorabilia, uniforms and skull-and-crossbones flags. They have nothing to do with pirates. The skull and crossbones has been the symbol of numerous rebellions here. Rebecca West describes an Easter Sunday procession in which a group of black-uniformed men, rifles on their shoulders, were headed by a venerable old warrior carrying just such a flag.[14] The symbol was taken up by the Četnik brigades in the Second World War and by some of the unofficial paramilitary units that operated during the wars of the early 1990s. These banners that are for sale on Knez Mihailova Street could be from any of these periods. It's impossible to tell unless you know the brigade numbers.

There are innumerable veterans' websites for the various units of the Croatian army, even dating back to the Ustaše units that were run by the Nazis' puppet government in the 'Independent State of Croatia' ('Nezavisna Država Hrvatska' or NDH) from 1941 to 1945. (These kind of online celebrations don't seem to exist for the Četniks, however.) A bitter debate continues to be conducted over the extent of the Ustaše's war crimes during the Second World War, and the number of people they killed. Numerous writers, including Robert D. Kaplan, have observed that Serbian estimates of how many people were killed by the Ustaše tend to be far higher than Croatian estimates, and the use of either set of figures identifies both the source of the information and the sympathies of the writer.

Turning again to the transcripts of the Eichmann trial, we find a Jewish survivor, Mr Arnon, who is in the witness stand and confirming something that our presiding judge thinks he must have misheard:

> Q. One more question: I am not sure that I heard correctly when you said that in one camp hundreds of thousands of Serbs were exterminated?
>
> A. Hundreds of thousands.[15]

Vesna Kesić's advice about checking news items from the Balkans three times can be disregarded, however, when reading non-fiction about the Balkans: a triple check is nowhere near enough. You need to read dozens of accounts before you even begin to understand how the authors might be reproducing, even unwittingly, the rhetoric of one side or another in the wars of the 1990s. This question of perspective, a writer's viewpoint and interpretation, is something that you have to develop a certain 'radar' for, coupled with a realization that no one is necessarily wholly correct.

This isn't simply an issue of the numbers of people murdered during the Second World War: every aspect of the complex history of these countries seems to be up for grabs. When Marcus Tanner, for instance, in his history of Croatia, describes Stefan Dušan, the Tsar of the medieval Serbian empire at its greatest extent, as 'a rustic monarch of the Balkan hinter-land',[16] the effect on most readers is, arguably, less to underline how impressive the city state of Ragusa (now Dubrovnik) must have appeared at the time Dušan visited it, than to aggrandize Croatian history and legit-imize its continuity at the expense of the Serbian. The opposite process would be equally easy to demonstrate in any number of accounts at the expense of Croatia, including Rebecca West's.

To give a more contemporary example, when Kate Hudson describes the eventual, if contested, defeat of Slobodan Milošević in the presidential election of 2000 as flawed *only* for having taken place under conditions of 'unprecedented western intervention,'[17] the effect is arguably to minimize the opposition movement in Serbia, which had somehow managed to sur-vive in spite of being, until that moment, effectively held in check by almost total state control of the media. It glosses over Milošević's continu-ing war of attrition on all political opposition, through his manipulation of police and other forms of state and unofficial violence and intimidation, which dated back to the literally murderous and heavy-handed suppression of the Belgrade protests of March 1991.

One of the postcard stands on Knez Mihailova Street has a very few cards left over from the period of the bombing, from the moment when the anti-war and anti-Milošević protest movements became, also, anti-NATO, and when many people in Belgrade wore targets on badges or T-shirts. 'F*** the coca, f*** the pizza, All we need is *šljivovica*' says one. Others are even more explicit. The wittiest of the cards, however, is a painstakingly precise paro-dy of the frontispiece to the *Asterix* comic strips: a cartoon map of Roman-ruled Europe with a magnifying glass over the Balkans rather than Gaul. A Roman standard is planted in Singidunum, as the Romans called Belgrade, but instead of Caesar's head there is Hitler's, together with a NATO logo and a US flag. The legend completes the perfect parody of Asterix: 'The year is 1999 A.C. Europe is entirely occupied by the Americans. Well, not entirely… One small country of indomitable Serbs still holds out against the invaders…'

These aren't the only reminders of the recent wars. There are limbless men who are obviously military veterans begging on Knez Mihailova Street. Some are walking around on crutches, others have empty sleeves pinned to their jackets. Their tragedy is replicated all over the Yugoslav successor countries. Many of the soldiers were conscripts who were not quick enough, or lacked the resources, to beat the draft. It's a reminder, however, that, by a certain grim reckoning, these are the lucky ones. At least they survived.

Estimates of total fatalities during the wars in the former Yugoslavia, including Kosovo, are reckoned to be somewhere between 250,000 and 310,000 people,[18] depending upon the source of the statistics. Human Rights Watch estimates that the civilian deaths during the NATO bombings in Serbia and Kosovo were around 500, although:

> The Pentagon has suggested that only 20 to 30 incidents resulted in civilian deaths during Operation Allied Force. The Yugoslav government has claimed that NATO was responsible for at least 1,200 and as many as 5,000 civilian deaths.[19]

The legacy of the NATO bombing is still very much at the forefront of people's minds, as well as before their eyes. There are reminders everywhere you look, and everyone has a story about a narrow escape. The outrage felt by the people of Belgrade at being bombed when so many were themselves trying to oust Milošević may take a long time to abate.

Other more material effects of the bombing have an even longer half-life. As we eat the inevitable heavy lunch of grilled meats, bread, salads and very spicy green chillis in the Little Paris café, a famous bohemian meeting point at the time of Rebecca West's visits to Belgrade, Boro Radaković jokes: 'I can guarantee that this food is free of genetically modified ingredients, but I can't guarantee it's free of depleted uranium!' We all laugh and cheerily knock back our glasses of *šljivovica*, but, if the reports about depleted uranium are reliable, it's not so funny for the people who live here. Industrial towns and areas on the outskirts of Belgrade, as well as further south, were apparently subjected to enormous pollution as a result of the bombing. It's not simply the depleted uranium that may be a cause for concern when an oil refinery or a chemical works is bombed. Countless toxins are released into the environment, contaminating the water table and entering the food chain. There's little discussion of the matter in the Belgrade media, but the as yet unknown effects of the bombing on a generation of children are becoming a source of some anxiety.

Others talk of a strange moment of cultural vacuum. Until the toppling of Milošević the protest movement was, or at least seemed to many observers to be, the authentic culture of Belgrade. The protest 'happenings' that saw up to half the population of the city banging saucepans on their balconies or blowing whistles at the same time every evening, driving at five miles an hour on a designated day, or distributing ironic ration coupons offering '1 Orgasm' to the military, were theatre on a previously unimagined scale, performance art with a purpose. The culture of resistance had culminated in the storming of the Parliament building at the other end of the leafy square, quiet now, outside the window of my room at the Splendid Hotel.

Since then, a certain cultural numbness, which several people comment upon, seems to have set in, the result both of a collective post-traumatic stress and of a nagging sense of anti-climax. Yet with the huge excitement generated by events like this literature festival, and the intense cultural appetite of the city generally, all us visitors in 2001 had the impression that something, somehow, would emerge to replace those popular theatres, those vast and ultimately powerful cultural manifestations. Even if we couldn't see what form that cultural expression would take, we could all sense that it wouldn't come from any expected quarter ('Why should we listen to B92 now?' someone asked me). The atmosphere of expectation, the optimism that visitors to Berlin in the early 1990s may well recall, is so palpable in the air of Belgrade that one is tempted not to doubt its future vitality for one second. Another of Rebecca West's observations of more than 60 years ago seems to echo the feelings of everyone I meet, resident and visitor alike:

> [The people of Belgrade] were certain in any circumstances to act vigorously; and it would be impossible to foresee what form that action might take... I asked myself in vain 'What will they do?' And I asked myself also the more important question, 'What would they feel that they could not do?'[20]

Later I hear that some of the Croatian writers who have come to Belgrade wrote on their return that the people of Belgrade were relieved that the finger of international blame was no longer pointing at them after '9/11'; relieved to no longer be the universal bad guy. Some people might have said this, but no one that I spoke to. The majority of conversations I'd had in Belgrade were not concerned with President George W. Bush's 'War on Terror' at all. Most people were too busy rebuilding their lives.

Take, for one example, the friend of a friend whom we shared a drink with, in the early hours of Sunday morning, after a cab ride down Jurija Gagarina Street. We bumped into him as we picked our way by moonlight over broken concrete and a half-finished oil pipeline to a little wooden floating bar called Skalar on the banks of the Sava in Novi Beograd. We walked up the gangplank, found a table and ordered the inevitable bottle of Macedonian red wine. Aside from football (he knew more about the English Premiership than I did), he was more concerned with a burgeoning career as an insurance salesman that he was using to supplement his taxi driving than anything else. 'Do you know,' he asked me, 'that one quarter of the population in Slovenia have taken out private pensions since the war? Five hundred thousand, out of a population of two million! We can have this here!' If really pressed, one or two people wondered, with a depressed shrug of recognition, whether the US government might now appreciate the full meaning of that glib euphemism employed during the bombing of Belgrade, and during all other wars of the 1990s and beyond: 'collateral damage'.

It is soon time to return to Zagreb. My appetite for this city and its people is undiminished, sharpened rather than satisfied. All us writers staying at the Splendid pack and leave our bags beneath the stairs in the hotel foyer, reclaim our passports and then go across the road for a final vast lunch in an old-fashioned restaurant with a beautiful Art Nouveau exterior on Terazije. I order what has become my favourite meal during the past few days, since the lunch at the Little Paris Café: grilled chicken livers wrapped in bacon – 'King's Morsels' – and a large bowl of salad with cheese and chillis. We drain a few more bottles of Tikveš wine and, unsure of the trade relationship between the Former Yugoslav Republic of Macedonia and Croatia, I fear that they may be our last.

Vladimir Arsenijević comes along to see us off. He tells us that the saturation media coverage that the festival has received will continue, with four or five TV programmes in the next week. He suggests that the festival seems to have reminded the people of Belgrade of something they'd forgotten, or heard about but perhaps not believed: that literature can be fun, not something you have to read for your own good or to satisfy some state agenda. He also tells me how important, historically, the relationships between Zagreb and Belgrade have been. He thinks that the culture of each of these two cities complements that of the other. The lines of communication have now been reopened and it seems as if no one can stop these conversations now.

We have train tickets but have to buy additional tokens to get through the turnstiles and make our way on to the platform. Sunlight streams in beneath the vaulted roof and our train is waiting at the platform.

It's undoubtedly true that any railway terminus can be a romantic place, in the broadest sense of the word, full of possibilities and metaphors for possibilities: the tracks, the points that can switch you from one route to another, the knowledge that you can buy a ticket to more or less anywhere you want to go.

Edi Rama, the visionary Mayor of Tirana in Albania, described by Misha Glenny as one of a new breed of politicians who might just be the future of politics in the Balkans, once described his country as being 'like a station where everybody is waiting for a train or a boat ... or a beautiful man or lady to take them away because they've lost confidence in the government and any possibility of a better life'.[21] I'm feeling a bit like that now, standing here and waiting at the railway station, because at this moment a part of me doesn't want to go to Zagreb. I feel something of a wrench at the prospect of leaving Belgrade so soon after I'd finally arrived here, as if I'm being pulled in two different directions at once.

I snap out of this moment of indecision when the guard walks past and sharply blows his whistle. Boro and Danijela are beckoning me frantically from the doorway of the carriage. I scramble up the steps and slam the door behind me just a second before the train starts moving.

Chapter Four
Zagreb II (2001)

The return journey back to Zagreb is slightly quicker than the outward one had been a few days before, although we're stuck at the border for some time while a Roma family in the next compartment are hauled off the train. They are brought back an hour later, enough time for their papers to have been checked exhaustively. I hear from various sources that there have been violent attacks on the Roma population of Zagreb, which tallies with an almost systematic climate of abuse and discrimination against Roma across the whole region, ranging from casual police brutality to numerous well-documented instances of out-and-out racism being spouted by self-seeking politicians everywhere from Greece to Romania.

When the train finally pulls into Zagreb Station we're all exhausted and hungry. Unfortunately none of us thought to bring Croatian money with us to Belgrade, and the restaurant car that was attached to the rear of the train when we crossed the border from Serbia would take only Croatian money, not deutschmarks or euros, and certainly not Serbian dinars. The unofficial informality relating to what is acceptable legal tender in Serbia is not shared in Croatia, but still neither the dinar nor the Croatian kuna is a viable currency on the foreign exchange markets. But a plan has emerged, and when we scramble off the train and leave the station we follow one of the festival's organisers, Kruno Lokotar, across the road and go down an escalator to a stunning, chromium-lined, subterranean shopping centre. One can practically smell the new paint in this example of the kind of investment in infrastructure that is already happening across Croatia, but may take years to come to Belgrade or the rest of Serbia.

We end up in the glitzy Hollywood Bar, listening to 1980s British pop music (New Order's 'Blue Monday'), drinking local beer, and eating from a huge communal tray of *ćevapčići* (which means 'little kebabs,' Boro tells me) with chips and focaccia. We all spear the food with the cocktail sticks provided, too hungry to talk. This is all very well: comfort, good food, and the suggestion of economic recovery on the brink of a world recession. Yet I find myself missing the rough and ready quality of a street café in Belgrade, and wondering how long it will be before I can sit on Skadarlija and enjoy a plate of grilled chicken livers with a chilli, tomato and cucumber salad, and a bottle of Macedonian wine.

The economic optimism that had seemed to be symbolized by the shining chrome and twinkling lights of the Hollywood Bar and the new shopping centre is not really borne out elsewhere in Zagreb, but the city is beautiful, and all life seems to take place on the streets rather than in its buildings. The 19th-century Viennese-style architecture that dominates most of the city centre survived the Second World War and is stunning in the light of the Indian summer that has travelled with us up from Belgrade.

The main square is packed with people. A man has set up a shoeshine stand facing the statue of Ban Josip Jelačić, the Croatian leader who was appointed by Vienna to counter the Hungarian revolution of 1848 and after whom the square is named. In an attempt to secure a sort of partial independence for Croatia, a detachment from Hungarian domination and a firmer link with Vienna – at a time when the seeds of Southern Slav unity were first being sown, just as Hungary was convulsed by Kossuth's revolution – Jelačić led an ill-prepared army against Hungary. He was either victorious or defeated, depending on which accounts you trust, and anyway was hung out to dry by the Austrians, whose promised reinforcements failed to appear. During the Tito era his statue was removed and the square was renamed, like most town squares across the then Yugoslavia, Trg Republike (the Square of the Republic). Under Tito, Jelačić's statue was even replaced, for a time, with a striking modernist sculpture of an Eiffel Tower-like pylon, a Tatlin Tower for Tito, which looks from photographs to have been built from painted plywood, and which, judging by its position, may even have been built on top of Jelačić's then redundant and empty plinth. By the 1960s the square, statueless, was largely given over to a car park.

Reinstating the statue following Croatian independence in the 1990s, when the square was once again renamed after Jelačić, Franjo Tudjman, the right-wing President who'd led Croatia into war, tinkered with history somewhat. When the statue of Ban Jelačić was first erected it faced Hungary. With his raised sword, Jelačić was depicted by the sculptor at that heroic moment when he set off on his ill-fated mission, rather than when he retreated to Vienna, where the Austrians gave Croatia back to the Hungarians in any case. Nowadays, instead of facing Hungary Jelačić faces south, and raises his sword at Serbia. I'd heard about this, but only recently found further proof in a photograph of a Partisan women's brigade that was taken in the square in 1945: in it, the statue clearly faced towards the north.

I take a seat on a concrete bench at the other end of the square. To my left blue and yellow trams run through it from end to end, while to my right a group of uniformed primary school children gather noisily around a small sunken fountain, throwing coins into the water and making wishes. The sun is hot and two backpackers stroll past in T-shirts. Behind me the city's official souvenir shop stands on the corner of Trg Ban Jelačić and Praška Street. Neon signs surround the square, some new, some old, some advertising brands I recognize, such as Ericsson, Panasonic, Technics, Ideal Standard or *Jutarnji List* (the main Croatian daily newspaper), others brands that I don't recognize: Dona, Končar, Iskon Internet, Partner Bank, Franck, Astra.

High above the square, above the awnings of Café Ban that advertise Jamnica mineral water, is an example of high 1960s camp: a stylized cartoon figure of a pedal-pusher-wearing Audrey Hepburn-like woman takes a photo above the legend 'Efke Foto Material'. A big screen behind the statue of Ban Jelačić shows constant adverts for Samsung, and an EU flag hangs outside the City Centar Varteks store. Elsewhere groups of students on their lunchbreaks sit on the sun-warmed stones to chat and smoke, while a man in red overalls washes down the pavements with a high-pressure hose and an elderly woman walks towards me carrying a tray of flowers.

I hear laughter behind me and turn to see that, just as the school group has moved away from the fountain, two equally young children, a boy and a girl, scruffily dressed and evidently not at school, have scampered down the steps. These two are not here to make wishes, however. The little boy immediately strips off all of his clothes, to reveal a tanned and dirty body, and then jumps into the small pool around the fountain. For a second or two I wonder if he's just doing this to cool down, since it is very hot, but then I realize that he's taking deep breaths and diving down to the bottom like a pearl fisher, surfacing every now and then, with a spluttering giggle, gasping and shivering from the cold water, to hand treasure to his co-conspirator. He's gathering up a morning's worth of coins. Maybe somebody has thrown in a penny and wished that one of Zagreb's invisible Roma families might eat today. Passers by have stopped to watch this joyful display of abject urban poverty and are laughing in the sunshine. A policeman saunters past, oblivious. By the time he's noticed the crowd and approached the fountain the little boy has dragged his clothes back on, and they've scampered away with their loot, their appreciative audience dissipating into the crowds.

Here too there are reminders of the recent wars, even if they're more subtle than the gaping holes in Belgrade's buildings. I'm staying in the Astoria Hotel in the middle of town. Ten years ago it was called the Belgrade.

Boro has arranged for us to meet Danijela, and we spend some time at the city's Art Pavilion, looking at an exhibition of works by Andy Warhol that is touring central and eastern Europe. The flowers that had been left outside the pavilion a couple of weeks ago in tribute to the victims of the '9/11' attacks on the USA have now gone, but the satire of Warhol's camouflage-patterned Statue of Liberty screen print is suddenly acute – even though its irony might have been better appreciated in Belgrade.

I'm due to give a reading at the Ivana Gorana Kovačića Library later that evening. Boro leads the way. The library is in the newer part of the city, on the other side of the railway tracks, an area that, judging by its architecture, was largely developed after the Second World War, during the Tito years. We duck through a low, graffiti-scrawled subway beneath the tracks and find ourselves surrounded, not by ornate stone buildings, but by concrete and glass. The reading is well-attended and, as at literary events everywhere, plastic cups of wine are being handed out. Plenty of the audience want to stay and chat afterwards, about books in general, or about music. One man, looking like a more dishevelled Jean-Paul Belmondo, takes his time coming over. When he does he asks me: 'How many cyclists are killed on the roads in Britain every year?'

Kruno Lokotar, who organized the event, has developed a good system. There is a small ticket price for audiences to attend FAK events and readings, but this kitty is then taken to a bar around the corner, called Limb, where it miraculously becomes a tab. We duly troop to the bar and, as we work our way through the door takings, I discover that the storm caused here by the FAK festival continued while we were in Belgrade.

Ivan Aralica is a Croatian establishment novelist who'd been a close associate of Franjo Tudjman. He was reportedly Tudjman's 'favorite writer, adviser, and eventually his ideologue of Islamophobia'.[1] He has just published a hefty denunciation of the FAK writers. Boro Radaković has also been invited to defend the Belgrade trip on national TV, to justify why Croatian writers should have anything to do with a country that until very recently had been 'the enemy'. The catch is that this TV appearance would see Boro facing two well-known nationalists, which he qualifies by explaining to me that one of them had published a list of 'traitorous', that is, not sufficiently 'pure' Croatian writers and other public figures during the war. Those kinds of denunciations needed to be taken very seriously during the 1990s, as they could lead to people being imprisoned, hounded from their homes or even killed.

At first this sours the evening. The prospect of defending FAK against such an uneven field seems impossible, a no-win situation, but people are starting to compose a letter in response. Then Edo Popović, one of the writers who'd also travelled to Belgrade, comes up with a more constructive plan of action: to ignore them. His idea seems too simple at first, a barroom solution that would never work. It's surprising coming from Edo, a skeletally thin writer with long, curly black hair who over the past few days seems to have positively revelled in taking an almost recklessly provocative and confrontational stance with almost anyone on just about anything. So much so that I'd wondered more than once whether he was actually looking for a fight. If anyone would be spoiling to annoy some nationalists it would seem to be him, but, uncharacteristic or not, the more his idea is discussed, the better it sounds. By refusing to participate in these loaded debates FAK will deny the nationalists a platform from which to further disseminate their dangerous rhetoric. The matter settled, for now, we can relax, and discuss our visit to Belgrade.

Miraculously the bar has several bottles of my favourite Tikveš-brand wine, a beautifully soft red from Macedonia. One of the people who have come to join us says, 'Look, I like this wine, it's called "Sorrow for the South", *T'ga za Jug* means "Sorrow for the South".' The patriotic sentimentality of the name seems somehow fitting. Sorrow for the south indeed, or at least for the south Slav dream that was Yugoslavia.

Boro interjects: 'You shouldn't listen to this stupid paratrooper! Actually better translation would be "Longing for the South"!' This ribbing goes on for a while. The 'paratrooper' and Boro both tell me that I should read the

Nobel Prize-winning author Ivo Andrić's novel *The Bridge Over the Drina* if I want to understand the former Yugoslavia.

Some time later, when I'm back in London, I hear the former Liberal Democrat leader Paddy Ashdown speaking on BBC Radio 4. Ashdown was the High Representative in Bosnia-Herzegovina from May 2002 to January 2006. This is a post that was created under the General Framework Agreement for Peace in Bosnia-Herzegovina (the Dayton Peace Agreement) in 1995, to 'oversee implementation of the civilian aspects of the Peace Agreement'.[2] Ashdown says that when people ask him what the Balkans are like, what they need to know before coming to work in Bosnia-Herzegovina, he simply recommends two things: that they read *Bridge Over the Drina* by Ivo Andrić and watch *The Third Man*, Carol Reed's film about corruption in post-war Vienna.

My contribution to the conversation with Boro and the 'paratrooper' in this Zagreb bar is, of course, to talk about Rebecca West. Neither of them has read *Black Lamb and Grey Falcon*, so I grope for biographical details, telling them that she was a brilliant novelist, journalist and essayist, easily the equal of George Orwell, of D.H. Lawrence, that she'd had a long-standing relationship, and a child, with H.G. Wells, and that she wrote the book following exhaustive travels around Yugoslavia on the eve of the Second World War with her husband and a series of guides, most notably a poet whom she called 'Constantin' in the book, but who was really Stanislav Vinaver.

'Ah!' says 'Paratrooper'. She was married to H.G. Wells? Perfect! So H.G. Wells was in Yugoslavia! I cannot believe it, but it is excellent news – this place is perfect science fiction.'

Of course, it was her banker husband Henry Andrews who accompanied West on her travels around Yugoslavia, not H.G. Wells, whom she never did marry, but the idea of the author of *The Time Machine* or *Things to Come* visiting the former Yugoslavia is too good to contradict. It seems so apt and funny, and just for a moment it feels as if it's enough for one person to believe something for it to be true.

With the bar to ourselves, and being full of Dutch (or Macedonian) courage, those of us who'd travelled down to Belgrade are all thrilled with the success of the festival. We remember the Serbian custom of kissing three times, and the Serbian salute, combining thumb, index finger and middle finger – both gestures representing the holy trinity. A few years ago, when Serbia and Croatia were at war, to do any of these things in public here in Croatia might have invited imprisonment – probably in the grim-looking, concrete police station opposite my hotel – or the attentions of a lynch mob, but now we joke about it. I use sign language to order two coffees from the bar. 'Are you sure that's enough?' one of the writers asks. 'Maybe we should get three!' The barmaid laughs.

The bravado stops when, shortly before closing time, some unfamiliar faces arrive. You never know who a stranger might be here. I, for one, am anxious not to cause another diplomatic incident and keen not to offend any more veterans.

I wake very early the next day, to catch my flight, and when I get downstairs Boro and another friend called Nenad are already waiting for me in the lobby. Nenad has brought his car and we drive through the deserted Zagreb streets, past the station, under the railway tracks and out over the River Sava.

'It's funny, you know,' says Boro. 'No one much goes to the Sava River in Zagreb, and yet for a long time there was enormous graffiti there.' He's stretching his arms as if he were a fisherman talking about the one that got away. 'Huge, all along this big concrete wall, and it said, "Irish Republican Army". I have never found out who did this. I cannot imagine who would come to Zagreb to do such a thing. It's truly the last thing you would expect to see here in Zagreb!'

We pass Boro's apartment building too. 'Look at that,' he says, pointing at the small park between the apartment block and the road. 'We planted those trees when Tito died. Everyone planted 88 trees, because that was how old he was when he died!' It didn't look as if there were 88 trees left there any more, but I imagine this being replicated across the country: 88 trees on every patch of grass.

Later, when I'm back in London, I come across a biography of Tito written by Milovan Djilas, his former deputy. Djilas fell out of favour in the early 1950s and became the former Yugoslavia's most famous dissident. His book contains some beautifully condensed and acerbic lines about Tito, about his lack of education and his use of party funds to build luxury villas, that must have been polished and perfected during Djilas's long imprisonment: 'He was as uninterested in fiction as he was interested in those who wrote it.'[3] It's superbly critical, full of a hilariously acute but always measured (drop by drop) venom. It reminded me of something I'd underlined in Trotsky's book on the Balkan Wars, and which I immediately reached for: '…the marked one-sidedness that is obligatory in the memoirs of all the public men who have been forced to take a back seat…'[4]

At the airport Nenad buys a newspaper, the *Jutarnji List*. The front page is dominated by a photo of an aircraft carrier taken from the cabin of a helicopter gunship. Beneath this is a grim-faced Tony Blair and the headline, '*Blair najavio početak rata*' ('Blair Announces Beginning of War'). Looking back on this now it's hard to immediately remember which war this was, but it was of course Afghanistan.

While I wait for my flight back to London, drinking an espresso and a big tumbler of *loza*, the Croatian grappa, I remember something that Andy Warhol said in the closing minutes of a documentary I'd happened upon when I switched on the television in my hotel room the night before. I'd been a little distracted, watching it half-heartedly for ten minutes while I mulled over those first few days in Belgrade, and tried to make some sense of that city where, as Rebecca West had suggested more than 60 years earlier, anything might happen. I'd looked at the TV again by chance, just before the closing credits rolled, and saw some black-and-white video footage of Warhol at a party some time in the late 1970s. A journalist is asking him how he'd like to be remembered after his death. His reply, which suddenly came back to me as I sat at the bar in the departure lounge at Zagreb Airport, seemed to me at the time to be strangely appropriate to cultures and peoples that were just now emerging from a decade of wars. 'What?' Warhol asks, incredulously, 'I've been dead for the past ten years. Why should posterity matter to me?'

Chapter Five
Belgrade II (2003)

Two years later I returned to Belgrade, having timed my visit to coincide with a presidential election. Serbia had been without a president since December 2002, with two previous elections, in 2002 and 2003, being annulled due to the Serbian law that requires a minimum turnout of 50 per cent for an election result to stand. A lot else had happened since I was last there in 2001. For one thing, the slow processes of post-war reconstruction and reintegration with the rest of Europe at least meant that I didn't have to obtain a visa for this visit as I'd had to in 2001.

Since then the embassy in London had moved to Belgrave Square from its previous location, which was in a leafy crescent a short walk from Kensington Olympia. Added to this, it was now the Embassy of Serbia and Montenegro, rather than of Yugoslavia.

It was another token of this process of normalization that nonetheless saw me visiting the embassy the night before my departure in order to attend a reception celebrating a week-long cultural festival that's brought a number of playwrights and 'creative industries' luminaries from Belgrade to London.

I wander around the dark expanse of Belgrave Square looking for the embassy. At last I see that one of the enormous white villas has its lights on. When I get closer I look up at the window and see a smallish wood-panelled library in which are assembled more women with long, straight, hennaed hair than would be statistically likely in any random group of Londoners. Wine glasses in their hands, they stand and chat to another surplus, of Byronic-haired men in green or purple velvet jackets. This is not quite what I'd expected to see. Walking up the steps, I stop in my tracks and almost laugh out loud when the brass plaque on the door glows orange in the street lighting and becomes legible. This is not the Embassy of Serbia and Montenegro, after all, but the National Spiritualist Association of Great Britain. I dig around in my bag, find my notebook and check the number I'm actually looking for: it's just a few doors down.

The curtains and shutters of the actual embassy are firmly closed, but I press the buzzer and I'm shown through to a newly decorated function room, its blue carpets as fresh as the white paint on the walls. I'm a little early, so I have an opportunity to look at a series of the historical paintings that are hung on the pristine walls before the rest of the guests arrive. A lot of the paintings are of men dressed in military uniforms of the 19th century. These are portraits of some of the people that I've read about over the years, and not only in *Black Lamb and Grey Falcon*, though that was of course the first place that I came across the names Obrenović and Karadjordjević, Serbia's two royal families. Until now, though, I'd never seen pictures of these founding fathers of the modern Serbian and Yugoslavian state. The portraits are much as you might expect of uniformed male heads of state from 100 and more years ago, all moustaches and medals, though in fact none of them seems quite as decoratively Ruritanian-looking as their equivalents in Britain might be.

I turn to a small avuncular-looking man who is standing nearby, snappily dressed in bold black-and-white tweed, with a well-trimmed goatee beard and salt-and-pepper hair to match his jacket. It transpires that he's a travel agent from Belgrade who's come to London to take part in a travel industry expo in a convention centre in the London Docklands.

I ask him where he's from and he tells me 'Yugoslavia.' Well of course it's not called that now, he says, turning to the young woman on his right, smiling, drawing her in to the conversation. 'It's true,' he says. 'We Serbs always called ourselves "Yugoslavs". Am I right?'

She nods, *'Da, da'* ('Yes, yes') and laughs. 'Even now,' he says, 'if you ask a Serb where they're from they will tell you "Yugoslavia"! Even if the country no longer exists!' This reminds him of a joke about two old women sitting on a park bench. One of them says, 'You know, I am well-travelled. I have lived in many countries!' She has never moved from the same park bench, it's just that borders and names have changed around her. He mentions that this is the first embassy party he's been to in Britain that has young people at it. In years gone by these events used to be full of elderly people who'd left Communist Yugoslavia for whatever reason: expatriates and ageing anti-Communists. 'Am I right?' The young woman nods again, *'Da!'*

I gesture at the white walls and blue carpets. 'What do you think of this new building?'

'Well, it's fine,' he says, 'and of course I'm pleased, but listen, our old embassy was beautiful. Our old king came to this country to set up an embassy many years ago. He found the finest architects and it was a truly beautiful building, am I right? But of course all overseas properties of Yugoslavia had to be shared out with the other new republics during the 1990s. Now, I don't know, it's maybe the Slovenian Embassy, or the Bosnian one. It's such a shame. We were so proud of that embassy.'

I tell him that I am flying to Belgrade in the morning. 'Ah! Excellent! Then I will see you on the plane! You are on the 8.30 JAT?'

JAT, pronounced *'yat'* is the old Yugoslav airline, which still flies from Serbia and Montenegro, but I tell him that, no, in fact I'm booked on the 8.00 British Airways flight.

'And how much did you pay?' he asks.

It was very cheap, I tell him: 100 pounds or so. He rolls his eyes and turns again to the young lady: 'What are they doing to us?' he asks. 'They cannot make any money like this! It's crazy! No one can compete with this. They just want to put everyone else out of business!'

Before I have a chance to introduce myself to anyone else there are speeches, initially from a smartly dressed and fresh-faced Englishman who works for the non-governmental organization (NGO) that is hosting the forthcoming festival. The speech is all about business and culture, networks and information exchange. He talks of bringing young media entrepreneurs to the UK to learn from their peers in London, of private 'networking' meetings going on behind the culture.

The speech ends in a slight moment of confusion, a Freudian slip: '…I'll look forward to a long and exciting history,' he says, then pauses with a slightly puzzled expression on his face.

It takes a couple of seconds before he realises that he'd said 'history' instead of 'partnership' or 'project', something banal like that. People laugh indulgently to themselves but keep straight faces. As if Serbia and Montenegro's history hasn't been long and exciting enough already!

The new Serbian Minister of Culture is here too. He's in London to promote *The Professional,* a film he also stars in. When I'm in Belgrade the next day I'll mention this to some friends – 'Ah!' they'll say, 'He is great movie star, brilliant actor, but not so brilliant Minister of Culture!'

Before I leave I pick up a selection of free publications that are fanned out on the lid of the grand piano, including an issue of a Belgrade-based glossy magazine that has been produced as a festival tie-in. I flick through an introduction that describes the Belgrade of a couple of years before as a cultural desert. I wonder whether this was the same city I'd visited. The basis for these patronizing comments seems to be entirely related to electronic banking: 'there were no functioning cash machines, credit cards were accepted in only a few expensive restaurants'.[1]

Well, at least the festival has energy and enthusiasm behind it, at least it's happening, though friends in Belgrade are all furious at the tone of this magazine when I show it to them the next day.

The Serbian Crown Hotel, where Rebecca West stayed, down by Kalemegdan Park, no longer exists. It was bombed in the first massive Nazi bombing raid on Belgrade in 1941. All of the international journalists who were staying there were killed, along with 20,000 civilians across the city. As an alternative, I tried e-mailing the Moskva Hotel, which, even when Trotsky came to Serbia to report the beginnings of the Balkan Wars, was 'the best in Belgrade', even if 'a vehicle approaching [it] sinks into a puddle up to the hubs of its wheels'.[2] Of course, the puddles have gone and there are certainly flashier hotels in town now. There needed to be, to service all the international journalists and politicians who came to Belgrade during the 1990s – not to mention the gangsters and paramilitary leaders who'd hold court in the hotel bars. These big, modern hotels, though, are just over the bridge in Novi Beograd and I want to stay in the city centre.

The Moskva is one of the most imposing buildings on Terazije, and I'm sure that if you have a room on the west side of the building you'd get a fantastic view down the precipitous hill that overlooks the Sava River and Novi Beograd. I'm convinced that I'll get a good deal at this time of year, but actually the rooms turn out to be more expensive than in a comparable hotel in Britain. Relative to the local economy, they cost only slightly less per night than the average monthly wage.

I decide to contact my old friends at the Splendid Hotel where I'd stayed in 2001. It may not figure in the literature, but it's very cheap and just as central as the Moskva.

Once I've checked in, I take the lift up to my room on the second floor. I'll unpack later. For now I throw my bags on to the bed and switch on the TV, then draw back the curtains and try to figure out how to open the windows. Outside it's nearly dark. Leaning out into the cool evening air, I can see the floodlit Parliament building over to my left, while what I now know is the Old Palace (Stari Dvor), on the opposite side of Dragoslava Jovanovića Street, is so close I could almost touch it. This is the palace that was built at the end of the 19th century for the Obrenović dynasty, one of the two Serbian and, for a while, Yugoslav, royal families.

The side of the palace that faces the Parliament Building, across what used to be a park, is floodlit. A bull-necked, black-leather-jacketed man is polishing a black limo that's parked beneath the portico, its passenger door aligned with the red carpeted steps to the front door. Turning to look at what had been a park the last time I stayed, I see that it has been replaced by a building site. There are deep excavations, exposing several basement levels that extend out from the palace beneath the area of the park. Directly opposite the Splendid a ramp is being built down into this exposed subterranean structure.

I wonder if these hidden levels once constituted the royal carparks, or some elaborate system of underground tunnels. But then had there been escape routes, King Aleksandar Obrenović and Queen Draga might have stood a chance in the early hours of 11 June 1903, when the officers who had assembled at the Serbian Crown Hotel arrived at the palace to kill them. If there had been a tunnel, Aleksandar and Draga might have escaped with their lives, rather than having to hide for some hours in a built-in wardrobe off their bedroom while the 86 conspirators searched the building. Looking at the palace now, I wonder which window it was that the officers threw their bodies from.

Rebecca West's descriptions of the events leading up to the murders, and of the murders themselves, are written – like much of *Black Lamb and Grey Falcon* – with all the suspense of a thriller. The various cock-ups and conspiracies, networks and significances are delineated in painstaking detail, but never to the detriment of a sense of horror and suspense, which grows as one reads. West builds up to the murders, withdraws, then approaches them from yet another angle as she explores the various chains of events and the clashes of personalities that culminated in the semi-clothed bodies of the King and Queen being thrown into the palace garden, just a few yards away from where I'm leaning out of my second-floor window in the Splendid Hotel.

West employs telling, almost cinematic details in relating this grim episode. The dead King's fingers were supposedly found clutching tightly at some blades of grass; his other fingers had been severed as he tried to cling to the balcony. In a final twist, West tells us that both he and his prime minister, Cincar-Marković, who was assassinated on the same night, died in ignorance of the plot against them: in their final moments, each thought that the other had ordered the killing.[3] Ann Lane suggests that it was at this time that 'the adjective "balkan" acquired the perjorative connotations which it has never shaken off'.[4]

Following the coup, the Karadjordjević dynasty – in the person of Petar Karadjordjević, who until that time had been living in Swiss exile after serving in the French army – was invited to take up the throne. Petar took up residence here in the same Old Palace until the outbreak of the First World War.

The Karadjordevic family now has its own website. It also has a living heir to Serbia's and the now non-existent Yugoslavia's now non-existent throne: His Royal Highness Crown Prince Aleksandar II.

When Serbia was invaded by the Nazis in 1941, another King, Petar Karadjordjević II was on the throne. He fled first to Athens and eventually to London, joining all the other heads of state and governments in exile who'd decamped there. This Petar was the son of Aleksandar Karadjordjević, and he'd succeeded to the throne when Aleksandar was assassinated in Marseille in 1934. However, at that time he was only 11 years old, so his cousin Prince Pavle and two ministers were appointed regents until Petar came of age. King Petar married during his Second World War exile in London where, in 1945, he and his wife had their first child, the current Crown Prince Aleksandar II. He was born in Suite 212 of London's Claridge's Hotel. The British Prime Minister, Winston Churchill, arranged for King George VI to declare the room Yugoslav territory in order that Aleksandar could be born in his own country. Some accounts suggest that a spade-full of Yugoslav earth was tipped under the bed, so that Aleksandar could be said to have been born on Yugoslav soil.

My imagination gets the better of me. If the rooms were declared to be part of Yugoslavia in perpetuity, then might not Suite 212 now contain the only few square feet of Yugoslavia that still exist anywhere on the face of the Earth?

The website of Claridge's Hotel briefly mentions Aleksandar's birth, but inevitably, perhaps, the more detailed discussions about the suite, and other such disputed territories and enclaves, take place elsewhere on the internet. One website proclaims itself 'an international open discussion list for finding, researching, photographing and discussing geopolitical boundary points, especially those of a tri-state or multipoint nature'.[5] A message posted on the site reminds the other users that 'the group had a discussion about vertical sovereignty some time back, and [Suite 212 of Claridge's] came up when someone asked whether Yugoslavia ended at the floor and ceiling'.[6]

I telephone Claridge's to see if they still have any records connected with the story of Crown Prince Aleksandar's birth. What I really want to do is to arrange a visit to the suite. I want to see if there is a plaque on the door, and if they know the full story. I wonder whether the decree was permanent and whether there is still a part of Yugoslavia in London.

However, when I try to speak to the hotel's marketing department and explain that, yes, I think they may be able to help me, the operator simply interrupts and tells me she doesn't have the faintest idea what I'm talking about.

When King Petar fled to London in 1941, he had been on the throne for just a few days following a coup that overthrew the previous government and the regency of Prince Pavle. The coup took place in protest after it became known that Prince Pavle and his government had buckled under pressure and signed a non-aggression pact with the Nazis. Petar Karadjordjević was still a minor at the time of this coup; he was a few months short of his 18th birthday at the time. Belgrade was mercilessly bombed, and ten days later Petar and the government fled, first to Cairo and then to London. In their absence the whole of Yugoslavia was occupied and divided up by and between German, Italian, Hungarian and Bulgarian forces. Within a few months a quisling regime had been set up in Belgrade, but this regime was no longer responsible for a Yugoslav entity.

Two resistance movements, General 'Draža' Mihailović's Četniks and Tito's Partisans, fought not only the occupying forces, but also each other, as well as the Croatian Ustaše, who'd returned from exile and used the occupation to set up both the Nezavisna Država Hrvatska (or NDH, the 'Independent State of Croatia') and their own concentration camps for the extermination of Serbs, Roma and Jews. There was near-civil war between the two resistance movements, with the Allies eventually deciding at the summit conference of Teheran in 1943 to switch their support from Mihailović to Tito. It's been suggested that this was because Tito's policy of direct engagement with the occupiers was strategically more useful to the Allies, as in fact it delayed and hampered Hitler's invasion of the Soviet Union, while Mihailović's tactics of infiltration and the avoidance of casualties saw the Četniks branded as collaborators. The switch of Allied support from the government in exile to Tito was a reversal that stunned Rebecca West, whose links and sympathies were with the government in exile, and with the pre-war monarchy, rather than with the Communists. She was profoundly suspicious of them and remained so for the rest of her life. Rebecca West saw the switch of Allied support to Tito as a profound betrayal that, she believed, was fomented, at least in part, by a Communist tendency among the British officials who had first advised the Allies to switch allegiance. She tried, with negligible success, to campaign against it. And even in later life still bitterly resented what she saw as the unnecessary vilification of Mihailović.

Following the Allied victory in Europe, and with the help of Soviet forces, Yugoslavia was liberated and Tito's Partisans switched smoothly from resistance to government, a process that they'd begun to put in place almost as soon as they'd begun to fight, setting up all kinds of civil and political structures between 1941 and 1945. Post-war Yugoslavia was refounded as a Communist state, but broke traumatically with Stalin in 1948. Then, in 1991, ten or so years after the death of Tito, there came the eventual dissolution of Yugoslavia into what we have now: Croatia, Slovenia, Bosnia-Herzegovina, Serbia and Montenegro, and Macedonia (FYROM).

Over 60 years after Rebecca West published *Black Lamb and Grey Falcon*, and since King Petar fled, the Karadjordjević family are now once more resident in Belgrade. Following the fall of Milošević in 2000, Zoran Djindjić, the then Prime Minister, invited them to return, not to take up the throne, but simply to live once more in Belgrade. [7] Crown Prince Aleksandar still calls himself the heir, taking the view that Tito's abolition of the monarchy was illegal and that King Petar never in fact abdicated.

Suite 212 at Claridge's was used once more in its official capacity as a 'piece' of Yugoslavia in February 2001. It was the location for the ceremony that conferred (or, depending how you look at it, recognized) Crown Prince Aleksandar and his family's citizenship of Serbia and Montenegro.

I check the 'Announcements' page on the Royal Family's website and see that two days ago, as I write, on 12 March 2004, Crown Prince Aleksandar joined the new Prime Minister of Serbia (and former President of post Milošević 'rump' Yugoslavia), Vojislav Koštunica, and other politicians in laying wreaths at a new memorial to Zoran Djindjić, the man who invited him back to Belgrade.

One year earlier, on 12 March 2003, Crown Prince Aleksandar had just returned from speaking to the Association of Families of Soldiers in Wars 1990–1999 at the Army Club in Belgrade, where he'd been presented with a diploma and a trophy in gratitude for his support during the war, when news came in of Zoran Djindjić's assassination. Aleksandar issued an urgent statement:

> The return of assassinations to the political and historical scene in our country is the worst possible situation one can imagine. In that respect, the victim of this crime is not only human and the political personage of the Prime Minister of Serbia, Dr Zoran Djindjić, but the whole country and all its citizens.[8]

The news of Djindjić's assassination flashed around the world, just as the news of King Aleksandar's assassination, when it had so sparked Rebecca West's imagination, had in October 1934. The international news coverage was broadly in agreement with Crown Prince Aleksandar – that Djindjić's assassination was a tragedy for Serbia, if not for the whole of the former Yugoslavia.

Neil Clark, writing in the *Guardian*, was a sole dissenting voice when he described Djindjić as 'a reviled western stooge',[9] for passing the legislation that kick-started the mass-privatization of those state-owned industries that hadn't already been sold off or given away by Milošević, and, most of all, for selling, as Clark puts it,

> the country itself. And in January [2003] Djindjić did just that. Despite the opposition of most of its citizens, the 'heralder of democracy' followed the requirements of the 'international community' and after 74 years the name of Yugoslavia disappeared off the political map. The strategic goal of its replacement with a series of weak and divided protectorates had finally been achieved.[10]

Clark's judgement is arguably unjust. Yugoslavia proper, the land of the southern Slavs, was the name, not made official until 1929, of the post-Ottoman, post-Austro-Hungarian federation of all the Southern Slav communities, the emergent nations, whether Croat, Slovene, Serb, Macedonian, Bosnian, Montenegrin, and as such hadn't really existed in fact or spirit since 1991, so it lasted only 62 years in all, not 74. Even though the union of Serbia and Montenegro had still officially been called Yugoslavia, it was more often referred to internationally as 'rump Yugoslavia'. It wasn't Djindjić who had wiped Yugoslavia off the map: it took a great deal of concerted effort by many more people, and two or three hundred thousand deaths, to do that.

Clark's assertion that Djindjić would be mourned by few of his countrymen and women wasn't borne out when vast crowds turned out and marched through Belgrade behind his coffin, a fact noted on *The Guardian's* letters page the next day, not least in a letter from Dr Vladeta Janković, the Ambassador of Serbia and Montenegro, who noted that:

> on the very day when the article was published the funeral itself was attended by hundreds of thousands of people from all over Serbia who gave voice to deep sorrow over the death of Zoran Djindjić.[11]

Just before I'd left for Belgrade I'd seen a press story in Britain which reported a new theory that Djindjić had been killed by marks*men* shooting from two buildings, rather than just one sniper, and that he'd been caught in cross-fire. What had drawn my attention to this was that the story went on to say that the supposed second marksman had fired from the upper window of an apartment on Birčaninova Street. That's a place I know well because it's where the Centre for Cultural Decontamination (CZKD) is located – the venue for the literary festival I'd attended back in 2001.

Birčaninova Street is one of the leafy, tree-lined, mainly residential streets that run parallel to the main boulevards in the city centre. The short cut from the centre of town is to walk south down Srpskih Vladara (Serbian Kings), the continuation of Terazije, and to turn right when you reach a large yellow building called the Student Cultural Centre, which stands on the corner of General Ždanova Street, where the CD market, the real student cultural centre, used to be.

The last time I'd visited Belgrade the pavement of General Ždanova Street had been lined with several dozen kiosks that looked like little wood-

en summerhouses but were crammed with CDs and software, all of it produced on the black market and on sale for pennies. I'd been tipped off
before this visit that the CD market was now gone. As part of the 'transition process' and the clampdown on organised crime that followed
Djindjić's assassination, these tolerated black markets were being closed
down. The days when 'pirate' culture dominated and was even semi-legit-
imate, when, for example, the Milošević-controlled TV channels would
screen pirate copies of new Hollywood movies before they were even
released – often to coincide with anti-war protests, an extra incentive to
stay at home – are long gone too.

A few yards down General Ždanova Street, past a gleamingly modern
bookshop that sells designer stationery, full-price CDs that few can afford
to buy, and novels by the likes of Nick Hornby and Tony Parsons, both in
translation and in English, you can walk through a leafy little park and into
Birčaninova Street, which is lined with trees and tall apartment buildings.
It's hard to equate this peaceful, leafy street, with Zoran Djindjić's sudden
assassination.

Beyond the southern end of Birčaninova Street, across JNA Boulevard
(the Boulevard of the Yugoslav National Army) lies the massive Hram
Svetog Save (Temple of St Sava), said to be the biggest Orthodox church
in the world. St Sava, originally Rastko Nemanjić, was the son of Stefan
Nemanja, the founder of the medieval Serbian state. Sava lived from the
1170s to the 1230s, and himself founded the independent Serbian
Orthodox Church. Following his death his bones were interred in a succession of Serbian monasteries until they were taken and burned in
Belgrade by the Ottomans at the end of the 16th century. The temple is
supposedly built on the spot where this took place.

Although a society whose sole purpose was to commemorate St Sava by
building a church on the site was first formed in 1895, it has taken more
than 100 years to achieve the near-complete state that the temple is now
in. The design of the building was decided in 1926 and building com-
menced in 1935, but it was stopped after the Nazis' first aerial bombard-
ment in 1941. It took a further 43 years before work on the building
recommenced, in 1984, but even then work more or less stopped between
1995 and 2000. Throughout the long history of its construction the
church has been funded by voluntary donations from a variety of sources,
including a consortium of the 30 biggest Serbian companies, whose repre-

sentatives gathered in 2001 in presence of the then prime minister, the late Zoran Djindjić, to pledge themselves to securing the temples completion. More recently still, Serbian football stars collectively donated a substantial sum of money, and in November 2005 a fund-raising dinner was held in the presence of the current Serbian President, Boris Tadić, who is also the latest head of the committee for that same Association for the Construction of the Temple of St Sava, founded 110 years ago.

I take a walk to Hram Svetog Save on a grey morning. It's not cold, but there's a fine, misty rain in the air. I'd seen the church, floodlit, the night before, from the window of a taxi. It's not so far from the Splendid Hotel to Hram Svetog Save, but it takes a while to walk all the way down Srpskih Vladara, and for most of the time the church looms in the distance, so big that it baffles one's sense of perspective: it hardly seems to be connected to the ground. The final approach to the church is up a steep, narrow, residential street that is in the process of being dug up from one end to the other. It's a bit like Birčaninova Street, with those same big, New York-style stoops, an occasional boutique or bank, a bicycle repair shop.

As I get closer, I can see that the landscaping of the area surrounding the temple has yet to be completed. Temporary fencing cordons off an area that is being used as a contractors' car park, and the contractors' notice boards, complete with artists' impressions of the completed building, are still lined up next to the gate to the site, although the building does appear from this modest distance to be almost completed. A 20-foot-high bronze statue of St Sava is mounted on a temporary plinth made of scaffolding and planks next to the gate. The front entrance is taped off, and builders are working on the steps up to the vast front door. I assume this means that I can't get in, that I'll have to phone somebody and arrange an appointment for another time, but when I mention this to friends later on, they all just laugh: 'Of course it's open to public! So they are working on the door, that doesn't stop you going in. Ah! You are so English – you're too polite. You should have just said you were going in! Told them to get out of the way!'

St Sava is so tall that it merits a reference on skyscraperpage.com, which is, as you'd imagine, a website for skyscraper fans. I found it when I was researching the Genex Tower, also known as the 'Western Gate', the big Goldfinger-esque building in Novi Beograd that I'd seen on my first visit.

I have several photographs of the Genex Tower on the pin boards behind my computer right now, pictures that were taken from the passenger seat of a Yugo taxi en route for the airport. They show the concrete of the tower bleached bone-white against a deep blue sky. You can just see where the enormous red letters spelling 'Yugotours' have been stripped from the city-facing side of the lift shaft. Autumnal trees, poplar, birch and gorse, line the verge beside the motorway.

'Genex' is short for 'General Export'. Since this tower was built in 1978 it had been at the heart of a business empire that controlled a vast number of companies, a continuous flow of deals. Yugotours, whose logo once took up nearly 12 storeys of the tower, was not even the half of it. Genex had divisions for agriculture, pharmaceuticals, chemicals, metals and oil, investments and engineering, textiles, leather and footwear, timber, paper and graphics, representation and consumer goods, information, and just 'business'. It also encompassed Genex Hotels, Aviogenex, an airline and, of course, Yugotours, the travel agency. Genex also owned the Inter-Continental Beograd Hotel and had its own finance division, the International Genex Bank. These are just the operations that were 'domiciled in Belgrade'.[12] There were 20 more offices, and still more operations, outside Serbia.[13]

It's not clear which bits of Genex, if any, are still trading, or who owns them these days. Various bankruptcy proceedings are documented, from 1998 and 2003. At one point, together with Yugobanka and Central Bank, Genex owned one of the richest mines in the country, the Rmhk-Trepča complex near Mitrovica in Kosovo, which alone had an estimated mineral-reserve value of US$5 billion, a contract for which was apparently sold to Greek and US holdings for a fraction of this amount.

I can hardly believe what I'm reading when I come across these stories about Trepča. I reach for the copy of *Black Lamb and Grey Falcon* that's on the floor next to my chair, and flick through the index: Gospodin Mac, Gospodin Mac, Gospodin Mac. When Rebecca West visited Mitrovica she went to these very mines. Back then they were being managed by a Scot, referred to by the loosely fictionalized name of *Gospodin* Mac (Mr Mac). She fell in love with the place, certainly (she says as much), but was also impressed with him. She's quite starry-eyed, eulogizing the country, the industry and the industriousness of the people. 'It's a fine mix-up of races and religions,'[14] Gospodin Mac says at one point, before describing (naively? she gives him the benefit of the doubt on this) how he plays on the antagonisms among Croats, Serbs and Albanians to divide and rule his workforce: 'This country's getting over its past nicely,'[15] he says.

In the late 1980s, during the build-up to the war and to the Kosovo crisis, the mines were at the centre of a strike[16] and at one point some accounts report the mines being occupied by Kosovar Albanians 'to protest about the policy of forced Yugoslav immigration',[17] although 'immigration' is not quite the word, since Kosovo was part of Yugoslavia at the time. On 24 March 1999, according to the Italian *Corriere economia*, 'on the eve of the NATO raids, Kosovska Mitrovica was the first place from which Albanians were deported en masse'.[18]

This is non-governmental organization (NGO) country. One of them, the European Stability Initiative (motto: 'Berlin – Brussels – Sarajevo'), has produced a comprehensive report on the Trepča of today, which says that the mine

> provided most of the region's employment. [...] However, plagued by poor management and over-employment throughout its history, it became divided as a result of the Kosovo conflict and by 2000 had almost entirely ceased production. With mountains of debt and unresolved property disputes, the future of Trepča is extremely uncertain. The result is a one-company town without its company. This is the most dramatic case of industrial collapse that ESI has found right across the former Yugoslavia.[19]

It's all a very long way from Rebecca West's proud vision of Gospodin Mac.

In early 2004, following the shooting in an apparently racist or, as the parlance goes, 'ethnically motivated attack'[20] of a Serbian teenager in a village outside Priština, the capital of Kosovo, and, the next day, the deaths of two Albanian children in the town of Mitrovica, much of Kosovo erupted in violence again.

The town of Mitrovica itself is split in two by the River Ibar, which roughly divides the communities representing Kosovo's two major ethnic groups: Serbs to the north of the river and Albanians to the south. More than this, Mitrovica is now home to fully half of Kosovo's remaining Serb population, which itself is estimated at only 100,000 across the whole of the province. At least 100,000 Serbs have left Kosovo during and since the crisis, most of them, it seems, forced out against their wishes. The Serbian population had been shrinking anyway, from 23.6 per cent of the population of Kosovo in 1948 to 13.2 per cent in 1981,[21] but statistics are not much use in Mitrovica, where, in a period of three days, there have been riots and attacks on people and property, numerous deaths, at least 500 injured, and attacks on symbolic, civic and religious buildings. Churches and houses have been burning, most of which are Orthodox churches and Serb houses. All of this prompted the Serbian prime minister, Vojislav Koštunica, to describe the violence as 'an attempted pogrom and ethnic cleansing'.[22] German, French and British peacekeeping forces were immediately flown in en masse to boost the numbers of K-FOR[23] troops in the area.

It's worth noting that analysts have blamed the rise of Milošević on his manipulation of the grievances that Serbs felt following the implementing of the 1974 Constitution of Yugoslavia, when the Serb minority in Kosovo had their right to self-determination effectively given away under a mechanism that gave Vojvodina and Kosovo, which were provinces of Serbia, practically equal standing in the Yugoslav Presidency with the six republics of the Federation, and therefore an effective power of veto over much of Serbian policy. The speech that Milošević gave in Kosovo in 1987 with its famously opportunistic cry 'You shall not be beaten again', had played into this grievance, allowing the Serb minority to see a way to regain their right to self-determination. Yet the result of all of this has proved to have exactly the opposite effect: the Serb minority in Kosovo is in a far worse position now than it was before.

Milošević's cynical and ultimately counterproductive manipulation of the Kosovo Serbs' grievances, and his use of them to construct his power base and oust his mentor Ivan Stambolić, mean that his rise and fall reads like a story by the celebrated 20th-century Indian novelist R.K. Narayan. One by one the dreams of a vain man are slowly demolished, until even the absolute worst-case scenario, which by then has come to seem like something worth aiming for, cannot be fulfilled. At present the future of Kosovo, and whether it remains a province of Serbia, seems to be completely up for grabs as all parties sign up for talks on the province's ultimate status which will commence in 2006.

One of the other tragedies of the unrest in March 2004 is that this wave of violence in Kosovo was blamed by the media on a gang of Serbs, who, it was said, had set a dog on the Albanian children in order to drown them in the river. This story, as if it provides justification, persisted for days after the violence erupted and was repeated hundreds of times around the world.

Reading the papers in March 2004, following the funerals of the children who had drowned, I came across a photo of an evidently distraught child. This, the caption said, was the boy who'd survived the attempted drowning of the children by the Serbs who'd set dogs on them and chased them into the river.

Although it hasn't been fully reported in Britain, the United Nations Mission in Kosovo (UNMIK) sent out a press release saying that the surviving boy had confessed to his parents about the matter: he and his two friends had been playing in the river because it was hot, but the current had been too strong and his two friends had been swept away; there had been no Serbs with dogs. According to UNMIK, 'this was definitely not true according to the account of the surviving boy'.[24] Whoever it was that started the rumour about Serbs and dogs, thus blaming the nearest visible minority group, a group that also happens to represent a hugely potent political bogeyman in Kosovo as well as around the world, had unleashed a province-wide lynch mob.

Rebecca West's optimism on the eve of the Second World War seems all the more remarkable now. She saw this mine as a heavenly idyll, an enchanted glen of good honest labour. It seems all too soon that they must leave, West, her husband and their chauffeur, oh so reluctantly, to be absorbed again by 'the dark, proliferating complexity of Slavonic life'.[25]

The tentacles of the financial deals tied up at the interface between Serbian business and politics during the 1990s stretched to Moscow, to France, to Cyprus. The US$5 billion-worth of mineral value at Trepča sounds like a lot, but these kinds of figures are bandied around liberally in discussions of Milošević-era business.

Whether it's the setting up of banks in France and Cyprus, vast credit deals with international companies, the selling off of state industries, or the alleged disappearance of the former Yugoslavia's currency reserves, the kinds of deals and networks, and the sheer scale of the payments that are exposed if you only begin to scratch the surface of business-finance-state collusion in Milošević-era Serbia are terrifying. The one-time Deputy Interior Minister, Radovan Stojičić, also known as 'Badža', was once quoted as saying, 'There is no organised crime in Serbia', but some reports alleged that 'when he was killed, in April 1997, he was carrying a briefcase containing 700,000 marks'.[26] In early 2000 the general manager of Beopetrol, one Zoran Todorović, was gunned down by an unknown assassin outside the company's offices in Belgrade.

I suppose that if a prime minister can step out of his car next to a government building down by Birčaninova Street and be assassinated, then it's not surprising that reports about Milošević-era business dealings often include the sudden deaths of mere businessmen, even ones who were or had been close associates of the Milošević family.

As we've seen, Zoran Djindjić's murder in March 2003 was followed by a huge crackdown on organized crime and graft across the country. Thousands of people were arrested. The drug dealers and the CD market would have been small fry in comparison with what the then biggest industry in Serbia was involved in. A huge criminal infrastructure does not disappear overnight when war ends and there's a regime change.

All of this makes me realize what was missing from Paddy Ashdown's reading list, his impromptu crammer for understanding life in post-Yugoslav Bosnia-Herzegovina, but which could just as easily apply to life in Serbia and Montenegro. The book that, along with Ivo Andrić's *Bridge on the Drina* and Carol Reed's film *The Third Man*, completes the picture and sums up Milošević-era Serbia is Bertolt Brecht's *Threepenny Novel*. Like *The Threepenny Opera*, which preceded it, it's the story of Macheath, the king of thieves, Peachum, king of the beggars, and Tiger Brown, the chief of police, and the graft, corruption and collusion among these pillars of the establishment as they embezzle and defraud their way, at any cost in human terms, through as many of the state's assets as possible. The fictional frauds perpetrated over government funds to requisition ships to help the war effort, in this case the Boer War, are extremely complex and labyrinthine. Vaster swindles are conducted. Worthless commodities are sold for extortionate prices while valuable ones are flogged to friends or temporary allies, drawn in way over their heads, for a peppercorn. Stooges, who spend half the period of their entrapment congratulating themselves on what clever businessmen they are, are lined up mercilessly to take the rap for everything.

Thirteen people are currently on trial for Djindjić's murder, although eight of those charged were not in court at the beginning of the trial. Charged *in absentia*, they were still at large for some time, including the man whom the police suspected was at the head of the conspiracy, Milorad Luković, also known as 'Legija', the former leader of the elite Serbian security force the Red Berets.

Even now that he is in court there's no certainty that Legija will speak.

Further down the alleged chain of command, at the bottom in fact, the one man accused of actually pulling a trigger has not entered a plea, and is refusing to recognise the legitimacy of the court, or even to speak or to answer questions. I've heard no more, either in Belgrade or London, of the theory about the second gunman.

Chapter Six
Belgrade III (2003), Split (2005)

In a few days the nearest kiosk to the Splendid Hotel will have run out of Telekom Srbija's 200-dinar 'Hello'-brand phone cards – with the reproduction of Christ crucified from a 13th-century fresco in the monastery at Studenica on the front – because I will have bought them all. I'm tearing at the phone cards' cellophane wrappers and discarding them with the obsessive staccato rapidity of discarded pistachio shells as I make endless phone calls.

Exhausted, I sit down at one of the tables in the Splendid Hotel's bar. It's a pleasant little wood-panelled place with pot plants, a television that's always on, and yellow tablecloths to match the curtains. Behind the bar there are bottles of *šljivovica*, gin and Johnny Walker, and an espresso machine that is hardly used because everyone orders '*Jednu kafu tursku*' ('One Turkish coffee'), which is prepared on the stove in the little kitchen behind the bar and comes in a little long-handled brass jug.

It is not crowded, but there seem to be one or two men who are holding court, taking a succession of meetings. Other men, dressed in slacks and short-sleeved shirts file in and sit down for their ten minutes. They knock back a quick coffee, *šljivovica* or lager, then make a move when the next appointment arrives.

The exception to this pattern is an elderly man in the corner who is haranguing a younger man in German. His gruff, rasping voice is booming above the sound of the TV and it's impossible to ignore. I can't make out what he's saying, apart from the odd word: 'Nazis', 'cocaine', 'George Bush', 'NATO', 'Albania', 'Columbia', 'Mafia', 'Hitler'. It crosses my mind that he might be some venerable figure who is briefing international journalists arriving in the city to cover the presidential election. Some camera crews are hanging around in reception, checking in great big flight cases full of equipment. I remember somebody once telling me that the Splendid was a popular hotel for journalists during the 'October revolution' that deposed Milošević in 2000, because it is so close to the Parliament building. I ask for my bill, speaking to the waitress in Serbian. Her reply begins in German, then seamlessly, almost mid-word, switches to Italian. She's scanning my face as she speaks, looking for some glimmer of comprehension, trying to find the language that's most likely to be understood. She finally plumps for French, by which time I have taken my wallet out and paid. '*Merci beaucoup*,' I say.

I stroll along to Kalemegdan Park, which surrounds the fortress above the river that is the historical heart of Belgrade. I pass a monument on the way, on the corner of Terazije and Trg Nikole Pašića (Nikola Pašić Square), by the pedestrian crossing. It's a bronze cast of a roughly hewn sculpture, about the size and shape of a large tree trunk. It has a bland, knobbly surface, which looks like roughly finished clay. It's only as I get closer that I notice the figures that are hewn in to the sculpture. Here and there, as if the figures are being excavated from the clay, I can see a backbone, the narrowing of a waist, the nape of a neck. There is writing too, though this is so roughly hacked into the clay that I can barely recognize the letters. The figures, such as they are, seem to be bound, there are cords around ankles, around necks. It's fairly obvious that it's commemorating some tragedy or other. It's been a while since I've looked at sculpture like this, sculpture that depicts something, so I'm not quite sure what to make of these bound figures imprisoned in the bronze. Later, back in London, I read in accounts of the Nazi occupation of Belgrade that Terazije was a favoured spot for public hangings. Now it is more like Belgrade's answer to London's Oxford Street.

I hadn't even noticed the McDonald's on Terazije, in Belgrade city centre, the last time I'd visited, or seen the huge neon McDonald's sign on the top of the Hotel Balkan on the opposite side of the road. Now it's hard to miss. There's even a huge stack of branded postcards in a tourist information display in the foyer of the Splendid Hotel. On the back is a map of Belgrade showing the locations of all the McDonald's restaurants in the city.

This kind of marketing of international brands is in marked contrast to the last time I was here. In 2001 the information display stand in the Splendid's foyer had simply been stocked with postcards advertising a local restaurant rather than a global chain. The front of that postcard was a montage of pictures of politicians and dignitaries who had visited the restaurant. The more famous of these included Mohammed Ali. Among the other images were a shot of the house band, and a picture of a small man in a blue shirt, drink in hand, with his arm around a tall grey-haired man in a green jacket and bold-patterned tie. In one picture a glamorous couple pose, while in another a group of men in suits stand around a long table, captured in the act of raising their glasses. In the top left corner is a photo that had meant little when I first picked up the postcard in 2001, but which makes me do a double-take when I look at it again. A bearded man in a polo shirt, arms folded, sits next to Zoran Djindjić. They are sitting in front of a big plant, both leaning inwards to get in the frame. Djindjić is wearing a black shirt. For some reason it's the only photo on the whole card that has reproduced well. All of the others are blurry and out of focus. The late Zoran Djindjić is looking directly at the camera and smiling quizzically.

The McDonald's postcards are an amazing example of globalization kitsch. They show an aerial photograph of Belgrade in which Kalemegdan is dwarfed by the golden arches and the new McDonald's slogan. This becomes an ironic running gag during the time that I'm here. We're all 'lovin' everything.

As I enter the fortress at Kalemegdan, crossing the wooden bridge over the moat, I notice some graffiti on the wall of the King's Gate: '*Jelena – Volim te! A.*' ('Jelena – I love you! A.')

The view is still as breathtaking as it was the first time I came here. Down below me, on the city side of the river, are grey apartment blocks that remind me of buildings on the outskirts of Genoa, and the roofs of what look like factories, though in Rebecca West's day they were barracks, where she watched soldiers in dress uniform performing parade drill.[1]

West likened this scene to a ballet, though she hastily made sure the reader realised that this scene, these young men, were not homosexual. That's a possibility that might not even have entered the contemporary reader's head if she had not mentioned it. West's occasional homophobia is probably no more than a period detail, but it's been commented that 'ethnosexual discourse'[2] of this kind is not dissimilar to the idea that all Serbs are rapists. It's been pointed out that, for all her obvious love of the former Yugoslavia, West was contrasting what had to be a fictional idea of a primitive sexuality – a land where 'men are men' – with an England that she saw as a nation of effete and ineffective men who were no longer in touch with either their masculinity or any sense of their own agency.[3]

There are no soldiers today, rather a steady stream of lorries and cars slowly making their way around the headland and up into the city. But I'm looking beyond them, at the bridges that cross the Sava. The distant apartment blocks of Novi Beograd and the Genex Tower are insubstantial in the haze. I try for a second to imagine what all this would have looked like when Novi Beograd didn't exist, when that peninsula between the Sava and the Danube was just swampy marshland, prone to flooding.

Next to me a man lifts his little girl so that she can see over the parapet, and as he does so he starts to sing, '*Plovi patka preko Save...*' I recognize the song and so does the little girl. They sing together:

> *Plovi patka preko Save,*
> *Nosi pismo na vrh glave,*
> *U tom pismu piše: 'Ne volim te više.'*

(Roughly translated: 'Duck swimming from across the Sava/ Carries a letter on the top of his head/ And his letter says: "I don't love you any more."') It seems somewhat harsh for a nursery rhyme.

Far below us a tugboat pushes a barge slowly down the Sava towards the Danube, past a large, flat forested island that I'd forgotten was here.

I check the map and see that this island is called Veliko Ratno Ostrvo. For a second I question my knowledge of Serbian: 'Great War Island'. It seems a strange name for an island that's best known for bird-watching and the sandy beach on its northern tip, but siege, invasion, war and bombardments have been a regular feature of life in this city, since before it was a city, for whoever occupied this fortress, this promontory. In fact, so many attacks on the fortress have been coordinated from 'Great War Island' – the Turkish siege, Karadjordje's rebellion at the beginning of the 19th century – that its name starts to make sense. The use of '*veliko*' in its name – 'big', 'great', 'major' – has nothing to do with the 'Great War', when the Austro-Hungarian army launched its assault on the city from there, but is to differentiate it from 'Little War Island', which is on the opposite bank of this channel.

Standing in Kalemegdan and looking out over these two great rivers, I remember that I am also looking out over what was once one of the great symbolic frontiers of the world, and not only a political frontier, but an imaginary one, in the sense perhaps that during the Cold War period the 'Iron Curtain' was an imaginary border as much as a physical one. This is where the *really* 'balkan' part of the Balkan peninsula was always held to start. Behind me, to the south and the east are the *real* imaginary Balkans, which isn't the oxymoron that it sounds. This side of the old border was beyond the pale even to the benign traveller, whether aristocrat or Communist. When Lady Mary Wortley Montagu travelled here in the 18th century her party stopped somewhere down there on the opposite bank, and she looked up and saw that there was a yellow flag flying from Kalemegdan fortress – a sign that the city was infected with plague.

Leon Trotsky gained access to Belgrade at this point too, from what was then Hungary, on the eve of the Balkan Wars in 1912.Taking a ferry from Zemun, he'd landed somewhere on the bank below me, as steamers passed by carrying Serbian soldiers down the Danube to the Eastern Front. Even though this wasn't Trotsky's first visit to Belgrade, he was still shocked by the sudden poverty, the unfinished nature of everything he saw, and by the disappearance of Hungarian opulence; the toothpicks wrapped in rice paper and the complimentary chocolates on restaurant tables.

Small lookout turrets are spaced along the perimeter of Kalemegdan. It is easy to imagine some shivering soldier keeping watch and seeing some massed enemy down on Veliko Ratno Ostrvo. The nursery rhyme doesn't seem quite so harsh now: quite the opposite, once you start thinking of the horrors that must really have crossed the Sava. It was never simply a duck with a note on its head, but an army, an empire, a culture, an alliance, with more malignant purposes than ending a relationship.

In the middle of the river is a timeless scene. A man is standing up in a small boat, fishing. He seems completely oblivious to the huge barge that's still making its way towards the Danube, but he must be able to hear it and will definitely feel its wake in a few minutes. I lean against the parapet and watch him for a while, increasingly becoming aware of the great monument that also stands here, next to me: Pobednik (the Victor).

The story goes that this great figure, a man with a sword who stands atop a white stone column, was originally intended to be sited somewhere in the city centre, but that the great sculptor Ivan Meštrović had been a little too generous in depicting his genitals, so, in order to spare the blushes of the women of Belgrade, the sculpture was erected here on top of the cliff, facing outwards. Certainly this is the story that West repeats, but the Victor is built on such a grand scale and seems so perfectly situated here on its column that it's impossible to imagine another location in the city where it might stand. It's a gesture that again seems both futile and defiant: he's retrospectively warning off the ghosts of invaders past.

As I turn to leave I hear the cheerful voice of an English woman from somewhere in the Home Counties. 'I think it's underground,' she says. 'Come on! This way!' I turn around and see an English woman in regulation jeans and navy blue fleece, a red rucksack on her back, guidebook in her hand, turning and beckoning, without breaking her stride, to three similarly rucksacked-and-fleeced teenage boys, signalling them to follow her off down the path, in search of what I don't know. I'm tempted to follow them down underground, into the network of cellars and tunnels that thread through the rock beneath my feet, to find out what it is they're off to see. I imagine Rebecca West striding around like this, with husband Henry Andrews in tow: 'Come on! This way!'

The lessons that Rebecca West drew from her visits to Yugoslavia were not just about war, but also about art, which she writes about at length in *Black Lamb and Grey Falcon*, and which she came to see as a means of personal as well as human salvation:

> Art is not a plaything, but a necessity, and its essence, form, is not
> a decorative adjustment, but a cup into which life can be poured
> and lifted to the lips and tasted.[4]

Many readers have referred to her absolute reverence for the art of Mozart, to her faith in the value of his ability to communicate the sheer joy of life and love. This was a faith that saw her playing Susanna's aria ('*Deh vieni non tardar…*') from Act IV of Mozart's opera *The Marriage of Figaro*, while London was being bombed, because the 'huge red star' of the bomb cannot 'consume the small white star' of the song, which is 'correct, permanent, important'.[5] She also suggests that art

> gives us hope that history may change its spots and become hon-
> ourable … No wonder we reach out to lay hold on such a force
> when we are beset with disgusting dangers.[6]

Given the importance that Rebecca West ascribes to art, the absence from *Black Lamb and Grey Falcon* of any serious discussion of Ivan Meštrović's work, save a few mentions such as this second-hand story about the prurient response to his sculpture of the Victor, begins to seem like an unlikely omission on her part. However, a closer reading of her text suggests that this is simply because she takes it for granted that the reader knows who she is writing about. Even the first time she mentions Ivan Meštrović she simply refers to him by his surname. Later she writes about 'those who knew Mestrovich's [*sic*] work only from international exhibitions'.[7] This is perhaps just a reminder of how trends and fashions can come and go in the arts. Certainly, figurative sculpture of the kind at which he excelled has been profoundly unfashionable for several decades, but in his time he was seen as the inheritor both of Michelangelo's skill with, and knowledge of, marble – his equal at depicting the human form – and of Rodin's expressiveness with bronze, and he was particularly celebrated in Britain. However, perhaps these trends in art can also be cyclical. Tate Modern displayed two relatively minor works by Meštrović in 2004, and there are in fact works by him in various British public collections, which may one day be exhibited again.

Ivan Meštrović was born in 1883 in the village of Vrpolje in Slavonia, where his parents happened to be doing seasonal agricultural work. He spent his childhood in the mountains of Dalmatia, in a village called Otavice near Drniš. A compulsive carver of wood and stone during a childhood spent working as a shepherd, he was sent to be a stone dresser's apprentice and from there to Vienna, where he studied with other great sculptors of the day and became a leading figure in the Secessionist movement. Moving to Paris, he began work on a never realised monument to Slav heroes. This was the beginning of an ongoing personal commitment to southern Slav liberation, and to the idea and realization of Yugoslavia. It was a commitment that wasn't confined to his artistic practice. In November 1914 he and two other expatriate Croatians living in Florence set up the 'Yugoslav Committee', which set itself the task of influencing policy in order to create a unified southern Slav state outside the Austro-Hungarian sphere.[8]

I'd seen various pieces of Meštrović's work all over Croatia, as well as here in Serbia, though in fact the idea that these two countries should now be separate entities profoundly contradicts what much of his work and life was devoted to.

In the centre of Zagreb there is a famous sculpture in the garden square surrounding the National Theatre. It's called 'The Well of Life': a group of old and young men and women circle a well, which is actually more like a font, filled with water. The young are lost in their love for each other and, soon, for their children, while an old man, alone now, is the only one contemplating the brightly reflective surface of the water. It's a beautifully simple piece of work, but amazingly moving. Art is no longer measured or appreciated according to its verisimilitude to life, but when one encounters an artist who really can make stone or bronze seem to possess the weight and tension of flesh, muscle and bone, no more no less, and to be filled with the real messy emotional force of life, to the extent that these figures seem to be still only because your glance has fallen upon them in the split second before they move again, it really does take one's breath away. 'The Well of Life' is set in a small, circular sunken terrace, which in the daytime is a favourite place for students to sit, and in places the bronze is polished to a golden sheen by decades of human contact, but still, these figures seem almost as alive as the generations of students who have made this little corner of the garden their own.

Visiting Zagreb briefly in 2005, I happen to mention 'The Well of Life' to the writer Edo Popović as a group of us are walking through the city streets one evening. We take a small detour to go and look at Meštrović's sculpture, now that it's dark and the students have gone. We all walk slowly round it, unable to stop ourselves reaching out to touch the figures, adding to the polished highlights. As we turn to leave Edo says, 'You know, I have seen this sculpture so often that I no longer notice it. You think, "Ah, Meštrović, so what?" But it *is* remarkable.'

The best place to see Meštrović's work is not Zagreb or Belgrade, but Split, far down on Croatia's Dalmatian coast, a remarkable city built in and around the ruins of the palace of the Roman Emperor Diocletian. When the nearby town of Salona was sacked by the Avars, in the mid- to late seventh century, a few of the surviving inhabitants fled to the islands off the coast, where they hid out and somehow survived for several years before gradually creeping back. Rather than trying to rebuild Salona, however, they took refuge in the basements and buildings of Diocletian's vast palace, which is itself larger than many medieval towns. Gradually, over centuries, they and their descendants built houses between the columns, in the walls and perched along the guards' walkways atop them. Even Diocletian's mausoleum, a huge octagonal structure near the western wall, was afforded no respect, being converted bit by bit into a cathedral. His porphyry sarcophagus disappeared at some point in the intervening centuries. Rebecca West imagined it lying forgotten in somebody's garden, but recent thinking has it that the stone of the sarcophagus was reused to build, among other things, the cathedral's fine baroque pulpit.

Split is also where, in the 18th century, British architect Robert Adam got his ideas for mixing vernacular brick and stone work with classical structures and detailing. Almost everywhere you look the scene is redolent with the absolutely ubiquitous and familiar forms of neo-classical Georgian architecture, as it is known in Britain. While in between these huge stone columns, often higgledy-piggledy, sometimes with measured precision, are the doors and windows of little houses. One of the main streets, just outside the palace walls, is named after Adam. I was surprised to discover that he hadn't just been inspired by these haphazard frontages, with their juxtapositions of the grand and classical with the everyday. Even the elegant pillars and simple Roman brick vaulting of the palace's vast and labrynthine basements are reproduced, or at least faithfully echoed, in the multi-levelled and terrace-long brick basements beneath Adam's signature Adelphi mansion on the Strand in London, which is still home to the Royal Society for the Encouragement of the Arts, Manufacture and Commerce (a coffeehouse debating society founded more than 250 years ago and now called the RSA) for whom it was built.

It's been many years since the city of Split was contained within the walls of Diocletian's palace. The city now extends far beyond even the area where Salona's ruins would stand, and its huge suburban area spreads right across to the foot of the enormous limestone mountains that provide the city with such a dramatic backdrop.

Visiting Split recently, I happened to mention to my companions that I'd seen a Meštrović sculpture just outside the palace's Golden Gate, and how much I was coming to love his work. When Rebecca West visited Split in the 1930s this sculpture had been situated in the small square, the peristyle, outside the mausoleum-cathedral, a situation so inappropriate to the scale of both the square and the sculpture that it gave her licence to dismiss the work almost entirely: 'Nobody can say whether it is a good statue or not,' she writes. 'A more ungodly misfit was never seen.'[9] Elsewhere she describes Meštrović's work as 'characteristic... in the uncertainty with which it gropes after forms,' and describes some 'terrible errors'.[10] But this is at least partly to allow herself to prove the point that 'Turkish occupation' and more recently 'Philistine Austria' had 'sterilized South Slav art for 500 years' and isolated it 'from all the artistic achievements that the rest of Europe had been making in the meantime'.[11]

Even now, when it's set outside the palace walls, it's hard to miss Meštrović's towering bronze. The statue is of Bishop Gregor of Nin, or Grgur Ninski, a bishop who tried in the tenth century (rather than the fourth, as West tells us) to introduce a Slavic liturgy. Accounts of Grgur Ninski's importance differ. Some say that he was a pioneer of South Slav unity, or even of Croatian nationalism, others that this matter of the liturgy was an ecclesiastical squabble between the bishoprics of Split and Nin. Ivan Meštrović, however, has certainly cast him in heroic mould. His Grgur Ninski is an imposing figure, some 25 feet tall, who holds a Bible in his left hand while he points up and away with the elongated fingers of his right. With this right arm slightly held back, it's as if he's pulling the string of an invisible bow: a gesture that suggests, again, that the statue is just about to burst into life, to loose the bow string and let fly with some thunderous sermon.

Instead of speaking his Slavic liturgy, however, this towering hero has to content himself with being the constant recipient of an affectionate but slightly patronising 'there, there' of a gesture, which has become a good luck ritual for the people of Split to perform whenever they pass by: everybody seems to want to touch Grgur's toe. Seventy or more years of this tribute have left him with a big toe that shines an even brighter gold than the heads and shoulders of those figures that are gathered around 'The Well of Life' in Zagreb.

When I mention the statue of Grgur Ninski to a friend, Nenad, whom I'm travelling with, he says, 'Oh, well. We should go to Meštrović Museum some time.'

'God,' I say. 'I'd love to. Where is it?'

'Here in Split. Just over there.'

Nenad Rizvanović, 'Rizva' to his friends (and not 'Rizla' as I mistakenly heard), was someone else that I met in Belgrade in 2001. A former music journalist, with an encyclopaedic knowledge of British pop and rock music of the 1960s, as well as the punk and post-punk eras, and an especial fan of two English bands, the Fall and the Kinks, Nenad is now an editor with one of the biggest Croatian publishing houses. He says nothing more about Meštrović, but after driving us up a steep coast road for a few minutes he stops and points at an elegant stone building at the top of a long flight of steps beyond an imposing gate and says, 'Here we are. This is Meštrović Museum.'

We get out of the car. Next to the side of the road where we've parked, olive and cypress trees, rocks and dry grass tumble down the hillside to an Adriatic that shines an impossible blue in the May sunshine.

Set above a broad, flat lawn, and terraces lined with lavender and fig trees, atop a wide stone staircase, is an elegant and near-minimalist two-storey mansion. Two square wings stand either side of an arcade that runs half the total length of the building, a welcome area of shade that hides behind eight stone columns. Built from a warm sandy-coloured stone, the design eschews decoration in favour of flat clean lines. Inside are large, airy galleries with cool, dark wood floors and staircases set symmetrically on either side of a large hallway. The tragedy of the house, because it was actually built as both house and studio, is that it was completed only in 1939, on the very eve of the Second World War when Meštrović fled the Italian occupation of Dalmatia.

There is such a lot of work to see here, so many sculptures competing for a limited amount of floor space. But there's something about the work, these figures carved in marble, the stylized wooden bas-reliefs, the plaster casts of huge clay sculptures, these bronzes and endless studies for bronzes, that each one pleads for your undivided attention.

I stop in front of a beautiful white marble sculpture of a woman. Face downturned, she sits on the floor and rests her folded arms on her knees, or rather, on a shawl or skirt that's wrapped around her shoulders and hips, stretched across her knees. The sculpture is entitled 'Contemplation' and must weigh several tons, but, despite this, the illusion of life, expressed in what appears to be the tension of the fabric that stretches across the flesh of her hips, the weight of her legs against the shawl, is so perfectly and delicately executed – so simply, with a sensitivity of line and shape, and perhaps a silk-like texture in the stone – that one almost feels that she could at any minute gather her skirts and stretch, before standing up and walking away.

On the first floor there are four monumental sculptures of the evangelists Matthew, Mark, Luke and John, but the real treasures here are a series of studies, on paper and sculpted, for a statue of Job. This figure is also seated on the ground, knees raised, but the sculpture is the antithesis of

'Contemplation'. I walk from one study to the next, and as I do so this haunted figure of a man becomes more abject until I turn a corner and am confronted by the larger-than-lifesize final piece, which is cast in rough black bronze. His feet and toes curl, he's hunched and contorted with pain, a hand half-raised in a gesture that is half beckoning, half supplicating, his neck twisted back as he howls at the heavens. The abjectness of this figure of Job, tormented by casually inflicted suffering, is underlined by his splayed legs, his absolute loss of dignity, which reveals a big heavy scrotum that makes me wonder if there wasn't some grain of truth after all in the story about the statue of the Victor in Kalemegdan being sited where it was to spare the blushes of Belgrade's womenfolk.

I discovered later that this was a work that Meštrović had made at the beginning of an exile that lasted for the rest of his life. After he'd fled Split for Zagreb, and been imprisoned there because 'he did not want his work to serve the occupier,'[12] (the 'occupier' being in this case, I presume, not so much the Nazis as the fascist NDH, run by the Ustaše), he fled along the escape routes to Italy and Switzerland, where in fact he made this sculpture of Job, fixed forever in his torment.

On the ground floor of the north wing is a huge and formal family dining room, sparsely furnished with a long wooden table and chairs, in which busts of family members line the heavy wooden sideboards. At one end of the room, taking up the whole width of the wall, is a huge brick fireplace undecorated except by two enormous marble caryatids supporting the heavy lintel above. You realize, stepping into this room, that this really was a house designed for Meštrović and his family to live in, and indeed for him to work in. The bricks behind the hearth are coated in soot – this room has been used many, many times – but Meštrović himself certainly wouldn't have been here for more than one year or so.

In the garden, at either end of the building, are two big studios. One of these studios is guarded by an enormous bronze Cyclops, who is poised to hurl his rock out into the Adriatic below. The room is filled with huge plaster casts, which look as fresh as they might have done when they were made. A patch of damp on an interior wall is about the only visible sign that this is now a building to be preserved rather than one that is still regularly used.

Back in Belgrade, there's at least one other Meštrović sculpture in Kalemegdan Park. I'd read about this, but it still catches me by surprise as

I pass the short avenue of topiaried, cone-shaped yews in which it's set. It's a monument to the French soldiers who died in what later became Yugoslavia during the First World War. The monument was built to acknowledge the probable fact that without those French war dead Yugoslavia might not actually have come into existence at all. Rebecca West describes it as a 'figure bathing in a sea of courage,'[13] but this figure doesn't look like a bather at all, even though in its proportions and its bulk, the outstretched limbs, there's a flavour of Picasso's painting from 1922, 'Women Running on the Beach'. What it does resemble is a huge and impossibly heavy cloaked figure, who seems to be stepping into some great wind, the huge folds of a cloak billowing out behind, through an atmosphere and a gravity impossibly heavier than our own, as if the thin, clear air that's blowing the last autumn leaves off the trees in Kalemegdan is too thin to support its weight. Below, on either side of the substantial plinth, there is a shallow and stylized bas-relief of infantry-men marching in close formation, their rifles pointing into the same wind. A legend carved on the back of the plinth reads: '*Volimo Francusku kao što je ona nas volela. 1914–1918*', which means, 'We love France as she loved us.'

As I leave the fortress, crossing the drawbridge again, the park is fuller than it was when I arrived. This glorious day in late autumn is already as hot as a summer's afternoon in England. People are reading in the sun, propped up in little nooks they've found in the battlements; teenagers are posing on the ramparts for photos, the buildings of Novi Beograd blue and hazy behind them. Elderly men, sitting and chatting on benches, eyes front, use their walking sticks to point at something only they can see, to set some-thing straight or make a point. Pigeons strut along the paths, picking at grit, flapping out from under foot, while sparrows bob and dart between the trees. Four busts set on a marble pediment beneath the castle walls, which had been vandalized, smashed, last time I was here in Belgrade, have been restored, and a small bouquet of long-dead flowers, wrapped in plastic, is laid on the white stone beside them. Smoke is curling from the chimney of a half-ruined building that looks ancient, seeming to be the relic of a previ-ous era, but appears to be the park-keeper's shed.

Everyone has come out for a walk: mothers pushing pushchairs, couples, an elderly man with a young woman who carries a yellow balloon. A police car, a four-wheel drive, slides past, and the young policewoman in the passenger seat turns to watch me writing. I try not to look at her sunglasses; I don't want to run the risk of catching her eye.

Interspersed through the trees are busts of 'the great and the good'. There are so many to choose from that I stop at random and look at one more closely. The name, 'Djura Daničić', and the dates, '1825–1882,' have been retouched slightly messily in gold paint. He's ornamented with streaks of bird droppings. Daničić was a philologist and educator, one of the researchers who worked on the formalization of the Serbian and Croatian languages (which would become, for a while, the Serbo-Croat language) during the mid-19th century. Daničić was a supporter and defender of the work of Vuk Karadžić, the writer who'd done most to formalize the language(s) of the South Slavs as they began their struggle for independence by reasserting national identities that had been subsumed by empire. Djura Daničić was also the head of Serbia's National Library from 1856 to 1859 and defined a 'collection policy' for the library that stated that it should include not only every book published in Serbian, but also every book published about Serbia or Serbian culture anywhere in the world.

On the footpath near the bust of Daničić is a popcorn stand that appears to be unmanned, but a man I'd seen out of the corner of my eye and assumed was sleeping on a nearby bench is obviously keeping an eye on it. He quickly gets up when someone approaches, scampers over, while wiping his hands on his trousers, and pops out from behind it as if he'd been there all the time. Other benches are turned into temporary market stalls. Though, the old women are no longer selling lace anti-macassars and table-cloths with *'Beograd'* knotted into the lace, as they had been when I was here in September 2001, but gloves, scarves and hats for the winter that, impossible though it seems, is just around the corner. Men are selling stamps, old coins and bank notes, and plastic-laminated pictures of the former Bosnian Serb leader and fugitive Radovan Karadžić.

I join the crowd waiting for a tram to pass, then cross and walk back into town along the pedestrianized shopping street of Knez Mihailova Street. I stop for a slice of *pizza s pečurkama*, pizza with mushrooms, at the *pekara* on the corner where half the city seems to have come for lunch. I eat standing at one of the tall round tables that are put out on the pavement and watch the traffic go past, the odd punk rocker or junk-shop New-Waver among the smartly dressed office workers and the labourers: occasional glimpses of bohemia. Last time I was here I bought protest postcards and saw stalls selling war memorabilia, which people seemed happier to part with their cash for than to give it to the veterans begging or swinging themselves along the street on crutches. This has all disappeared, at least for today.

In my room I open the windows and turn on the TV. I switch to B92, the television channel that grew from the once dissident student radio station, in time to see adverts for British and American bands that are visiting Belgrade in the coming weeks: the Tindersticks and Blondie, only two of the many international acts that now regularly visit this city.

The commercial break ends and the programme resumes: the daily live transmission from the International Criminal Tribunal at The Hague. It's almost too abrupt, this transition from pop songs to the courtroom where Milošević is on trial. The proceedings being televised today are concerned with the massacre of seven or eight thousand Bosnian Muslim men (estimates vary, but these are the usual figures cited) from the UN's 'safe area' around Srebrenica. The tribunal resembles a modern office. It's neat and there are computers everywhere, white walls and tasteful furniture. It's not at all like the footage of crowded war crime tribunals in Nuremberg – the closing stages of which Rebecca West covered for the *Telegraph* – after the Second World War.

Slobodan Milošević, who refused representation in the court until it was made mandatory, is cross-examining a witness, Lieutenant Colonel Franken, who was one of the deputy commanders of the Dutch Battalion that was protecting Srebrenica. Some videos are about to be shown as evidence. The contextual comments being made by Mr Nice (the prosecutor's real name) are hard to concentrate on, as there's a time lag on the dubbed translation. I'm finding it hard to listen in two languages, but what they're talking about is how the Dutch Battalion, or 'DutchBat', seem to have lost control of its posting at Srebrenica and was forced to move, with a large number of refugees, to a 'compound' at Potočari, a village just to the north. With only 200 troops, DutchBat was hopelessly outnumbered and the 'safe area' (rather than 'safe haven') policy was not vigorously supported by other UN members. DutchBat is reported to have had access to only about 16 per cent of the arms and supplies that even this small number of troops would normally expect to need, but was still charged with protecting about 30,000 civilians, most of whom were refugees. All the while the Dutch soldiers were being threatened with being shot at, both in and outside the compound, by Bosnian Serb forces of the VRS (Vojska Republike Srpske, the Army of Republika Srpska), if the UN didn't stop the few tentative air strikes that were taking place elsewhere. Some Dutch soldiers had even been taken prisoner. The DutchBat troops had barely enough food and water for themselves, while the so-called 'compound' was actually an area marked off with red-and-white tape, and, as events demonstrated, there was nothing secure about it.

Aerial photographs are shown to the court, 'white oblongs'[14] pointed out. These are the buses that were being brought in by the VRS to take people away once the civilians had been divided up. The women and children were put onto the buses, while the men were being 'processed' in some way in a building referred to as the 'white house'. General Ratko Mladić had told DutchBat that this was in order that the men could be checked to see if they were 'war criminals'.[15]

In his alarm, Lieutenant Colonel Franken started to write down the names of as many of these 'prisoners of war', the men in Potočari, as he could, and faxed the lists[16] to The Hague and to other UN personnel at Tuzla, before being made aware that the Bosnian Serbs considered 6,000 of the civilians there to be 'prisoners of war'. By the time events overran him Franken had managed to note down the names of just 251 of them.

Some of the exhibits that are shown to the court include video clips. It's not clear who's behind the camera: the tapes were allegedly purchased 'in Serbia' by journalists from a Dutch current affairs programme.[17] The footage shows meetings between General Mladić and Colonel Karremans, the Dutch commander, in the Hotel Fontana in Bratunac, a town just north of Srebrenica itself. These few minutes of video evidence are included in the transmission from the courtroom in The Hague.

The Dutch soldiers (and the Dutch government, which in fact resigned *en masse* over the catastrophic failure of DutchBat to prevent a genocidal massacre) received more than their share of blame for the atrocities that took place at or around Srebrenica, and this seems to go hand in hand with the popular mistake of referring to the status of Srebrenica as a 'safe haven' when actually it was a 'safe area', which was something quite different. Jan Willem Honig and Norbert Both remind us that:

> The difference under international law was that safe havens need not depend on consent of the warring parties and could be enforced, while safe areas were based on consent.[18]

International troop numbers were also at issue, with estimates of how many would be needed to protect the safe areas ranging from a 'heavy option' of 34,000, to a 'light option' of 7,600. The safe area policy that was agreed involved opting for the latter. But even this began to seem an unrealistically high figure as, one by one, for various reasons, and with the exception of the Dutch, the UN's member states declined to commit troops to defend the safe area. The initial Dutch deployment was of only 570 troops, but even this total was depleted by the time of the massacre, and even the light arms that had been designated as appropriate for such a peacekeeping mission did not all arrive.[19]

The Dutch were hopelessly outnumbered then, and under-resourced, and, having pushed for Srebrenica to become a protected enclave, they found that no other countries would commit troops in support of that. Ultimately, the 'safe area' status (again, rather than 'safe haven') meant that no one else was obliged to. In effect it seems the other UN member states hung the Dutch out to dry. Eventually, increasingly desperate, the Dutch persuaded Ukraine to commit troops to Srebrenica and relieve the Dutch personnel in mid-July. In the event the safe area didn't last long enough for this to happen.

Despite the fact that I'm watching the video evidence on a fuzzy little hotel TV, watching a screen within a screen, and having to concentrate incredibly hard above the noise from the builders outside, this short clip is one of the most disturbing things I have ever seen. One segment shows video footage of a meeting attended by a number of VRS and DutchBat officers, and Bosnian Muslim civilians.[20] During the meeting, which took place late on the evening of 11 July 1995, General Mladić says that the civilians can '*survive or disappear*', that they have until 10 am the next morning to tell him which they want.

On the live transmission Milošević makes a comment about this, just before it's shown, and refers to a document[21] that the court is addressing and that summarizes the content of the clip. He says that the document is wrong, that Mladić is making a slip of the tongue, that he didn't mean to say 'to survive' (*opstati*) but 'to stay' (*ostati*); that the words are very similar and that the next time he says this, it's quite clear that he's saying *ostati*.[22] In other words, Milošević is seeming to imply, this was not a threat.

In the footage Mladić appears to be more than just imposing, he's at the height of his power, and his awareness of this power is terrifying. Sitting there at the table, his meaty arms folded across his chest, he's practically bursting out of his uniform. Civilian representatives have been asked to attend the meeting, and one is sitting just to the right of Karremans, facing Mladić. He's a small man, a teacher called Nesib Mandžić. Mladić is addressing this comment (whether 'survive or disappear' or 'stay or disappear'), not to the Dutch Colonel Karremans but to Mandžić, the civilian. He reinforces the severity of the comment by then saying that 'the future of his people [is in Mandžić's] hands,' that 'the Muslim army [should] turn themselves in,'[23] and giving him the deadline of 10 am the following day. You can see the terror in Mandžić's eyes:[24] he can barely speak.

But that's the whole point. Anything Mandžić might say in this meeting would not be of any interest to Mladić. It's clear that Mandžić is not in any position to negotiate for himself, let alone for the 30,000 civilians trapped in Potočari. He couldn't possibly speak for the remaining members of the Bosnian Army who are in the compound. He certainly couldn't speak for the Dutch peacekeepers who are being held hostage at this point. Colonel Karremans looks afraid himself. Mandžić is not even in a position to report back the content of the meeting to the 30,000 people in Potočari. But even if Mandžić were in a position to do all of those things, he'd still be unable to speak, because he's not there to speak. He's there to listen and to be terrified. Besides, whatever Milošević is saying here in courtroom one at The Hague, when he picks up on this issue of translation, this possible slip of the tongue, whether Mladić meant 'survive' or 'stay', is not the point. The truly terrifying part of the sentence is the word 'disappear'.

Everyone who has had any access to news media since that date knows roughly what the word 'disappear' came to mean the very next day, 12 July 1995. Whatever Milošević says about a slip of the tongue, whether Mladić was saying 'survive or disappear' or 'stay or disappear', doesn't really matter, because 'disappear' was the operative word, and seven or eight thousand men between the ages of 16 and 60 were very precisely 'disappeared'.

Srebrenica is no longer just the name of a town but the name, now, of the worst single civilian massacre in Europe since the Second World War. In June 2005 the Srebrenica-Potočari Foundation published the best list it had been able to assemble of those who were killed at Srebrenica, and this lists some 8,106 men reported missing.[25]

Yet the *fact* of Srebrenica isn't the issue here at The Hague today, and it's not General Ratko Mladić who is on trial. He's still 'at large' at the time of writing. The question for the Tribunal would be whether Milošević was, at the time of the massacre, effectively in command of the VRS forces. They appear insignificant next to the shock of the videos, but there are one or two little asides during today's proceedings that are used by the prosecution to suggest that there was some command structure linking the Serbian government in Belgrade and the VRS troops, even though there had been a serious rift[26] between the Milošević government and the Republika Srpska leadership of Radovan Karadžić since the previous year. One of these asides is when Franken confirms that, when DutchBat was having trouble getting access to vehicles from Serbia itself, one of Mladić's men was able to clear that access 'with a single phone call'.[27] In contrast, a few months later Ian Traynor reported in *The Guardian* a general concern that Milošević had 'left no smoking gun' to link him with Srebrenica, and thus with the charges of genocide and complicity with genocide.[28]

It would seem, however, that VRS personnel were not the only troops who took part in the massacre. There is an ongoing controversy about Greek volunteers being present; a Greek flag being raised over the town once it had been overrun. During June 2005 a short video tape was shown at The Hague, and was also released to Serbian and international media. This new clip purports to show members of an elite Serbian (rather than Bosnian Serb) military force known as the Skorpions actually participating in the massacre, executing a small group of Bosnian Muslim boys and men. Within a day of its broadcast most of the former Skorpions who are shown on the tape had been arrested. The lengthy and complex process of liaison needed to identify these military personnel and track them down had evidently all been undertaken before it was screened. It's been suggested that the timing of the release of this videotape had itself also been orchestrated to take place during the run up to the tenth anniversary of the massacre, in order to prepare elements of the Serbian population for the imminent arrest of Ratko Mladić. Yet that arrest has still not happened.

The domestic climate does seem to have changed, however. Since the beginning of 2005 the official line coming out of Serbia and Montenegro about cooperation with The Hague has been backed up by a significant number of arrests and extraditions, though always it seems that the two most wanted are not among them. In fact a number of notional deadlines for the arrest of Mladić and Radovan Karadžić have come and gone during 2005, following a catalogue of (so far) failed attempts.[29] The events marking the tenth anniversary of the Srebrenica massacre on 11 July 2005 offered one such deadline, although the date passed without an arrest. Later in the year, on 22 November, the celebration of the anniversary of the signing of the Dayton Peace Accords was another. With both of these dates slipping past and no news of any arrest forthcoming, attention shifted to the next of these notional deadlines, 12 December 2005. On that day the Serbian daily newspaper *Večernje Novosti* quoted anonymous government sources who reportedly said that the whereabouts of Ratko Mladić was now known and that he would be arrested by the end of the year.

Chapter Seven
Belgrade IV (2003)

I telephone the novelist Vladimir Arsenijević to make sure that he's still expecting me at around seven o'clock. Yes, sure, he says, but then he asks if I can ring him in half an hour to confirm, to let him know that I'm on my way. I make a note to do this, but somehow it slips my mind once I've gone to get some supplies from a supermarket in a side street off Trg Republike: two bottles of T'ga za Jug and a bag of 'Bombay mix'. I'd been wondering if cheap Macedonian wine could really be as good as I remembered it being. I'm reminded of a scene in *Black Lamb and Grey Falcon* where Constantin rhapsodizes about some local wine and Rebecca West's chauffeur Dragutin dismisses him by saying simply, 'I think you must have been young and happy when you drank it, for the wine here is not very good. But we can try it.'[1]

I hail a cab by the National Theatre to take me to Vlada's place, which is quite a way down Bulevar Revolucije (Revolution Boulevard). It's about seven o'clock by now, and it isn't till I'm in the cab that I remember that I was supposed to phone again. The traffic is quite heavy, as it's still the rush hour, so the taxi crawls past the Parliament building and the main post office. To the right of the cab, at the corner of Kneza Miloša, are the usual kiosks, the official and, more often, unofficial newsagents and tobacconists that are scattered across the city, clustered at street corners. Some of these kiosks are now seen as design classics. One particular range of modular, moulded-plastic kiosks known as model K-67, which were designed in the late 1960s by a Slovenian architect named Saša J. Maechtig, are included in the contemporary design collection at the Museum of Modern Art in New York. They are not unlike slightly enlarged telephone boxes, with a canopied serving hatch on one side. The standard moulded fittings can be adapted to provide hatches, doorways, windows, or to 'dock' (the space-age terminology is not inappropriate) with other K-67s in order to create bigger facilities for shops, or ticket offices at bus stations. I've seen K-67s in red, blue, orange, yellow and white plastic.

There's even a website for K-67 fans[2] that has been set up by a group of Dutch architects called Public Plan. It catalogues photographs of these K-67 kiosks from all over eastern Europe and beyond, even as far afield as Japan. K-67s were also, apparently, among the most successful exports of the former Yugoslavia. Fans can upload photos to the site and they are added to the archive, which also includes links to documentation of K-67s being used in contemporary art.

During the era of corruption and instability in the 1990s the number of kiosks on the streets of Belgrade increased enormously, and they were not all design classics like Maechtig's K-67, creating a proliferation of informal urban architecture that is such a feature of the Belgrade streets that one can't imagine the city without them. It almost feels as if this motley collection of temporary structures must have always been here. A group of artists called Stealth have been documenting the growth of this social and architectural phenomenon. They exhibited their archive in New York during February 2004.[3] They use photography to document how these kiosks can sometimes literally take root in a location through the secret excavation of basements beneath street level. I imagine the owners of these kiosks emptying handfuls of dirt from their trouser pockets, as if in a version of *The Great Escape*. Some kiosks even gained attached living quarters and other extensions.

As the cab pulls up at the traffic lights I notice that one of the kiosks on the corner is cordoned off with blue-and-white police tape. There has been a move here in Belgrade to outlaw the illegal kiosks, but there has been some resistance. The woman who runs this particular one had been in the news a couple of days previously. She'd barricaded herself into the kiosk in protest at the new measures, and had threatened to blow herself up if the authorities tried to move her and her kiosk. There must have been a police raid in the meantime, because as our cab pulls away I can see that the kiosk is deserted.

As we drive down Bulevar Revolucije we enter a different zone of the city. The imposing buildings of state have given way to a more residential inner-city architecture. It's a busy street, with lots of activity on the pavements, lots of kiosks, of course, and all kinds of shops. It has a slightly New York flavour to it, like 4th or 5th Avenue way down by 7th or 8th Street, or like the livelier bits of Shepherd's Bush in London.

Vladimir Arsenijević is called 'Vlada' by his friends, the ending of the Serbian masculine diminutive being 'a' rather than the Croatian 'o', as in 'Boro'. This small cultural distinction has itself been used by critics of Radaković's writing, who have referred to him as 'Bora' Radaković, as if this might be sufficient criticism of his writing. Vlada Arsenijević, then, is one of Serbia's best-known novelists. Translations of his writings have been published around the world since he wrote *U Potpalublju*, the first contemporary Serbian anti-war novel, back in the early 1990s, a novel that won the then Yugoslav equivalent of the Booker Prize. Translated as *In the Hold* when it was published in English, it maps the fragmentation of friendships and society at the beginning of the war, through conscription, draft-dodging, petty crime, heroin addiction and, no less grim, natural causes. It's fairly inevitable that it would be quite a dark story.

Vlada lives in a street that's about two or three miles down the Boulevard. The cab driver can't find it for ages and has to stop a colleague at a street corner to ask directions. We make it eventually and I knock on the door.

Vlada appears after a couple of seconds. He's tall and dressed in the universal slacker mode – old T-shirt and combat trousers – and peering through his glasses. The ponytail he had the last time I saw him has gone. 'Hey, Tony,' he says. 'Great to see you. Come in! Come in!' Then, as I follow him through the hallway into the living room, he says, 'Wow I wasn't expecting you. I thought you were going to phone?'

I can see that Vlada is in the middle of packing; there are clothes draped and drying above all the heaters. He's flying to Berlin early the next morning to speak at a conference called 'Landscapes Undergoing Radical Change', which is bringing together writers from central and eastern Europe to look at the symbolic geography of the region in the context of EU enlargement. It's completely mystifying how Vlada exudes such a relaxed air. It belies his manic energy. He doesn't sit still for a minute until about two hours after I arrive, when his daughter finally goes to bed, but even when he's doing ten things at once, talking all the while, as he is for most of these two hours, he appears to be ambling along. It's as if he's moving in slow motion through his own life, in order to cram more things in.

I'm fortunate to catch him on a night off, although with the imminent trip to Berlin, a new book in progress, a daughter to look after and a publishing house to run, time off is obviously something that he rarely has, if ever. He offers tea, switches the volume off on the TV, introduces me to his partner and to his daughter, checks her homework, sorts through some things that he's taking with him to Germany, shows me the latest books he is publishing, and puts some music on, all in one smooth traverse across the room.

Rende, his publishing house, was set up immediately after the fall of Milošević to take advantage of the liberalization of the media that followed. *Rende* means 'grater': its publications are designed to be abrasive. It publishes new writers from across the former Yugoslavia and beyond, with an emphasis on literary and experimental fiction, as well as pop culture. The latest is a novel by a cult rapper from Zemun called Voodoo Popeye. Vlada pulls a stack of books out of the bag he's packing for Berlin to show it to me and puts one of Voodoo Popeye's CDs on.

I've been unable to avoid a fair amount of Serbian hip-hop on TV, though what I've seen so far has been largely derivative of US 'gangsta rap' – all gold chains, jacuzzis and skinny, bikini-clad models wiggling their behinds. It's a style that, transplanted to Belgrade, seems to feed directly off the four-wheel-drive-and-an-Uzi glamour of the sanctions-busting gangsters and militia leaders of Belgrade in the 1990s – many of whom were shot dead in the lobbies of the hotels where they held court. Arkan is probably the most famous example. Voodoo Popeye is different, Vlada tells me. His lyrics aren't about girls and guns. It's eccentric material, 'bedroom music', in the sense that a lot of the music that the late John Peel used to play on his show on BBC Radio 1 was made by teenage boys playing with drum machines and samplers in their bedrooms.

Voodoo Popeye raps quickly, testing my knowledge of Serbian to its limits. There are odd lines that I'm able to follow, such as *'Mi smo slobodni i zgodni/ Kao Del i Rodni...'* ('We're free and handsome,/Like Del and Rodney...'). It sounds smoother in Serbian obviously, and it rhymes, but it's funny how big *Only Fools and Horses* is in Serbia. It's massively popular. It is a British TV series, but the subject matter is hardly foreign to an international audience, let alone audiences in the former Yugoslavia. Maybe it's partly the 'ducking and diving' of the characters, their getting by on dreams rather than on money. Or that the fictional Peckham tower block, Nelson Mandela House, where Del and Rodney live with their Uncle Albert, belongs to a school of architecture that is ubiquitous across the former Yugoslavia and therefore doesn't evoke quite the same class-based prejudice that it does among some viewers in Britain. If *Only Fools and Horses* portrays a way of life that largely no longer exists in Britain, across the Yugoslav successor republics almost everyone lives in a small flat in an apartment block or a tower block with older generations of their family.

Vlada returns with mugs of tea and two plates of cakes, and skips the CD forward to a track he likes, which is a good example of Voodoo Popeye's eccentricity. To the tune of 'Lollipop' he lists all his shoes, but in Belgrade slang, which, like the slang of the Paris suburbs, operates by switching around the order of syllables in words. It's impossible to translate into English, but he's just rapping this list: sandals, trainers, slippers…

I notice that there's a note of the print-run inside the back cover of Voodoo Popeye's book: 500 copies. I'd noticed this in bookshops too. Vlada tells me that it's the relic of some Communist-era print tax. 'You don't have to publish that information in the UK?' he asks.

Vlada tells us about another Rende's publishing projects, which has grown from a long-standing collaborative web project. It's an encyclopaedia of the popular culture of the former Yugoslavia, called *Leksikon Yu-mitologije* (*Dictionary of Yu Mythology*). The project had existed as a website for a number of years, and was open for anybody to post entries onto, and hundreds of people had done so. Their entries, ranging from short notes to lengthy essays, cover all aspects of seemingly inconsequential popular culture, but precisely those aspects of Yugoslav life that have now vanished. The website and now the book contain myriad entries on everything from the TV series *Smogovci* – a comedy shown in the 1980s that followed the exploits of a family of brothers who lived in a Zagreb tower block and were bringing themselves up in the absence of their dead father while their mother worked as a *Gastarbeiter* ('guest worker') in Germany – to the boxer Mate Parlov, who won an Olympic gold medal and in the 1970s was Yugoslavia's equivalent to Mohammed Ali: while he is still described in Croatia as 'the most successful boxer of all times',[4] elsewhere he's largely forgotten.

The catalyst for Vlada publishing the *Leksikon* was when he mentioned Parlov's name to one of the younger members of staff at the publishing company who had absolutely no idea who Mate Parlov was. Vlada is insistent that this is not an exercise in so-called '*ostalgie*', that 'nostalgia for the East' that sustains, for example, the retro night clubs in the former East Berlin, where the staff dress as border guards and serve vintage brands of food and drink in a strange fetishization of period detail. For him it's an important social project that has grown out of a collective desire to at least document cultural phenomena that were completely taken for granted in Tito's Yugoslavia, but have already been forgotten by a generation that came of age during the wars of the 1990s. 'It's completely democratic, you know. It's all what people have posted on the website, what people want to remember. It's also very funny.'

Others are less convinced. A Serbian friend in London says, 'Of course it's about nostalgia. The 1970s and 1980s were like a golden age in Yugoslavia – people now in their 30s or 40s grew up with money, with the possibility of international travel, with access to music, film, whatever. All of that disappeared for the next generation. Yes, there is cultural value to the project, but we can't pretend it's not also about this privileged genera-tion getting sentimental about a time when life seemed much simpler.'

Vlada tells us that the *Leksikon* is to be published in book form on 25 May. The date is significant, of course: 25 May was Tito's birthday.

The conversation turns to how I've spent my day in Belgrade. I mention that I'd watched B92, and switched on just in time to see the Srebrenica segment of the Milošević proceedings, including 'the Mladić video'. Vlada has seen it too.

We begin talking about Sarajevo after this, because the only other doc-umentary footage I can think of that's at all comparable to the Mladić video, in actually portraying Mladić or Radovan Karadžić *in situ* and at the time – rather than in more managed and conventional bits of news footage of photo-opportunities, speeches, press conferences – is the film director Pawel Pawlikowski's BBC documentary *Serbian Epics*.

'Ah, yes!' says Vlada. 'The film with Limonov! I remember it. That was brilliant film – total indictment of all of them. The scene where Limonov is sniping – he was total pariah after that. But you know before the war, like in the 1980s, Limonov was an absolute cult novelist in Serbia. He was seen like kind of contemporary Charles Bukowski, you know, or Céline. Everyone was totally into his work.'

I remember from conversations at the time that *Serbian Epics* was a per-sonal affair, that it had come about because Pawlikowski knew and loved

Yugoslavia, and had friends there. He reminds me that, 'on the surface it was presented as a pretty straightforward affair, while for me it was a multi-layered mystery that I wanted to get closer to and explore.' Film-making for Pawlikowski is 'anti-journalism' which can throw reality into some kind of relief. To an extent he was reacting to the fact that the media were 'flattening' the war, repeating the same ideas over and over again. He and his crew spent several weeks in Bosnia-Herzegovina, and captured some of the most extraordinary and disturbing footage to come out of the war. Pawlikowski tells me that while he and his crew were in Bosnia, 'it was a permanent struggle to get near the man himself. It wasn't an "interview" film. I didn't need to be "attached" to Karadžić. I was hunting for significant and revealing scenes. We struggled and struggled and eventually got three very short bites at the cherry.' When it was broadcast in 1992 the criticism was resounding – the main thrust of it being, absurdly, that to document what Karadžić was doing was to be a collaborator. 'I wanted to make something timeless and universal,' he continues. 'A reflection not just of Balkan nationalism, but all forms of nationalist mythmaking and the ethnocentric reinterpretation of history.' I can still remember scenes in the film such as the 'war cabinet' meeting at which Karadžić and his generals discuss their breaking of the recently imposed 'no fly zone'. Their response – 'We'll just tell them that it's our National Flying Day' – demonstrating the disdain in which they held the international community. The other particularly memorable sequence, the scene that Vlada remembered, showed the once-fashionable émigré Russian novelist Edward Limonov enthusiastically taking a turn on the high-powered machine gun to snipe at the streets below. The novelist Miljenko Jergović, who now lives in Zagreb, was living in Sarajevo at this time. When he saw Pawlikowski's film Jergović realised that the date of Pawlikowski's filming coincided with the day he'd been sitting and writing in his Sarajevo flat and a salvo of bullets had crashed through the window and embedded themselves in the wall above his head. Jergović's response was to write a short story entitled 'Limonov is Shooting at Me'. Limonov is not so well-known in Britain, but he had been a great hope of Russian literature who had emigrated to the USA and written a nihilistic, semi-autobiographical 'beat' novel called *It's Me, Eddie.* Since then he'd become more interested in right-wing politics, and at the time of Pawlikowski's filming he'd just returned from a stint fighting with the VRS elsewhere in Bosnia.

When I'm back in London, I telephone Pawlikowski to ask him about Limonov. He describes him as a 'kind of self-styled Hemingway of the right', and says that it was bizarre, because when Limonov went to Bosnia to offer his support to the VRS and to fight with them, he was just about the only international 'intellectual' on their side. Karadžić himself was once a poet, and even now, from wherever he's hiding, he has recently published a novel called *Miraculous Chronicle of the Night* and a collection of his recent verse. But when Limonov appeared in Bosnia in the early 1990s, it was perhaps obvious that Karadžić's leadership would embrace him – an international literary figure! This was, however, in spite of the fact that they were deeply offended by the decadent nihilism and the portrayal of homosexuality in his novel. A scene in which the novel's protagonist performs oral sex on a well-endowed African American in New York was apparently particularly difficult for them to come to terms with. Pawlikowski tells me that when Limonov wasn't in the room members of Radovan Karadžić's team would talk about his writing and shake their heads in bewildered disgust.

More recently Limonov has been the leader of an ultra-fascist party in Russia called the National Bolsheviks, whose emblem is a hammer and sickle inside a white circle on a red background, and whose activities include a mixture of what someone once described to me as 'politics, posing and conceptual art'. In fact Limonov has only recently been released from prison, where he wrote a new novel, though this hasn't been translated yet.

As the title *Serbian Epics* suggests, Pawlikowski's film also traces how the old Serbian epic poems, such as the ones that document the Serbs' defeat at the Battle of Kosovo Polje in 1389, were invoked to suit the increasing nationalist sentiment during the build-up to the war, just as in Croatia Franjo Tudjman used rhetoric about Croatia 'the thousand-year state'. The Serbian epic tradition was necessarily oral, and survived the centuries of oppression by the Ottoman Empire, before being mobilized in the early 19th century when there was need of a literary tradition and a genesis story to back up the Serbian independence movement.

There are shots in Pawlikowski's film of Karadžić sitting playing the *gusle*, a one-stringed instrument played with a bow, and singing some of these epic poems. It's a scene that Karadžić presumably hoped would seem timeless and cast him in heroic mould. Someone once told me that, while the rest of the Southern Slavs think of the *gusle* as a Serbian instrument, in Serbia it's seen more generally as a Montenegrin tradition. More recently, in November 2005, it was widely reported that a bid by an independent organization called the Serbian Cultural Institute for UNESCO World Heritage status to be granted to a collection of field recordings of medieval Serbian poetry was hastily withdrawn after it was discovered that among the historical material were some more contemporary poems, which parodied the original poetic form in order to sing the praises of Radovan Karadžić and Ratko Mladić.

The value of Pawlikowski's film seems clear enough now: it is one of very few records that exists of Karadžić at the height of his power. It's no wonder, then, that segments of this film have also been screened at The Hague, during the proceedings to indict Karadžić *in absentia*.

It must be the talk of politics, conceptual art and posing, but my conversation with Pawlikowski then turns to an art movement called *Neue Slowenische Kunst* (NSK) that emerged in Slovenia when it was still part of the former Yugoslavia, during the post-Tito 1980s.

Comprising an 'art wing' known as Irwin and a 'music wing' (i.e. a band) called Laibach, NSK's work has been described as being concerned with 'analyzing the relation between art and ideology, working on the internationalization of the art scene in Slovenia, linking different media of art'.[5] In plain English, that meant adopting a kind of fascistic fancy dress, which was perhaps intended to expose the nationalistic tendencies that were beginning to be liberated following the death of Tito, as well as Yugoslavia's own fascistic movements, such as Croatia's Ustaše or some of the groups that glorified the Serbian Četniks, as well as the civil wars that had engulfed Yugoslavia during the Second World War but had been 'airbrushed' out of the Tito era's official version of recent history.

Retrospectively, NSK's critics describe an attempt to expose the connections between art and politics by looking backwards. This is referred to as a 'retro principle', used to reappropriate politically sensitive imagery in a country where, at the time, you had to be an officially sanctioned artist to be exhibited abroad. In practice this taboo-breaking reappropriation meant, among other things, wearing very extreme Nazi-like uniforms.

Nearly 20 years later NSK is still active. The group's 'musical wing', Laibach, continues to tour Europe, while the art collective Irwin is still making work and showing it on the international gallery circuit. By coincidence I was in Manchester recently and came across a new exhibition by Irwin.

The exhibition comprised some large colour reproductions of contemporary re-enactments by Irwin of conceptual artworks by a group of artists called Oho, which was active in the former Yugoslavia in the late 1960s and early 1970s. One photograph is of a carefully scored performance, 'Night, Bow, Burning Arrows', which sees two members of the group on either bank of a river – possibly the Sava – letting fly with flaming arrows in set patterns from one bank to the other. It seems Leni Riefenstahl-esque, mock-heroic. Another, 'Wheat and String', shows a piece of rope being stretched across a wheatfield, bending the corn stalks – a crop line, perhaps, rather than a crop circle. A third shows a map of the night sky that's been traced in nightlight candles across the contours of a ploughed field, like a low-tech planetarium, with a white Catholic church in the background.

Elsewhere, archive footage of the original Oho actions, rather than Irwin's reconstructions, is on display. The documentary aspect of these archive works is sometimes more interesting than the actions themselves. One jokey short film that's being screened when I visit the gallery, shows a man in a suit walking briskly through Ljubljana, climbing over increasingly improbable fences and walls that get in his way, eventually scaling a huge castle wall. The tone of this slow-burning joke is mildly funny, but it's the fragmentary views of the city of the time that are really affecting: the Yugo cars parked in the cluttered yards of apartment buildings, the stiffly formal passers-by looking curiously at the camera, the washing hanging on a line.

Slovenia may now have joined the European Union, but the country's secession from the former Yugoslavia in 1991 has left a legacy of domestic problems, which are an uncomfortable reminder of that traumatic period in the region's history. When Slovenia declared its independence from the rest of Yugoslavia in 1991, there were, as you might expect, considerable numbers of people living there whose 'ethnic' or cultural origin was in one of the other Yugoslav nations. They were Serbs, perhaps, or Albanians from Kosovo, Croatians, Bosnians, Macedonians, and there was a large Roma population as well. Shortly after independence the new Slovenian government passed a law that required all citizens who were not ethnic Slovenes to reapply for citizenship. This application process had a strict deadline.

People who didn't apply by a certain date to become citizens of a country that they had already been full citizens of, with historical rights to self-determination, would no longer have a right to citizenship. In their haste to extract themselves from Yugoslavia both Slovenia and Croatia made mistakes, and one of them was to define themselves as the nation states, not of all their citizens, but of their majorities, the Slovenians and the Croatians respectively, thus instantly disenfranchizing sizeable parts of their populations.

In Slovenia many people didn't register in time for the deadline. Some fled; others were perhaps mistrustful of the motives for this re-registration process, and didn't sign because they thought it might lead to a forced 'repatriation' from their own country, or at least expulsion. Others may not have heard about it in time: perhaps they were temporarily out of the country, or they didn't have access to sufficient information about the changes. This is an explanation that seems to be particularly relevant to Slovenia's Roma population. Those who didn't register became non-citizens, no longer entitled to passports or driving licences, to official employment or health care.

In early 2004 there were estimated to be tens of thousands of these 'erased' former citizens living in Slovenia. According to the European Roma Rights Centre:

> government figures from June 2002 [show that] 29,064 persons were erased. However, an internal document of the Minister of Interior from 1996 mentions a number of around 83,000 'new aliens'. According to the Ljubljana-based Helsinki Monitor of Slovenia [HMS], the figures vary from 62,816, which was the figure provided to the HMS by the Ministry of Interior in December 2000, to the HMS's own estimate of 130,000 persons.[6]

More recently there has been significant opposition to the law being repealed, even though it was estimated that retrospectively regranting citizenship *and* financially compensating 'the erased' would have cost far less than it did to hold the referendum on the measure,[7] on 4 April 2004, which resulted in a vote against 'the erased'.

Maybe this result is no surprise, but it should be, because it's still shocking to see that the right-wing opposition campaigned against restitution of citizenship on the basis of its cost, and from the position that the 'erased' don't deserve to be citizens. The result is held to stand in perpetuity, regardless of electoral turnout – which in this case was around 31 per cent. Of course the erased themselves weren't able to vote in this referendum, but something like 95 per cent of an admittedly low turnout voted against restoring citizenship.

But even with the referendum result this issue is not resolved at the time of writing. The referendum may be overruled, and the state of limbo in which these people find themselves may just be perpetuated by endless constitutional arguments. It's extraordinary that, in particular, a resolution of the position of 'the erased' was not one of the transition criteria attached to Slovenia's joining the EU. International press coverage of this complex issue was almost completely absent when coverage could have been used to apply pressure to the Slovenian government to rectify such a bald abuse of human rights. There are obviously a lot of compelling stories competing for column inches in the British press, but all too often it's the proverbial 'skateboarding duck' that gets through: '38,660 Croatians simultaneously [eat an] identical breakfast in bid to set new world synchronized breakfast record'.[8]

In light of the referendum result regarding the 'erased', the most unintentionally potent part of the NSK exhibition in Manchester comes in a section that's devoted to another current project: opening 'embassies' in various cities around the world and issuing 'passports'. The 'erased' may well have finally been rubbed out by the Slovenian electorate (or rather, that section of it that turned out to vote), but it's good to know that, if they want to, they can always get an NSK 'passport', and become part of its transnational and conceptual 'Art State'. It looks as if that might be the only kind of passport they can hope to get, now that this act of 'bureaucratic ethnic cleansing'[9] seems to have been completed and ratified. The file is closed, leaving anything from 18,000 to 130,000 people, depending on the source, with no civil rights whatsoever.

Pawel Pawlikowski tells me that before the war he travelled through different regions of Bosnia which were clearly in the grip of three different nationalisms. 'Only in Sarajevo could you kid yourself that this could be a mature multi-ethnic society.' He visited an exhibition of NSK's art works in an isolated Franciscan monastery near Mostar. 'There were a few Nazis there,' he tells me, 'or there were at that time. Those Croat bits of Bosnia were kind of the heartland of the Ustaše. These monks, I mean, they were sweet, you know, typical monks, drafted from the peasantry, playing football and drinking *šljivovica*, but their political views were extremely nationalistic, as far removed from Christ's teachings as you can imagine. Every day they would pray for the fatherland. I asked them if they prayed for their enemies too, as Christ commanded, and one of them took me aside and said, "You know, don't worry, Bosnia is all going to be Croatian soon."'

Pawlikowski goes on to suggest that he can't help thinking that part of the reason for the build-up to the war was that there was 'no truly responsible dissident intelligentsia responding to the evaporation of Communism in Yugoslavia. None of them carried any authority.' He adds that, 'It's fine to be conceptual artists in a historically empty landscape, but doing that in such a historically loaded landscape was just irresponsible. They were all very cool, you know, these artists, and name-dropping New York galleries, but none of them seemed really seriously engaged. I blame them for the war as much as the idiots who were doing the shooting. I'll never forget those lazy exhibitions they were doing at that time. They were just posing, playing with nationalism and peasant culture, irony all over the shop, wonderful! It was really cool. Seriousness is what was lacking.'

Vlada Arsenijević has, at the time of our meeting, just finished a new novel called *Ishmail*, which tells the story of a young Yugoslav teenager's coming of age in the late 1970s, his discoveries of punk rock and the hitherto secret life of an uncle whose activities as an *avant garde* artist in the 1960s is revealed by an absurd suicide. This novel was written in part in collaboration with other writers and artists. Borivoj Radaković (Boro), the novelist and playwright from Zagreb, who is an expert on the literary cultures of the various Serbian and Croatian dialects, has written dialogue for one of the characters, while elsewhere the novel is illustrated with incredible ink drawings and comic strips by the artist Aleksandar Zograf. 'Zograf' is literally a pen name: 'Its meaning is simply "painter" (or, literally, "the one who makes things alive by drawings"). All of the authors of icons and fresco paintings were adding the word "Zograf" to their first name.'[10]

Comics are called 'strips' in Serbia, and Aleksandar Zograf is a strip artist rather than an icon painter. Everyone seems to know his work, partly because of his e-mails telling his network of friends about his view of NATO's war against Serbia, but I'm interested in what he's doing now.

Aleksandar, or Saša for short, lives in Pančevo, which is on the other side of the Danube, and the river must be crossed by means of a huge iron rail and road bridge. The quickest way to make the journey is to go to 29 Novembar Street in Belgrade, which runs all the way practically from Trg Republike and out of the city along the bank of the Danube river. The street commemorates 29 November 1945, the date on which a new Constitutional Assembly proclaimed the re-formation of Yugoslavia as a 'Federal People's Republic' and abolished the monarchy,[11] following the overwhelming success of the Communists in the first election after the Second World War. The *Leksikon Yu-mitologije* records that this date was not just commemorated by a street name in the former Yugoslav capital, but was also a popular food brand, which produced, among other things, 29 Novembar pasta.

Just by the slipway that leads to Pančevo bridge from 29 Novembar Street there's a real bustle of activity, with cafés, minicab offices, shops selling fishing bait, bus stops, and lots of people milling around and waiting for one of the numerous buses into the city that stop at this point. This is also the place where, if you can catch the eye of the right person and join an unofficial queue that's threaded innocuously through the queues at the official bus stops, you can catch a semi-legal minibus out to Pančevo. They don't leave regularly, just when enough people have assembled to fill the van. You pay your money in advance and sign a piece of paper (perhaps it's a disclaimer of some kind), then all pile in and off you go.

The bridge was, perhaps inevitably, considered a major target during the NATO bombing, and it became the site of many protests during that time. There were nightly vigils there, as well as rock concerts, but in the event it wasn't bombed. Saša Zograf tells me that he saw some NATO officials on television confirming that, as with the Gazela, which crosses the Sava River on the other side of the city, it was the French who vetoed the selection of this bridge as a target for NATO bombing. It's actually one of the few bridges across the Danube that wasn't bombed by NATO, although I find out later that it was itself in fact a replacement for an older bridge that stood on this site and was bombed by the Nazis in 1941.

Saša Zograf is often the main character in his 'strips'. Like this thinly fictionalized version of himself, he is a good-humoured man who wears his dark hair in a kind of pudding-bowl cut, and is softly spoken and rather amusing company.

He shows me through to the room where he works. The radio is on, quietly. The room is cluttered, but still feels incredibly tidy. Everything is in its place, as if we've just come back into a room that has been locked up for ten years, the dust-covers only now taken off. There's a stillness about the room, which is in marked contrast to Vlada's apartment. I can imagine that most of the time the only movement in here is the minute scratching of Zograf's pen on paper.

Zograf's drawing board is set up next to the window; there's a half-finished drawing on it. An arm's reach away are pens and pencils, a pile of scrap paper, parcel tape. Next to the drawing board are a computer, a fax machine, a printer and a scanner. There are framed cartoons on the walls. Every inch of space seems to be used, filled with either heavy dark-wood furniture or the accumulation of a lifetime's worth of culture, most of which has come directly into this room. There are cassettes of John Peel's shows on BBC Radio, and a video of a Jacques Tati feature film. A small tapestry mat, a souvenir of Skopje, the capital of Macedonia, is draped over the back of a chair. 'It's a bizarre souvenir,' Zograf tells me later. The inscription, which you can see if you unfold it, reads 'Skopje until 26 July 1963'. The image woven into the tapestry is of one of the buildings that were destroyed in a major earthquake that happened that year – the year in which Zograf was born. Next to an old typewriter is a globe from 1934 with all the inscriptions in Cyrillic.

When Zograf sits back down at his desk, where he must spend most of the day and night, with the light from the window falling on the side of his face, the scene suddenly resembles a Vermeer painting, one of those tableaux, another variation of woman, table, jug, arranged next to that one window in Delft. I think about the one time I went to The Hague, not to sit in the public gallery during Milošević's trial but to see the 'blockbuster' Vermeer show of the early 1990s – the first time that so many of his paintings (25 out of 35) had been assembled in one place. I remember that as I walked through the crowded galleries of the Maritshuis Museum I started thinking that there might be narratives operating between at least some of these extraordinary paintings. In one of them a woman stands at a table: she's opened a letter and has taken out a pearl necklace. In the next the same woman is wearing the necklace while she writes a letter. Seeing those paintings next to each other, it was as if they were frames in a storyboard, or a comic strip.

Zograf's latest strips are for the Belgrade news magazine *Vreme*, which is well-known here for having been consistently critical of Milošević while he was in power. The strip, a regular feature, is about a different subject each week. The one that he's just finishing now, and that's pinned to his drawingboard, is about people who are positively influenced by the Balkans, people who ignore the pejorative usage of that term, and draw something positive from the region and its cultures. He talks about how his generation was inspired by British culture, particularly the popular music of the late 1970s. It was punk rock and 'new wave' that really excited him. He and his friends all used to read the British music journals *Melody Maker* and the *NME*, and listen to John Peel on the BBC World Service. Zograf tells me about another strand of work he's doing, based on forgotten books that he finds in Pančevo's famous flea market. He uses these historical texts to cast contemporary events in a new light. On his last visit he found some police books from the 1940s that went into prurient detail about the crimes of the time, when everyone was so poor that thieves would steal your shoes, or maybe your pen, your suitcase of clothes and underwear. Nobody had anything else to take. It's funny now, he says, that the criminals are richer than the politicians. 'At least now they're not interested in our underwear and pens, ha!'

Even more recently Zograf has written to tell me that he has turned up two remarkable documents at the flea market. One was a copy of the newspaper *Politika*, dated 6 April 1941, the morning of the Nazi's first massive bombing of Belgrade. Hardly any copies of this particular issue survive. There would have been barely enough time for the papers to roll off the presses before the printers and the rest of the city were bombed. On the same day Zograf also found the memoirs of an anonymous Belgrade journalist in which the last entry is dated 5 April 1941. Gathered together as these documents were, it's not unlikely that the journalist author of the memoirs had hurried home with his copy of what he surely knew was an historic edition of the paper he worked on, but that he didn't survive the bombing.

Zograf is so prolific that the comic and magazine publishers can't keep up with him. Many of the strips that he produces are then self-published: *The Hypnagogic Review* – a diary of the images he sees between sleeping and waking – and improvised collaborations with comic artists from all over the world. He's also a magnetic field for comic activity. Pančevo has recently hosted the Second International Festival of Authors' Comics.

Zograf goes and gets me a copy of the catalogue. There's a story about the comic artists who carried on working in Belgrade during the Nazi occupation from 1941 to 1945, some of whom – but not all – were executed as collaborators when the city was finally liberated. The article is illustrated with reproductions of their strips. Some are fantasy reworkings of Germanic mythology, others are pin-ups or children's comics. Most toed the official anti-Semitic and anti-Communist line that was sanctioned by the Nazis' 'Propaganda Department Southeast'.[12] There's also a reproduction of an ultra-cheaply produced Partisan comic strip, a reminder that the Partisans weren't just a resistance movement, but the mobilization of an entire society, underground, with national and local governments, and a newspaper – *Borba* (Struggle). The Partisan movement was as much about establishing a viable form of government for the moment after liberation as it was about achieving liberation itself.[13] The strip that's reproduced, 'Kapljice', which means 'tiny drops', is about some mischievous little raindrops that together make a mighty storm (presumably), but are frightened by the wind, who rides through the clouds on a great horse.

I have a cup of tea with another writer, called Milena Marković. On the wall by her kitchen door is an amazing framed photograph of Milena's grandmother, who looks very like her. It's a beautiful photograph. She's wearing traditional Montenegrin costume: her face is framed by her long dark hair and a beautiful lace headdress that has coins hanging from it.

Like Vlada Arsenijević, Milena is incredibly energetic. Unlike Vlada, though, there's no casual air about her. Spotting that I've noticed the picture, she tells of her grandmother, who, having been born in a ditch while her family were fleeing from the Bulgarian army, survived numerous migrations and massacres during the Balkan Wars and then the First World War to become an actress. Milena is of a line of strong women.

However, she is anxious about how she and her writing might be represented in the UK. She tells me that she completely disagrees with the exoticization of cultures from small countries and would never participate in anything of that sort. 'We're not exotic at all,' she says, 'just we've been in extreme situations, and we think we're more important than we are. Look,' she says, pointing at the rooftops outside, 'you know what it is like, the further south you go it gets more and more eastern in every way. We are small city, maybe we could be like Atina [Athens]; you know, small eastern city. Would not be so bad.'

Milena talks about much current writing in Belgrade as tending towards the phoney; about writers imposing superficially universal, contemporary or urban themes onto literature, which in her opinion leads to an absence of authenticity. She tells me that she always comes across young writers and playwrights who are trying to write some gritty sexual drama. Because of the current economic and political situation they are actually too poor not to still be living at home, and are writing these 'contemporary' (they think) dramas while still sharing small flats in Novi Beograd with their parents and not having any sex at all. They don't have the confidence to write about these experiences, however, about their own lives. Because of this, she thinks, because these writers copy western dramatic styles without living western dramatic lives, they usually completely miss where the dramatic heart of the writing actually is; they just can't see it. 'You have to be honest in everything,' she tells me, 'in your writing and in your personal life. That is what being grown up means. I have a child, I cannot behave like I did when I was younger.'

There's a measured pessimism about Milena Marković, which is refreshing in several senses. 'Nothing is changing in this country,' she says. 'We are heading for great poverty.'

While she expounds this view an Englishman called Jonathan Boulting arrives. He is wrapped in an improbable number of scarves and jumpers. It takes him a while to unwrap himself. He teaches at the University of Belgrade and has been translating some of Milena's poems into English. He has come to show his translations to Milena. Jonathan talks about how he thinks that Serbian society is more matriarchal than any man here would ever have you believe. Boys, he insists, are brought up to be their mothers' little princes, and this creates an illusion that the power really resides with the men. It's no wonder that it's a matriarchal society, he says, when you consider that a quarter of the population died in the First World War. Who else was going to run the place when so many men were killed?

I telephone Zoran Živković to tell him that I'm on my way. This is not the politician who succeeded Zoran Djindjić, but a Serbian science fiction author.

The Enjub Centar, where Zoran Živković lives, is a mixture of shops and flats directly over the road from the former Chinese Embassy, which itself is surprisingly huge and looks more like a factory than an embassy, or like the headquarters of a multinational that might just as easily be sited in some sprawling business development along the M4 Corridor, one of the international corporate HQs that you see from the train between London and Slough. The Chinese Embassy was hit by two Cruise missiles during the NATO bombing and the damage is still very visible. Živković had covered this for the *Independent* in London. He was the only writer who'd actually been close by when it happened. He tells me that he and his family had been at home when it was bombed. So great was the noise that they thought that their own building had been hit, and that they were done for.

Zoran Živković is dapper, with smartly cropped salt and pepper hair; he's wearing steel-rimmed glasses and a white T-shirt. 'I thought I had better come down and meet you this time,' says Zoran, 'so that next time you will know which way to go. Come, this way.' He ushers me into a lift.

When we're up in his flat, and he's sure that I'm completely comfortable in one of the big leather armchairs, he goes through his files to show me a clipping of his article about the embassy bombing. The flat is immaculate, tastefully decorated rather than haphazardly accumulated, and almost completely lined, from floor to ceiling, with books. I can't imagine anyone living here, and it comes out in conversation that he and his wife and their family actually live in the flat next door, and use this one for work. This room is his office.

His wife's office opens onto this one, and while we chat she is working on a translation of a 'chick lit' novel, *The Devil Wears Prada* by Lauren Weisberger. She pops her head around the door to ask my advice about the occasional word. This seems to be out of politeness, it's a way of reinforcing their considerable hospitality.

Zoran himself sits at the other end of a big coffee table, elbows on the arms of his chair, hands loosely clasped and chin resting on his thumbs; thoughtful, measured. He speaks slowly and precisely, authoritatively. I'd wanted to come and see him because he has quite a reputation on the international science fiction scene. Among other things, he co-edits a respected online literary journal. I remember a conversation I'd had the first time I went to Zagreb, when someone mistakenly thought that H.G. Wells had travelled to Yugoslavia with Rebecca West in the 1930s and had said, 'This place is perfect science fiction.' I'd wanted to ask Zoran whether he agreed with this half-joking statement.

Events have overtaken us, however, and there will not be time to have a conversation. It turns out that just a couple of hours ago Živković learned that he had won an international literary prize, the World Fantasy Award, for one of his books. 'You did not know this?' he asks, surprised.

'*Odlično!*' ('Excellent!') I say, thinking that my detachment from international news media, let alone from science fiction news lists, must be self-evident. 'Congratulations! I had no idea! You must be delighted!'

There's a measured formality about his perfect English, beyond that which comes from speaking a second language, and which I recognize from his writing, which is delightful for this reason. He has a slightly old-fashioned literary style, and writes elegant (if, by the time they're translated into English, slightly ponderous) self-referential novels that remind me very much of Italo Calvino, perhaps, or Stanislaw Lem, and in which, for example, the very book you are holding in your hands and reading might actually also be the narrator and protagonist.

There's a solipsistic aspect to Zoran's writing as well, something born of isolation, and he knows this. 'Yes, you may indeed be asking yourself,' he says, suddenly holding up his right hand because he senses that I'm about to speak, 'what it means to a Serbian writer, a writer from such a small isolated country, a writer who spends all his time in this flat – sitting at this very desk! – to be so honoured with this award.' His hand is still poised to stop me interrupting. 'Well, I have to tell you that I am delighted, of course, to have received such recognition.'

I offer hearty congratulations. I'm delighted for him. He deserves the recognition of his peers in the international science fiction and fantasy community. We perform the universal writers' ritual, a book swap – 'All I ask is that you read it.' He kindly offers to drive me back into town.

Chapter Eight
Belgrade V (2003)

Sunday 16 November 2003 is presidential election day in Serbia. The bar at the Splendid Hotel is more packed than usual, and all the camera crews I've seen checking in over the past couple of days are either hurriedly finishing the last of their omelettes, queueing at the reception desk to hand in their keys, or standing around with their flight cases and bags of cameras and lights. They're getting ready for action, to go off and film the usual election day performances. As with any election there will be numerous stage-managed news opportunities taking place across the city for the rest of the day and night: party leaders casting their own votes with their families, press conferences, pollsters, counts.

The small Turkish coffee doesn't quite kick-start me as I'd hoped. I decide to escape the journalists and camera crews, and go for a walk down the road to Trg Republike, to the café in the Knjižara Beoizlog (Beoizlog bookshop), and find something stronger – a double espresso.

There's not much sign of the elections on the streets, apart perhaps from a few more police than usual, and one or two soldiers standing at street corners. There are also camera crews walking around, looking at their maps, talking on their mobiles. They look lost.

I'd been meaning to go back to the bookshop anyway. I'd kicked myself for not buying any books in Serbian last time I was here, or any in Croatian when I was in Zagreb. Croatian, Serbian: no longer Serbo-Croat, though the only differences between the two are academic to the beginner, and until recently were more the reflection of small though significant dialectical variations. More recently the languages have diverged through legislated change, which has seen the Croatian government introducing anachronisms and neologisms, and some Germanic constructions in order to reinforce both the cultural connection with the medieval Croatian civilization and the distinction from Serbian. However, the most noticeable substantial difference between the literatures of these two countries is one of price. Quite simply, books in Croatia are very expensive, while books in Serbia are cheap.

Beoizlog is bustling. The first thing I see in the children's section is a pocket-sized hardback edition of *Mali Princ*, a translation of Antoine de Saint-Exupéry's *Le Petit Prince* (*The Little Prince*).

Looking up I notice a tiny old woman come into the café where I've found a table and spread out my things. She looks unbelievably poor, and her clothes are worn and greasy. She doesn't have shoes on, just rags wrapped around her feet and, judging from her posture, her frailty, the tiny bowlegged steps she's taking on the sides of her feet, I guess that she could be in her 80s or 90s. She's holding a small cardboard folder and it's obvious that she hasn't come here to buy a coffee. Instead she makes her way slowly around the tables at the other end of the café. At each one she hands over the folder, which I can see is actually a makeshift portfolio full of extremely faint drawings on sheets of very thin, cheap paper. Some people are embarrassed and shake their heads, or wave her on. Others leaf through the portfolio as if they were connoisseurs or collectors in the print room of a gallery in Cork Street, back in London, discussing which one they'd like. A woman holds two up side by side so that she and her companion can make an informed choice. Of these two pictures, the one that I can see, albeit faintly, looks like a 'Vorticist' drawing of an apple tree, executed in bold lines with a red pencil, all angular outlines of clumps of leaves decorated with lozenge-shaped fruits, perhaps apples or plums. The drawing is boldly shaded and, even if the cheap coloured pencil doesn't do justice to her line, it's obvious even from here that she's a draughtswoman. The drawing is quite beautiful. The couple eventually choose this one and hand over a few very low-denomination notes.

She has the appearance of a ghost, this artist selling her work for the equivalent of a few pence. She looks over at the area where I'm sitting, and I put *Mali Princ* aside to smile and beckon her over, pointing at her portfolio, but she hasn't seen me and turns for the door. I'm anxious to see her drawings, talk to her, buy the whole portfolio. How much could it cost?

I wonder how her drawings would reproduce, and whether I could use them here, in this book. They could be dotted throughout these pages like

Cora Gordon's little pen and ink drawings in *Two Vagabonds in the Balkans*: 'The Gipsies', 'Turkish Interior', 'Serbian Railway Carriage'. I wish that I hadn't spread out all my things on the table. It takes me an age to pack everything and, because I'm rushing to catch her before she reaches the door, I drop my notebook, and my pen rolls under the chair. I throw on my coat and stuff everything in my bag, then go and pay at the counter before turning to catch her up. I'd caught sight of her shutting the door behind her a few seconds ago, as I was trying to catch the proprietor's eye and settle, but by the time I've got my change there's no sign of her. I walk briskly through the café towards the door, thinking that she can't have gone far at that speed, but when I get there and step out into the fresh air of a still relatively quiet Trg Republike she is nowhere to be seen. I walk quickly round the square a few times, looking for her among the few shoppers and standing on tip-toe to see further down Knez Mihailova Street. She has completely vanished.

Instead, I stroll a hundred yards up to the taxi rank just where Terazije curves around into Kolarčeva. I give the address in Novi Beograd, and soon I'm crossing the Sava and being driven down Jurija Gagarina Street. I recognize a chicken restaurant, a line of shops and the tram platforms in the middle of the dual carriageway. This is the turning for the Gandijeva district, named after Mahatma Gandhi himself, a series of low-rise apartment blocks set alongside parkland and the Sava River.

There's a low winter sun, and red and yellow leaves are still on the trees. A beautiful golden light catches on the tiled concrete and some of the windows in the upper floors of the buildings. The road ends with a gate and some trees, a red-and-white-striped radio mast, beyond which is the Sava, but we turn left into Gandijeva before this. A few more turnings and we're pulling up outside a five-storey apartment building, alongside parked cars, Yugos and a Volkswagen Beetle. The upper storeys with their yellow awnings are visible through birch trees.

I'm spending election day in Novi Beograd. As I get out of the taxi I bump into Ivan, a friend and near-neighbour of Gordana Stanišić's. He tells me that a lot of people are going to go to the polling station together and perhaps I should come too. Ivan is an editor and he works for *Borba*, the one-time Partisan newspaper, which is now published from a big grey office building on Trg Nikole Pašića, just around the corner from the Splendid Hotel. The day before, when I'd walked past the office, there were photocopied notices taped to the glass doors at street level, declaring: *'Štrajk'* (strike). The paper is currently being privatized, a process that has recently been kick-started with the appointment of a new managing director who wants to increase efficiency and raise the paper's increasingly woeful sales. There is talk of redundancies and because of the strike there's been no edition on the stands for almost a week. Two days later another newspaper, *Politika,* will report that the police had to raid the *Borba* offices in order to break up the strike and rescue the new MD, who had barricaded himself into his office. The headline, *'Borba u Borbi',* is a great pun on the name of the paper that is worthy of a British tabloid (*'borba'* means *'struggle'*), and translates as 'Struggle at *Struggle'.*

I've been promised lunch – some home-made *gibanica* – and I can smell it cooking, the homely smell of *kajmak,* as we enter the apartment.

The table is laid in the narrow dining room next to the kitchen, and a TV on the dark wood sideboard is tuned to a news channel. When it comes the *gibanica,* with its layers of flaky pastry filled with cheese and egg, is astonishingly delicious and incredibly filling. It's washed down with drinking yoghurt in china mugs, then the *rakija* (brandy) is brought out – some clear *loza.*

While we enjoy lunch one of the presidential candidates, Dragoljub Mićunović, is being interviewed on the television. He's the favourite to win the election, in fact. Mićunović fronts the reform coalition, led by the Democratic Party, so he is pro-Europe and anti-nationalist, standing for the reforms that had been symbolized by Zoran Djindjić when he was the Democratic Party's leader. I'm surprised by Mićunović's appearance. He looks very old; too old to be standing for President, certainly.

Somehow we end up discussing the defining characteristics of the Serbs – something called *inat,* which is usually translated as 'spite', but which, after some thought, Gordana and Ivan decide is maybe more like 'in-spite-of-ness', which is quite different. Ivan comes up with another one, which might sound unlikely to those whose impressions of the country were formed by news coverage during the wars of the 1990s: generosity or, perhaps, hospitality.

Ivan tells me that there's a saying: *'Svakog gosta tri dana dosta',* which means, literally, 'Every guest, three days, enough.' This is less a word of advice to hosts, more what you'd say as a guest when someone asks you to stay longer, as a polite way of refusing the hospitality. Ivan is really laughing: 'We have some great sayings. "Like the rain around Kragujevac" is a good one, it means like you don't get to the point – Kragujevac is this small town surrounded by mountains.'

'Like "beating around the bush,"' I say.

'Yes, that's it – and we have another saying: "to know which bush the rabbit is hiding in" which means you can go straight to the point. *"Govori srpski da te ceo svet razume"* (speak Serbian so the whole world will understand you) is another. I don't know what it means.'

We set off to the polling station, which is in the local primary school. It's only a few minutes walk away. There's a network of paths and narrow roads that crisscross the Gandijeva district, past playgrounds and pizza restaurants. It's a little colder than it had been the day before and a breeze is blowing from the river, which is only a couple of hundred yards away.

As we walk Gordana talks about the day off they had every year for Tito's birthday on 25 May: how a big relay race, with ceremonial batons, was run across the country, and the whole school had to go and wave flags. A friend of hers had recently confessed that as a child he'd wanted more than anything to carry that baton for Tito, that for him at the time it seemed like the pinnacle of human existence to do so.

I was wondering if, for all Tito's supposed brilliance, 'the flood of idolatory and the radiance of his power,'[1] there had been a single moment when the veneer had fallen away from the personality cult: whether, as Milovan Djilas says,

> in front of his villas, in his drawing rooms, flanked by his horses and dogs, surrounded by his inner circle… Tito came off as a kind of Latin-American dictator.[2]

When we reach the polling station there's a steady stream of voters going up the steps and into the school hall. Maybe it will be a good turnout all over the country. Ten minutes later everyone has voted and now we can go for a walk along the river, a route that I'd only walked in the pitch dark before.

The banks of the Sava at this point are extraordinary. The slow-moving river is as wide as the Thames in central London. The opposite bank is lined with trees, this bank with dozens and dozens of boats, floating bars, as densely packed as the houseboats at Chelsea Wharf. They're built on barges, pontoons or rafts, and they range from the ramshackle to the classy. Some are futuristic constructions of tubular steel and blue glass that look like fun-fair rides. We pass one called the *Pingvin* (Penguin), then, a few yards further on, the *Stari Pingvin* (Old Penguin). Someone tells me that a whole series of these floating bars turn out to be owned by the same person, each catering to a slightly different idea of what constitutes a great night out – something for every leisure subculture. We walk away from the city for at least a couple of miles without running out of floating bars. You're never more than about ten yards from the next gangplank; the next gulp of grog.

On the way back to Ivan's apartment we go to the off-licence and buy some *pivo* (beer). We pick out a couple of large bottles of BIP, which was the brand of the old state-run brewery. Ivan tells me that they all used to call it 'Bad Imitation of *Pivo*', but that now, with privatization, foreign investment and actually having to compete in the marketplace, it's not so bad. It's fine, in fact.

Ivan's friend Pavle is in town and comes over a little later on. Pavle comes from the Gandijeva district too, but hasn't voted today. He's been working in the night clubs of Greece for the past few years, this summer managing an island bar, serving drinks to British and German tourists. He speaks almost perfect English, but he wants to be able to do so with no hint of an accent. 'This is one of my many ambitions,' he admits. He says that there are no opportunities for him in Belgrade, so why should he stay?

He's been hanging out with lairy English tourists for too long – his conversation is a ghastly stream of sexist and racist jokes, and swiftly turns into a monologue about the former Yugoslav nations and their failings: Montenegrins this, Albanians that, Bosnians the other. My obvious discomfort, my failure to laugh, is internalized by Pavle as an indicator that the jokes he's telling have not been funny or extreme enough yet. He ups the ante and talks about Essex girls, tells some 'rape' jokes and a couple of 'blonde jokes', and asks me if I know any. I say that I'd never even heard of 'blonde jokes' until I'd read in the paper recently that they'd been banned in Bosnia-Herzegovina. I go further and say that they don't really have any currency, that they're not 'a thing', in England. Pavle puts me straight: 'No, they definitely are – these English guys who come to my bar are always telling me blonde jokes.' He can't help telling another one. I recognise it of course, but when I heard it, years ago, it wasn't a 'blonde joke', it was an 'Irish joke'.

Ivan starts playing all the records he owns by the former Yugoslavian rock band EKV – short for *Ekatarina Velika* (Catherine the Great) – which recorded between 1984 and 1993, and which more recently has been documented with its own extensive section in the *Leksikon Yu-mitologije*. While we wait for election news on the television we listen to practically every record the band made, while I do my best to translate the lyrics printed on the inner sleeves.

One track from the first album, *Katarina II*, is played a few times: *'Geto'*. Everyone starts talking about Novi Beograd, debating whether or not it was a ghetto. To someone from England it certainly looks like the biggest, most run-down 'council estate' or social housing project imaginable: decaying post-war utopian apartment blocks surrounded by unkempt parkland that now looks more like wasteland. Yet a knee-jerk reading of what in London would be considered by many as warning signs of a 'no go area' – overgrown walkways, tower blocks and low-rise flats, bad lighting, graffiti, subways, back streets – would be wrong. These things don't mean the same in Novi Beograd as they would in England. Novi Beograd seems to be one of those places that people have a real affection for and that those who live there seem to love. Everyone asks me how much I'm paying per night for a hotel room in the centre of town and says, 'Next time just let us know when you're coming – it's crazy paying that much. You could rent a flat here in Novi Beograd for a month!'

'I like Novi Beograd because it once meant something,' someone says, then, later, 'We are from ghetto and we are proud of it.'

There's still nothing on the television about the election. The absence of news is starting to worry people: 'My God!' says Gordana. 'It must have been disaster!' As Ivan flicks to another channel we see a graphic image of a map of southern African states, overlaid with some statistics. 'Ah!' someone says. 'At last! The election results from Botswana!'

Finally, when we're all giving up hope of seeing anything about the election until tomorrow, there's a news flash. The results are in: reform candidate Dragoljub Mićunović hasn't won; the Serbian Radical Party's candidate, Tomislav Nikolić, has come first by quite a margin, with 1.2 million votes, but doesn't have a sufficient majority either; and anyway the result won't stand because the turnout needed to be at least 50 per cent and only 38.5 per cent of the electorate voted.

Everyone is shocked and a feeling is voiced that there must have been a low turnout in the cities specifically, as the nationalistic parties traditionally have stronger support in the rural areas.

Ivan laughs: 'You know, we have another saying, *"Obrali smo bostan"*, "We have picked our melons"!' I suppose that this is analogous to the British saying 'You've made your bed, now you'd better lie in it.' In this case however, luckily, the result won't have to stand.

In spite of this reprieve on a legal technicality, the news is sobering and the evening is over. Nobody is in the mood to stay up longer and chat, and the beer ran out long ago. As my cab drives along a Terazije that is more or less empty of other traffic, I wonder if it's just my imagination that there are more police on the streets than usual.

When I venture out the next day not only are there armed police on every corner and more soldiers than normal walking the streets, but here and there on Terazije – outside the Old Palace and down near Trg Republike – there are clusters of black 4x4s and limousines parked haphazardly on pavements or in the middle of the road, and surrounded by policemen and security guards. Inside there must be press conferences or emergency meetings taking place, responses to the election results being agreed upon and delivered up to waiting journalists. The other thing that has changed is that overnight the city has been saturation-flyposted with hundreds of strikingly designed red and yellow posters bearing the legend *'Sada je vreme za Otpor'* ('Now is the time for Otpor') and the old protest symbol of a clenched fist. I learn later, watching the news, that some of the leaders of the anti-Milošević protest movement Otpor, which had been so active in the 1990s, had decided to launch a political party with the same name. I also learned that the reform coalition that had united behind Dragoljub Mićunović has imploded following the humiliation of the previous day's result. I wasn't going to be around for long enough to see what the new Otpor was proposing, or how long it would last, but it would probably be fair to say that the addition of yet another party to the already crowded and factional Serbian political scene would do little to create a coherent front in the seemingly perpetual struggle against the would-be inheritors of Milošević's nationalistic and right-wing policies. Hopefully though, the results of the previous day's election would scare up a larger turnout when another presidential election was called, and this time the result might be more positively in favour of reform, reconstruction and the rebuilding of international relationships.

In fact, it takes until 27 June 2004 for a successful presidential election to be held. The 50 per cent turnout law has been overturned in the intervening seven months and, in spite of Serbian Radical Party candidate Tomislav Nikolić's share of the vote rising to 45 per cent (with 1.4 million votes, as against the 1.2 million he received in November 2003), Boris Tadić received 53 per cent of the vote, suggesting at least, as the International Crisis Group put it, that 'a slim majority of the electorate wants to see Serbia on a pro-European reform course'.[3]

For a treat on my last night in the city we go to Kafana Manjež (the Carousel Bar), just off Birčaninova Street. Inside it's an architectural period piece of dark wood and high ceilings. A lattice screen divides the red-formica-topped bar tables in the front from the smartly set tables at the rear. A uniformed waiter asks if we are here to eat or to drink. Well, maybe a little of both, but we choose the informality of the front. A young man sitting and reading at another table looks up and nods at us in silent greeting, before returning to his beer and his book.

'What shall we drink?' Ivan asks, then breaks into song:

> Još litar jedan dobrog vina dajte nama vi,
> Zapevajmo sada složno svi!

'Is an old song,' he explains. 'Means literally, "Another litre of your good wine you give us,/Now we all start singing together."' He sings it again when the waiter comes, and that's precisely what we order, together with a huge plate of succulent *ćevapčići*, bread and chips, and a small bowl of salad. *Ćevapčići* are usually eaten with small cocktail sticks, since the minced and spiced pork and beef is tender enough for these dainty implements to suffice as fork and knife.

I can see why Manjež is so popular. It's not just nostalgia for the old Yugoslav architecture of the place, the food is wonderful too, good enough to take the place of conversation for a while. By the time we're spearing the last few chips, wiping the plate, both bar and restaurant are crowded.

'Ah, he is famous journalist,' says Ivan, looking over his shoulder at two diners in the corner, 'having dinner with politician. It's always like this here.' The political upheavals of the past 24 hours, the dramatic presidential election and the collapse of the reform coalition, seem to have been forgotten, at least for tonight, as all around us people laugh and talk and drink.

The next morning I settle the Splendid Hotel's very modest bill. I've become used to my little room overlooking the Old Palace (Stari Dvor), and will miss it. I order a cab and carry my bags the few yards along to the corner of Terazije. The driver will pick me up outside the Putnik office.

Before the collapse of the former Yugoslavia, Putnik ('Traveller') was the big state-owned travel agency and its impressive headquarters on Terazije was obviously appropriate to that task, which in those days would have included tourism along the entire Croatian coastline. Now, when all it can sell is tourism to Serbia and Montenegro, this impressive office on Terazije seems anachronistic. Inside, uniformed assistants stand behind Putnik's long counter, while behind them a photographic mural of strikingly beautiful landscapes stretches along the wall. I must have walked past the Putnik offices dozens of times while I've been here, but I've never seen a customer in there, and I can't imagine what the employees find to do all day.

The taxi arrives a few minutes later and I throw my bags onto the back seat of the Yugo. Soon we are speeding down the hill towards the Gazela bridge. I'd been hoping that the 20-minute drive to the airport would give me the opportunity for a last bit of conversation in Serbian, but the driver insists on speaking in English and talking about the congestion charge in London.

We speed past the construction sites, sports stadiums and half-built motorway interchanges that mark the edge of Belgrade. In the distance is the Genex Tower, the 'Western Gate', that huge Goldfingeresque tower block with its enormous central arch. Oh well, I think to myself, settling back in my seat as it looms closer, I will at least get a photograph as we drive through the middle of it.

To my surprise, though, the motorway does no such thing. Instead of going through the 'Western Gate' the motorway simply goes past it. I wonder why everyone kept telling me that the motorway went through the middle. Maybe it was just an error of translation on the part of everyone who'd insisted that it did. I'm more puzzled than disappointed – a skyscraper is a skyscraper, even one as extraordinary as this – but as the Genex Tower finally slips past my window beyond the screen of birch trees I take some photographs anyway. I'll pin them above my desk when I get home.

Chapter Nine
The Dalmatina and Zagreb (2005)

While I'm travelling, Rebecca West recedes into the distance. Her book remains largely unreread while I'm in Croatia and Serbia, although I'd taken it along with me, more as a kind of talisman than as a daily work of reference anyway. It's a fact, though, that when it lies in my hotel rooms in Belgrade or Zagreb *Black Lamb and Grey Falcon* becomes as monolithic and unapproachable as the vast range of enormous and absolutely barren mountains that line the horizon when we set off on the drive from Split to Zagreb. We're on the new motorway, the Dalmatina, which has been 40 years in the making, and has only now been completed in the summer of 2005.

After our initial climb out of Split we are forced to take a short detour because the last few miles of the Dalmatina are still being built and the road is not yet opened. It's no inconvenience, other than when we get stuck behind the occasional tractor, because this older road travels through some beautifully lush agricultural land that's a delight to see. We track alongside a cultivated valley some ten miles long, which, according to a sign by the side of the road, is called Donje Polje, meaning something like 'Lower Field'.

This orderly mosaic of vineyards, fields and olive groves must have been cultivated in this way for hundreds of years. Hanging from the branches of an occasional broom or olive are some pendulous off-white globes, which must be cocoons or nests of some kind, whether of insects or birds I'm not sure, but which look like a type of bizarre and dessicated fruit.

At one point an ambulance overtakes us, sirens blaring. Ten minutes later, with Donje Polje some miles behind us, we catch up with it at a crossroads that divides a flat and otherwise deserted area of heathland punctuated only by big grey rocks. As one we all wince and there's a sudden collective inhalation. The ambulance is parked next to a white car that's crushed and mangled beyond recognition, while a few yards away three or four people stand or sit beside the road near another car that's barely scratched. They're staring into space and one of them is smoking a cigarette. The paramedics must be in the back of the ambulance, treating the people from the white car. These survivors look shocked by the inequality and the injustice of what seems to have just happened, this arbitrary meeting at an otherwise empty crossroads.

We drive past this strangely static aftermath just as, a few miles further down the road and back on the Dalmatina, we drive past the turning that leads to Knin, which during the wars of the 1990s was the capital of a breakaway Serb republic in Croatia. *Krajina* means 'borderland': for hundreds of years this region, the Vojna Krajina, was just that, the swathe of territory where the Ottoman and Austro-Hungarian Empires faced each other. The Austrians initially resettled Serbs who'd fled from the Ottomans in this region, to form a line of defence. As many writers have pointed out, the Krajina Serbs at that time had a degree of independence from both Zagreb and Budapest, being governed directly by Vienna.

A friend in Belgrade once told me that there's a common perception that the Serbs in Bosnia-Herzegovina and in Croatia consider themselves to be more truly Serb than the Serbians who live in Serbia. Certainly the very existence of these border Serbs was long defined by a need to defend themselves and therefore, like Rebecca West's farm cats, they could not 'let themselves be gentle'.[1]

In 1991 Franjo Tudjman and his Hrvatska Demokratska Zajednica (Croatian Democratic Union, or HDZ), which had come to power in May 1990, proposed the creation of an independent Croatia that would be the sovereign state solely of Croats, rather than of the Croats as well as of the other constituent nations (in the Yugoslav sense) that lived in Croatia. Understandably, this rang all kinds of alarm bells for Serbs who lived in Croatia. The HDZ government also adopted political symbols that had been associated with the Ustaše, such as the Šahovnica, that ubiquitous red checkerboard I'd seen on flags and car numberplates during my first visit to Croatia. The government claimed that it was merely reviving the symbols of medieval Croatia, but they also evoked, or were used by Serbian politicians to evoke, memories of the Second World War and the atrocities visited on Serbs and others in the region by the Ustaše, in the name of the fascist 'Independent State of Croatia' (or NDH). A section of the Krajina

Serbs rebelled and tried to hold a local referendum on their constitutional status, a process that was declared illegal by the government, which then attempted to send in extra police and special forces to restore order. This didn't work, and by August 1990 the borders of a state within a state had been drawn, and the roads into this part of the Krajina region, which the Dalmatina motorway now cuts across, had been barricaded. By the spring of 1991 the area had been named the 'Serbian Autonomous District of Krajina' (SAO) and then 'Republika Srpska Krajina' (RSK). Milan Babić, the dentist who had proclaimed himself President of the RSK, was removed from office in early 1992, in favour of Goran Hadžić, but remained as 'Minister for Foreign Affairs'. During the few short years of the RSK's existence there were offensives against Croats and other non-Serbs who lived in the region, resulting in the removal of tens of thousands of non-Serb civilians. Croat villages such as Kijevo, 'an enclave within an enclave',[2] were bombed and atrocities were conducted for which Babić has since been convicted and sentenced at The Hague.

Babić didn't need to be hunted down and arrested in order for case number IT-03-72-S to be initiated: he made contact with the ICTY himself in October 2001, one month after he'd been mentioned in the 'Croatia Indictment' that formed part of the charge sheet against Slobodan Milošević. Babić testified during the Milošević case and was then indicted himself in November 2003. He initially entered a plea that he'd been an 'aider and abettor of a JCE [joint criminal enterprise]',[3] but this claim to have been only an aider and abettor was not accepted. In January 2004 he entered a second plea that he was a 'co-perpetrator' of a JCE that had had as its goal 'the forcible permanent removal of the majority of Croat and other non-Serb populations from approximately one third of Croatia in order to transform that territory into a Serb-dominated state through the commission of crimes'.[4] These crimes included 'the extermination or murder of hundreds of Croat and other non-Serb civilians',[5] 'the prolonged and routine imprisonment and confinement' of such civilians, their 'deportation or forcible transfer[, and the] deliberate destruction of homes and other public and private property, cultural institutions, historic monuments, and sacred sites of the Croat and other non-Serb populations'[6]; that is, that Babić 'formulated, promoted, participated in, and encouraged' these policies and actions, and indeed encouraged them simply by 'remaining in his office and exercising functions associated with it'.[7] During the presentation of Babić's plea all parties agreed that, even if he 'had no knowledge of the specific murders charged',[8] he was aware that these crimes were being committed, and 'realized from his own observations that such killings were the likely outcome'[9] of these policies. Babić stated at the ICTY that he had continued in this way because he wanted to 'preserve his political position despite his knowledge that his actions or omissions would lead to ethnic strife and war, and the associated crimes'.[10]

The Krajina Serbs had the support of Milošević. Indeed, Babić argued at the ICTY that he 'co-perpetrated' the JCE as charged through the exercise of a power that was 'limited and undermined by the creation of a so-called "parallel structure" in the SAO Krajina, which he said included people who were ultimately controlled by Slobodan Milošević'.[11] The support of Milošević and his power structures could prove to be illusory, however, or at best pragmatic: as easily removed as given. Certainly by 1995 Milošević had hung the Krajina Serbs out to dry. When the Croatian army launched a huge offensive, *Olvja*, or Operation Storm, to retake the region, the Krajina Serbs could not count on any support from Belgrade. Hopelessly outnumbered, they fled in their tens of thousands.

Babić remains notable for the fact that he turned himself in and that he admitted his guilt, rather than pleading not guilty. He is currently serving a 13-year prison sentence.

Part of me wants to ask if we can take the turning for Knin, to drive the short distance to the RSK's former capital to see what is happening there, now that those same Serb refugees are being invited back or, rather, being invited to apply for permission to return to their properties in Croatia. We are expected back in Zagreb, however, so we continue to speed north along the Dalmatina. Always in the distance are these great white mountains, stretching from horizon to horizon, so far away that they remain as static in relation to our position as the moon glimpsed from a car window.

Like those mountains, Rebecca West's book can seem vast, distant and magnificent. It's impenetrable, not in the sense that it's difficult to read, but that it's difficult to get to grips with a work of art that's so enormous and accomplished. This is not just because of the sheer scale of her achievement in writing the book, her synthesis of the personal, the political and the his-torical, and her construction of such a convincing and necessary argument against Nazism, for beauty and honour rather than pointless self-destruc-tion, but also because her terms of reference are so much of her time. As

Vesna Goldsworthy observes, this is the point of the book, West's stated aim being to describe the feelings and thoughts of 'a typical Englishwoman'[12] on the eve of the Second World War. In so doing West was 'obliged to write a long and complicated history, and to swell that *with an account of myself*' (my italics) in order to 'show the past side by side with the present it created'.[13] It was as if, she wrote, a Roman woman had 'realized why [Rome] was going to be sacked and what motives inspired the barbarians and what the Romans, and had written down all she knew and felt about it'.[14] There's nothing typical about Rebecca West, however, and perhaps her stated ambition should be modified retrospectively to putting on paper what an *extraordinary* Englishwoman felt and thought at that time.

Goldsworthy goes on to point out how surprising it is, then, that *Black Lamb and Grey Falcon* should be turned to primarily as a reference work, to be 'interpreted almost exclusively by those interested in Balkan history'[15] or even to be seen as primarily 'a "Balkan" travel book',[16] both of which readings neglect the book's value as a seminal 'modernist travel narrative'[17] and a 'testimony to a British woman writer's attitude to the Second World War – with its plea not in favour of mindless courage but against dishonour'.[18]

Black Lamb and Grey Falcon certainly achieves its professed aim, but in doing so the book also achieves much more. It succeeds in this even where it rather fails to provide a truly plural description of the former Yugoslavia, although West is far from being alone in this failing. Indeed, it must almost be expected. As with any other complex subject, if one wants to gain as complete a picture as is possible, one must read everything. This frequent criticism of West, born, as it must be, from the naive expectation that any one source could provide a complete and comprehensive account of anything, is itself fatuous. Yes, read Rebecca West, it's as good a place as any to start reading if you want to understand the former Yugoslavia, but don't expect that understanding to be complete. *Black Lamb and Grey Falcon* is primarily a work of literature rather than of reference, and it is a great work of literature, which is as much about love, literature and art as it is about Yugoslavia. The book even satisfies West's own demanding criteria for what constitutes a great work, as she writes about the 'complex nature of all profound works of art':

> An artist is goaded into creation on this level by his [*sic*] need to resolve some important conflict, to find out where the truth lies among divergent opinions on a vital issue. His work, therefore, is

often a palimpsest on which are superimposed several incompat-
ible views about his subject; and it may be that which is expressed
with the greatest intensity, which his deeper nature finds the
truest, is not that which has determined the narrative form he has
given to it.[19]

Rebecca West's book should be read for its lessons about life, rather than
for the narrative form that she gave to the story of how she learned those
lessons. Like any great work of literature, it should be reread, and then
reread again; be studied rather than generalised about.

At times, I'd argue, West's terms of cultural reference can be difficult for
contemporary readers to engage with. A cultured person in the 1930s
might have been able to take it for granted that Mozart's music is extraordinary, for example, but to me, born in the 1960s and educated in the
1970s, the kind of education that produced such certainties seems as distant and unlikely an aspect of 20th-century life as flappers or the habitual
wearing of hats by men. Yet the central image in West's Epilogue, her rab-
ble-rousing finale, of her playing Susanna's aria from Act IV of Mozart's
The Marriage of Figaro during the Blitz, in order to reassert the importance
of beauty in the face of destruction, is actually very moving.

The late Serbian novelist Slobodan Selenić mercilessly satirized West's
enthusiastic appreciation of Macedonian folk art – the costumes and
embroidery that she found on her first visit (the one sponsored by the
British Council) – and her deployment of it as an illustration of the rich-
ness of lives lived in struggle, which she counterpoints with a vilification
of the Austrian women who then forced her to disinfect the garments and
thereby ruin them. In his novel *Fathers and Forefathers* Selenić uses a very
close paraphrase of her words[20] to paint West herself as exactly the type of
do-gooder she argues against in the preface to *Black Lamb and Grey Falcon,*
suggesting that the Yugoslavia she saw was an Arcadia that she conjured
from her dreams. He then asks whether it was not Austrian culture, after
all, that produced her beloved Mozart.

In contemporary culture the idea that we could, or should, all unques-
tioningly appreciate Mozart seems slightly anachronistic. Perhaps it's our
loss, but thinking about culture has changed. For many people the horrors
of the Second World War put paid to certainties about progress, and to
faith in what the postmodernists subsequently called 'the grand narratives'
of the Enlightenment, since these, they and others argued, had been cor-

rupted by progress itself being used to perfect the arts and sciences of destroying people. These uncertainties were reflected in the arts, which displayed what George Mallen has called a 'pervasive sense of failure, that somehow or other the great achievements of European art, by many assumed to be the pinnacle of human culture, had counted for nought when the great social catastrophes of the 20th century unfolded'.[21] It's a small irony that the victory that West counted on to preserve what was right and good in the world was won precisely at the expense of some of her certainties, of any consensus about what constitutes cultural value.

But then, in spite of these inevitable anachronisms, and the vast and teeming complexity of West's work, whenever I do pick up and reread *Black Lamb and Grey Falcon* I'm plunged right back into the work itself, the nitty-gritty of its stories and arguments and diversions, its real wonders, as well as West's opinions on art, politics and life, which are readily given, rather than its myth.

Similarly, when driving along the Dalmatina, through Zagora, the Dalmatian interior, those mountains aren't so impossibly distant after all: the road suddenly rises up to meet them and plunges us directly through the most terrifying mountain of all, Velebit. This is an enormous and almost theatrical series of bare crags that stretches up to heaven, like the elongated and beseeching hands on Meštrović's sculptures of Job, and that seems almost to have been carved from the exposed white rock for this purpose. It's like the stage set for some grand and terrifying opera.

This tunnel under Velebit was the first section of the Dalmatina to be built, in 1995, when the idea of the road was revived, having been initially promoted as part of the 'Croatian Spring' movement, a resurgence of nationalism that had emerged in Croatia during the 1960s. The plans for the Dalmatina were revived soon after the wars of the 1990s ended, this time not only as a means of linking the north and south of Croatia, but also, perhaps, as a way of bypassing the road and rail junctions that centred on vulnerable Serb-dominated areas such as Knin. Approaching Velebit, I wonder if the tunnel was also built at least partly for its symbolic value, so sublime is this particular rock face. There must be points in this huge chain of mountains that would have been easier for the engineers to tunnel through. But symbolic gestures were a major aspect of Franjo Tudjman's presidency, whether renaming the streets of Zagreb that commemorated Yugoslavia's victory in the war against fascism after the agents of Croatian nationalism, adopting the Šahovnica as a new national symbol in a stroke of reappropriation that was worthy of *Neue Slowenische Kunst,* or turning the statue of Ban Jelačić around so that he faced a new enemy, Serbia, instead of an old one, Hungary. It's almost tempting to believe that this site was chosen simply *because* it was the most obviously dramatic and difficult point at which the Dalmatina could cross the mountains. However, cross the mountains it does and, whether it's intentional or not, the theatricality of it all, and the crags of Velebit, are stunningly sublime in those few moments before we plunge into the darkness of the tunnel.

We emerge suddenly into a transformed upland landscape of beautiful and lush forests that is so completely different from the arid rocks we've just left that it's scarcely credible that it's in the same country. Looking around I see trees in every direction, even covering the landward slopes of the mountains we've just travelled beneath. I remember that it was in *Black Lamb and Grey Falcon* that I first heard what every Croatian learned at school: the sides of these mountains facing the Adriatic coast are completely barren because the Venetians, who controlled this coast at one time, cut down all the timber for use as the very piles upon which Venice was built.

Before I can properly begin to imagine what the Adriatic coast might have looked like if it were covered in dense, dark and beautiful forests such as the ones we're driving through, I start to notice village after village where half or most of the houses stand derelict and empty, roofless and semi-demolished. Those houses that remain are freshly whitewashed, with red-tiled roofs that stand out brightly against the trees. I realise that we are in Lika, the area where the war started, and very near to that part of Croatia that subsequently saw the worst ethnic cleansing of Serbs, during the notorious Operation Storm in 1995. This, the countermove to the atrocities that were committed in the name of the RSK, was the single largest forced migration of the war. The architect of Operation Storm, a former French Foreign Legionary and, subsequently, a general in the Croatian army called Ante Gotovina, was at the time of my visit still at large, despite the issuing of an indictment against him by The Hague in 2001. Rumours of his hiding in Croatia were strongly denied by the Croatian government, although their protracted failure to arrest Gotovina, and an apparent dissembling and undermining of international support lent for this task by factions of the Croatian security services who remained loyal to Gotovina, was for a time the single biggest obstacle to Croatia entering talks about EU accession, and the reason for those talks having been cancelled in early 2005. Talks resumed only in October 2005, when the international community could be satisfied that the Croatian government was doing all it could to arrest him. At the time of his eventual arrest in Tenerife, in the Canary Islands, on 7 December 2005, Gotovina was still, it is said, considered by many in Croatia to be a national hero rather than a criminal. Indeed, bill-board posters proclaiming '*Neznanje i nesposobnost: Nećete plaćati Gotovinom*' and giving the web address www.antegotovina.com, were, according to B92's news website, still on display in Split and Dubrovnik on the day of his arrest. The first part of the slogan means something like 'Ignorance and incompetence'. The second part is a pun on the word *gotovina*, which also means 'cash'. '*Nećete plaćati*' means 'Don't pay in cash', or, in this case, 'You will not pay with Gotovina'.

This loyalty to Gotovina, reminiscent of the loyalty to Mladić and Karadžić still apparently displayed by some Serbs, persists in spite of the joint criminal enterprise for which Gotovina has been indicted, and which includes the murders by certain personnel under his command of around 150 elderly residents of these Krajina villages who'd been simply too old to run. However, the Croatian government's insistence that he was not hiding in Croatia during his four or more years at large seems to have been borne out by the myriad of stamps in his forged passport, which, according to some accounts, show him to have been hiding in a succession of countries including 'Tahiti, Argentina, China, Chile, Russia, the Czech Republic and Mauritius'.[22]

As we drive past these villages, someone else in the car, another English visitor, says, 'This is such a mysterious landscape, don't you think?'. Someone answers, quite correctly. 'What is mysterious about the land-scape? It's just a normal Mediterranean landscape, no?'

In Zagreb I'm fortunate to meet up with a journalist called Drago Pilsel, columnist for the newspaper *Novi List*, who at the time war broke out had been a Franciscan monk in Bosnia-Herzegovina. How he went from being a monk to being a journalist is a story in itself. Drago believed that it was necessary to return to his original profession in order that he could become a witness of some of the worst atrocities that took place during Operation Storm, and in fact it's a story that he's writing himself, having been encour-aged to document his experiences in a book, so I can be brief.

We meet for dinner in one of Zagreb's best restaurants, at the suggestion

of Boro Radaković. I agree to this suggested venue only on the understanding that I will pay, at least for my share. Given the exchange rates and
the relative buying power of sterling in Croatia, the cost of a good meal
will be much cheaper for me than it would be for Boro, with his hard-
earned kuna.

The restaurant is set up on the crest of the hill on which the old town
stands, and from the terrace outside you can see right across the city, but
we choose a table inside and have what amounts to our own room. We
order food and wine, and pretty soon we're all helping ourselves from an
enormous platter of ham and cheese, which is followed by some wonderful grilled fish.

It's only really then, as the meal comes to an end, that Drago starts to
speak. He's a slight man, serious and very quietly spoken. He certainly
seems more suited to the monastic life than to that of a soldier, though
that's what he became at one point during the war.

I mention that I'd been told by the film-maker Pawel Pawlikowski that
some of the Franciscan monks in Herzegovina were very right-wing at the
beginning of the war. 'Yes, of course. Pawlikowski is correct,' he tells me. 'But
the worst thing is that there is a resurgence of that feeling now among sections
of the Croatian population in Herzegovina. There are even some in positions
of power who want a Croatian state in Bosnia-Herzegovina, you know, like
Republika Srpska; a third republic. These thoughts are very dangerous.'

As we pick the last of the delicate white fish from the bones on the plate,
he haltingly tells me his story. He speaks very quietly and slowly, eyes
down-turned for part of the conversation. He tells me that his brother
Branko was fighting in the 4th Brigade of the Croatian Army in the early
years of the war. Officially he is still missing in action, but everybody
knows that he's dead, and that he and others from his company were on a
boat that was shelled near the island of Šipan. Drago tells me that the families of those who were killed there even attended a memorial service
recently, on a boat that was anchored as near as they could reckon to the
spot where his brother's boat went down, but that some bureaucratic
convention of war means that until the Croatian Army's books are
balanced with those of the Serbians it is impossible to absolutely, finally
and officially account for those soldiers who were killed in this action.
Unfortunately, he adds, there is no immediate prospect of this kind of
cooperation.

At the time, however, Drago's response to the tragedy of his brother's death was not to grieve, but to leave the monastery immediately and enlist. Not only that, but he joined up in his brother's place, in the same unit, or what remained of it.

He didn't last long, his faith, or perhaps his humanity, forcing him to leave the army and become one of the founding members of a Croatian branch of an international human rights organization, the Helsinki Committee. It was then, however, that his worst experiences of the war took place. Following in the wake of Operation Storm at the beginning of August 1995, in the path of the Croatian armies that retook the Krajina region from the Croatian Serbs and forced this single largest exodus of the war, he came across village after village where all that remained were the corpses of the elderly. These crimes continued for months after the 'success' of Operation Storm.

Drago tells us that the one scene that he cannot escape and which haunts him to this day was that of two elderly Serbs who had been shot dead on the doorstep of their home. From the posture of their corpses he'd been able to deduce quite clearly that the woman, who, it turned out, was 91, had been shot as she'd tried to shield her son from a bullet, to throw her body across his. Before she was shot she had reached behind herself with a protective arm. The couple were frozen in this gesture of love as surely as the petrified victims of Pompeii.

It was perhaps inevitable that when he started publizising what he'd seen, Pilsel soon found himself denounced on television:

> We were eating dinner and watching the news, and suddenly my face was there! We were terrified, but I tell you half an hour later we'd packed and were on our way to Sarajevo. I disappeared completely for two months, until it was safe to come back.

We're listening in silence. All thought of the glorious meal that we've just eaten is forgotten as Drago tells us that he buried these traumas, these losses and these visions of Hell, so deeply that it took him almost eight years to have the nervous breakdown that was probably inevitable.

Outside we bid goodnight to Drago and walk back through Trg Ban Jelačić towards my hotel. I idly ask Boro whether Zagreb has a flea market. I sometimes think of flea markets as the soul of a city, the place where the hidden stories of a place enter the public domain. Normally I can just wonder around a city and chance upon the flea market. It's as if my antennae are somehow tuned to such places, but here I haven't found one yet. He just laughs: 'You want to go to flea market? You are in luck! Tomorrow is Sunday. We will go to Hrelić. Let me phone Edo and see if he wants to come too.'

Edo duly arrives outside my hotel, the Jadrana (Adriatic), at ten in the morning, and we drive over to Boro's apartment building (*'Preko puta Plive,'* as I've learned to tell taxi drivers – 'opposite Pliva', which is a pharmaceuticals factory). We don't go and knock on his door, rather we go to a small bar with a rattan-shaded verandah to drink coffee and wait for him.

Hrelić is a short drive out of the city, east of Novi Zagreb on the other side of the Sava River, which is as wide here as it is in Belgrade, although without the armada of floating bars.

We're not the only ones who've decided to come to Hrelić. As we get out of the car and climb to the top of the steep embankment that lines this southern side of the Sava I'm astounded to see a column of people trudging along the embankment ahead of us, almost as far as the eye can see. It's a sight that inevitably draws comparison with those other columns of people who've crisscrossed this country at one time or another, although these are not refugees, of course, but people looking for bargains.

It's a long walk from Youth Bridge, where we've parked, to Hrelić. Eventually Edo points at something on our side of the river and laughs: 'You see this hill?' he asks. 'Well, it's not a hill. It's made entirely of refuse. Can you smell it yet?' Actually the wind is behind us, so as we finally draw nearer the smell of rotting garbage is bearable, but still an occasional gust carries with it grit and a smell of dustbins that you can almost taste.

The market itself is huge, covering a site that must measure in the tens of acres. We pass a second-hand car market and a modern building that houses a Chinese supermarket. Beyond this we pass through a broad gate, along a roughly asphalted track and into the market proper. There are stalls selling the usual post-Communist tat – enamel badges, discontinued military uniforms – while others display discount clothes, cheap jeans, bicycles or telephones. Some stalls are in fact tarpaulins laid on the ground that seem just to be piled high with filthy broken junk that looks as if it's been tipped out of the back of a truck, while yet more sell furniture and huge brass and glass modernist chandeliers, just like the ones in the bars and vestibules of Tito-era hotels such as the Splendid in Belgrade.

I'm determined to buy something, a souvenir of some sort, but my indecision is not productive. At one stall I see a big green plastic binder that's full of seven-inch singles, dozens of Yugoslav-era pop records, interspersed with the occasional imported Beatles single. I hesitate for a moment, unsure if I'll be able to carry this comfortably before deciding that I probably could, but when I return to the stall it's been sold. Similarly, at another stall my eye briefly passes over an amateurish oil painting, a miniature of a greyish bird of prey, but I don't quite register what it means, and it's only half an hour later, when I see a little toy lamb, the black plush it's made from now matted and filthy, that I realise I've passed up a kitsch prize beyond measure: my very own black lamb and grey falcon. I'm never going to find the painting again now, and one is useless without the other. At one stall back near the gate I briefly pick up a small and roughly cast brass ashtray that's hidden among some slightly out-of-place Egyptiana, then, exhausted and empty-handed, we go for coffee, Boro and I taking turns to look anxiously at our watches. 'Excuse me,' says Edo, after knocking back his espresso, transparently enough for me not to notice, 'I just forgot something.'

It's a long walk back to the car, and once again we're part of a huge column of human traffic that stretches for two or three miles along the embankment. There are hundreds of people and most of them are carrying various bits of booty: a car bumper, a cash register, bags of food. Someone is wheeling a children's bicycle.

Back in the car we cross Freedom Bridge, heading back to the city centre, where Boro has promised to take me to the best *ćevapčići* shop in town. As we wait at a junction Edo reaches into the pocket of his green army-surplus-style jacket and without a word hands me the little brass ashtray that I'd briefly examined on one of the stalls.

Chapter Ten
Istria (2004)

Istria is a tiny India-shaped peninsula that hangs off the northwestern coast of Croatia just south of Trieste. Despite its large Slavic population, Istria wasn't actually part of Yugoslavia when Rebecca West visited that country in the late 1930s. It had been part of Italy since the end of the First World War, when Italian troops were sent in. Italy used the formulations of the Treaty of London (1915), which had offered Italy much of the Adriatic coast, to stake its ambitions to take control of borderlands previously controlled by the Austro-Hungarian Empire. During the Second World War, however, the resistance to Nazi and Italian occupation, and to the fascist NDH (the 'Independent State of Croatia'), ensured that Istria, which was not part of Pavelić's fascist puppet-state, became part of the post-war Yugoslav state-in-waiting announced by Tito and the Partisans at Jajce in Bosnia-Herzegovina in November 1943.

Accordingly, following the Allied victory in the Second World War, and the Communist victory in Yugoslavia's first post-war election two years later, which led to the declaration of the Federal People's Republic of Yugoslavia on 29 November 1945, Istria became part of Croatia and part of the Federal People's Republic.

I'd decided early on to understand my self-imposed brief ('in the footsteps of…') very loosely, and not to follow Rebecca West too closely, if at all. Rather I would try to see what was happening now in those former Yugoslav republics that I was able to visit, and to take my lead from whatever I encountered and from conversations with artists, writers – anyone but politicians – that I met along the way. In spite of this more modest approach, I'd come to feel slightly more cut adrift from West than I'd expected. Although Rebecca West never visited Istria, I reasoned to myself that my own visit to the region might provide a way to gain some small measure of sympathetic insight into her grand project, if only because I was coming here on a sort of official visit. Admittedly, my hosts were not government officials, as West's were, but the Istrian Tourist Board, but an official tour is an official tour, and in the course of my time here I was to be chauffeured around with all manner of guides and local dignitaries, shepherded through a rich sightseeing itinerary designed to give me a flavour of Istria. I wondered if this VIP treatment might not at least give me some little understanding of West's journeying, and allow me a glimpse of what she'd experienced, or rather of *how* she'd experienced it.

The flight that I take from Zagreb to Pula is not direct, but it's the quickest way in the off season. First we must fly down the coast to Zadar and then hop a couple of hundred miles back up north to Pula. A tiny propeller-driven plane, perhaps a 20- or 30-seater, is waiting on the tarmac at Zagreb Airport. There is no room inside for hand luggage, so my bag is flung into a webbing-lined cupboard as I take my seat. We take off and quickly climb above Zagreb. As we do so the city looks far bigger than I'd remembered. The two spires of the cathedral are initially hard to locate amid the post-war sprawl that stretches along and across the Sava River. Brooding behind the city, as the rubbish heap is to Hrelić, is the Sljeme mountain, a great forested mass far higher than anything else in the surrounding landscape. Even on the sunniest days it always seems to be cloaked in darkness. It's impossible to focus on the slopes, whether from the plane or on the ground. Sljeme defies scale and perspective, and the conifers that forest its slopes seem to absorb all light. This great mountain seems as insubstantial as a shadow or a storm cloud that looms over the city.

I've never flown in so small a plane before. Once we're airborne the plane buzzes and bounces its way up to a few thousand feet. As we climb, the red roofs of the villages that cluster on green hilltops in the countryside around Zagreb gradually thin out.

The first part of the flight is quite short, a matter of 40 minutes or so, and the wind is behind us. Beneath us the countryside gets drier, browner, and gradually more sparsely populated. It becomes hard to see any sign of human habitation at all, apart from an occasional road winding through a parched valley. As we fly over what at a certain point during the wars of the 1990s had been called 'the Bihać pocket', in northwestern Bosnia-Herzegovina, I can make out a series of crisscrossing straight lines etched into the dry, rocky soil far beneath us. This, the pilot tells us over the inter-com, is Bihać Airport. I've read about it: it's a former military facility, dat-ing from the days after the Second World War when many of the facilities of the Yugoslav National Army (the JNA) had been sited in Bosnia-Herzegovina precisely because of the inaccessibility of so much of its ter-rain. Together with a robust civil defence programme, this distribution of military and industrial facilities was part of Tito's policy to make any future invasion from the east as difficult as possible, but it had the unfortunate outcome of creating a ready infrastructure for civil war. From this height Bihać Airport looks like a Nazca drawing in the Peruvian desert – five run-ways sketching out an inverted triangle with a cross on top.

A few minutes later we start to climb higher, but the ground rises too, and some bald and rocky mountain tops rise up to greet us. Like Velebit, they are eroded by wind and weather along the lines of geological stratifi-cation. From this height it looks exactly like the sort of model terrain that a wargame enthusiast like 'Balkan Dave' might build in his living room or garage to exercise his carefully painted armies and military strategies upon. Just as I'm becoming used to these stark outcrops, suddenly, breathtaking-ly, the mountains fall away beneath us in a vertiginous tumble of rock, dusted here and there with only the very occasional twisted tree. Flying out over the crest we hit a sudden but prolonged burst of vicious turbulence, which must be caused by the intense heat that rises from these sun-baked rocks to meet the easterly wind. As the plane bounces around like a small fishing boat on a choppy sea, I wonder if these bald rocky slopes facing the Adriatic are a product of geography and weather, of the easterly winds that pour over this lip of rock and are instantly superheated by the vast, west-erly-facing rock faces.

As we clear the coastline, to bank and turn and begin the descent to Zadar, the turbulence stops, and far below the plane I catch the first real sight of the Adriatic. A road follows the coastline, and small towns and vil-lages hug the rocks on what little flat ground there is at the foot of these great mountains. Approaching the town and harbour of Zadar, I can see its yachts and its apartment blocks. Below us the sea is a deep blue, the rich-ness of which is only emphasized by pale ochre and sand-coloured rocks that plunge straight into the water. Perhaps half a mile from the harbour walls a lone speedboat draws a long, lazy arc of foam in the calm water. As the plane turns for our final descent into Zadar Airport, the bright midday sun suddenly catches the tip of every wave and ripple in the water below, throwing up a reflected glare so bright that it makes it impossible, too painful, to even look out of the window.

The runway at Zadar is surrounded by fields of ripe orange pumpkins, and by vineyards. We stay there just long enough to allow one or two people to get off the plane, one or two more to get on, and to watch two men pick up the nose of a two-seater plane and wheel it into its parking space. I glance at the in-flight magazine and see puffs about the beauty of Istria, about wild asparagus that grows in every hedgerow, about truffles and wine, about *'agriturizam'* (agri-tourism) and churches with incredible frescoes.

Once we are airborne again my window faces out into the sun, and below us, if I squint hard against the glare, I can see the numerous islands, big and small, that made up Croatia's Adriatic archipelago. What is surprising is that from this height these tree-covered and beachless islands are far from the jagged outcrops that I'd expected to see. They're almost surreally curvilinear, like blobs of melted wax in a lava lamp, or coral atolls in some imaginary South Pacific. I shift to a seat on the shady side of the plane, in order to see the coastline and those islands nearest to it. I see the same rounded treasure-map shapes, but these islands are completely bare and treeless. I go back to my original seat to make sure I hadn't imagined it, but sure enough the islands I can see from the left side of the plane are densely forested, while the islands nearest to the coast are as naked and rocky as the mountain tops we'd flown over an hour before.

It's not long before we swing further out to sea in order to make the approach to Pula, a harbour city at the southern tip of the Istrian peninsula. What little I know about the city has been gleaned from conversations with friends who've been here for flying visits: it has a Roman amphitheatre, James Joyce once lived there, and the former world champion boxer Mate Parlov now has a bar there.

As we turn in over Pula's harbour I catch sight of the amphitheatre. I'd expected this to be a rough semicircle of ruined terraced seating out in the countryside somewhere, but what I see is an almost completely intact, Colosseum-sized building of six or seven storeys, situated right in the heart of this little city's centre, surrounded by rooftops, narrow streets and railway lines.

I'll have to wait to explore these cluttered back streets and step out into the gladiatorial arena, as all tourists do, because I have been told that we're staying in the mountain village of Motovun. As we touch down and taxi at Pula I notice that the grass growing along the runway verges has been harvested and built into curious haystacks that use the trunks of trees as a central support.

I'm being met from the plane, and this time someone is actually holding up a sign with my name on it: a man called Ozren – slim, with short black hair and steel-rimmed glasses – whose family background is half-Croatian and half-Kenyan Asian, and who works for the Istrian Tourist Office. Our group for this official tour then reaches its full complement with the arrival of two other writers: György Dalos, a Hungarian now resident in Berlin, and Josef Haslinger, an Austrian novelist who is most famous for writing a thriller called (in English translation) *Opera Ball* about a terrorist attack on Viennese high society. György is small and stocky, with severely parted and damped-down hair, and he wears the light, many-pocketed casual clothes of the seasoned traveller, while Josef, in jeans, white T-shirt and black jacket, with spikey blond hair, has the slightly dissipated air of a rock star from the 1980s. Also travelling with us is a woman called Egle (pronounced 'Ay-glay'), who works for the Pula Book Fair, the organization that, together with the Tourist Office, is playing host for the week or so that we'll be here. Egle is acting as translator and general facilitator to the group, while Ozren, who always has a fat sheaf of papers and a mobile phone in his hand, and an itinerary in his head, is doing the organizing and the driving.

It doesn't take long, however, just a few minutes of conversation about our schedule, before my fantasies about being driven around Istria in chauffeured luxury turn out to be slightly hollow. Our hosts are certainly enormously generous, and they have lined up some amazing things for us to see and people for us to meet. Istria is so beautiful that it almost seems tinged by magic. In spite of this generosity and these wonders, the experience of being chauffeured turns sour because during those few minutes our group finds and settles, unshakably, into its *lingua franca*. This turns out to be German, a language that four out of five of us have in common. Unfortunately, I'm the odd one out. It means that the only translating that Egle has to do is to try and summarize for me, every five minutes or so, a continuous and complex German conversation that won't really stop until we get back to Pula in a couple of days' time. Unable to keep up with this conversation I sit in the back of the car like a sulky teenager and look out of the window.

There's an unexpected echo of Rebecca West's visits here after all. In *Black Lamb and Grey Falcon* West uses the German and Austrian tourists she meets as ciphers, as caricatures, their continuous, crass social violences providing West and the reader with evidence of the threat of Nazism. Now, in spite of the fact that I'm disappointed by this persistent low-level hum of German conversation, there's no need to deploy György or Josef as caricatures to prove a point. Austrian and Hungarian they may be, and thus in some sense descendants of the imperial powers that dominated Croatia up to the early 20th century, but I'm not going to ascribe any metaphorical post-colonial value to this chance conjunction of nationalities. They turn out, like Ozren and Egle, to be thoroughly charming and intelligent company. György in particular is hilarious, continually cracking jokes, even if the true wit of some of these is lost in translation: 'What is the definition of Middle Europe? A place where all the public buildings are yellow!'

'OK,' says Ozren, looking at his watch as we throw our bags into the large and slightly battered burgundy Mercedes that he has parked outside. 'We will drive to Motovun. I really want you to see this place before it gets dark. It's one of the most beautiful sights in Istria. If we go straight there we will make it.' Then he pauses and thinks for a second. 'I don't know, maybe you'd like a coffee somewhere on the way?'

We're barely out of Pula when Ozren's plans for a grand unveiling of Motovun before dark start to come unstuck. His knowledge of Istria is impressive, and his love for the region infectious, but his enthusiasm frustrates his choreography. He points to a Venetian church tower at the centre of a nearby village: 'Maybe we should stop here? This church has an amazing collection of mummies, relics, you know.' Then he thinks for a second or two and adds, 'It's OK, we have plenty of time to get to Motovun before dark.'

None of us is stupid enough to pass up the opportunity to see something macabre in our first half-hour in Istria. Of course we insist on stopping. As we pull up in the village square I learn that the church is a smaller copy of the church of San Francesco del Deserto in Venice.

We'll come across a lot of Venetian architecture over the next few days. Lions of St Mark stand on almost every important building. It's a reminder that at one time, indeed for a couple of thousand years, this area was far more important to the seafaring peoples of the eastern Mediterranean than to anyone else, and that this process began a few centuries before the Slavic tribes arrived from the east and began to settle in the interior.

A grey-haired man in light blue shirt and beige slacks is standing behind a table at the far end of the nave, to the left of the altar. In front of him are arrayed souvenir booklets, postcards and kitsch Catholic trinkets of various kinds. Ozren asks him if we can see the mummies; they talk *sotto voce* for a few seconds. He nods and comes around from behind the table, shakes our hands. '*Deutsche?* English?' he asks. 'I speak. Which you…?'

'*Da*, English. OK.' He gestures around him. 'This largest church… in Istria! We have saints! Only *Rim*,' he says. 'Only… *Rome* has… so many. Only Rome. Two hundred eighty saints! This is place… of pilgrimage.' He leads us behind the altar to a semicircular choir that is covered by a low canopy made of thick red velvet. A small red table lamp and a cassette recorder with two portable speakers are set up on a stool in front of a wall of glass cabinets, while behind the glass are stacked numerous smaller glass cases, not so different from the kinds of display cabinets that pubs might use to display stuffed pike, but these are not filled with angling trophies.

He points to the church's main attraction, which is a large and dessicated section of a human torso, comprising neck, shoulder, back and arm. There is no head. Veins and tendons protrude from the stump of the neck, from the arm, from the ragged edges of torn skin where the flesh of the back has been roughly torn. He points at it triumphantly: 'Can you feel…' he asks, so close that I can smell his breath, 'the *bio-energy?*' He pronounces it 'bee-oh enn-err-ghee'. I can smell it, I think, but I just raise my eyebrows, nod and shrug all at the same time. 'Is St Sebastian.'

'Ah,' I say, jabbing at my chest in an attempt to mime the action of piercing arrows, 'That St Sebastian?' I peer more closely at the dessicated corpse behind the glass – it's the right side of St Sebastian's back and his right arm. There are no puncture marks, but I suppose they would have been on the front of the body.

'Yes… St Sebastian. After… arrows… they … tear him apart. Head from body.' He leans in closer again: 'There is kind of *bio-energy* here. Can you feel? Is miracle! People come!'

He points at more glass boxes, more saints, none with quite such obviously violent origins as the brutally quartered St Sebastian. The other boxes contain arms, vertebrae and finger bones in tiny glass and silver vessels. 'Here is St Leon Bembo… St Noolosa Bursa… St Johannes Olui… Undecayed without being… embalm-ed. It is miracle.' My head is spinning from too much information, or maybe it's the bio-energy, but I lose track when he talks about someone, one of these saints, being the officer in charge of Diocletian and Maximilian's bodyguard. I think he's talking about St Sebastian. He stops and points at the cassette recorder: 'We have tape.'

The recorded commentary begins, but I get lost just looking at all the boxes. One contains the leg of St Barbara: the voice on the tape says '…her body intact and a very pleasant smell emanating from her grave'. Tiny glass bottles, jars and boxes are stuffed with cotton wool, fragments of bone and tiny illuminated paper scrolls. One of them contains the undecayed tongue of St Mary of Egypt, who, the recording tells us, 'worked as prostitute in Alexandria for 17 years'. Many of the 350 relics were spirited out of France during and after the revolution of 1789, and kept in Venice until 1818, when they were brought here.

As we make our way back out into the nave, where Ozren has been waiting, late afternoon light fills the space, and I see that a young couple and their two small children are next in line to see the relics. They smile.

'Deutsche? English? Italiano?' the curator asks them. 'I speak!'

'Nederlands,' the man says.

We stop for a very quick coffee a few miles further up the road to Motovun, Ozren discreetly glancing at his watch while we wait for the waitress to take our order. The village is called Sveti Vićenat, but the name is pronounced 'Savicente'; a reminder that there has been an Italian presence in Istria for hundreds of years.

At the centre of Sveti Vićenat is a huge ruined castle, the Kastel Morosini-Grimani. Ozren asks the waitress if she knows where the woman is who holds the key for the castle, then excuses himself to go and look for her. I'll soon find out that Istria is like a big village: everybody knows who has the key to every historical site. He returns a few minutes later with an enormous iron key that is at least a foot long: 'You want to have a look?' he says. 'There is amazing theatre festival here in the summer – in the castle itself. International theatre. You cannot move here, the whole town is so busy. It's nice to be here when it's quiet.' That is an understatement. The town is like a deserted film set. A couple of cats, some pigeons roosting in the castle windows up above us, and a small child riding up and down the deserted street on a bicycle are the only signs of life, at least until we walk past the open windows of some of the houses and hear voices inside.

'Look,' Ozren says, gesturing through an open front door at some beautifully cut yet unornamented stone, set against dark wood. 'Stone and wood. These are traditional building methods that you'll see all over Istria. The tourist board is really promoting that. You know, we have learned that we should make the most of what we have, these traditional methods, rather than build hotels or holiday homes that could be located anywhere in Europe.'

Inside the castle there is not much to see – a patch of grass and stone the size of a football pitch, surrounded by high, light-coloured stone walls – but nonetheless we wander around hopefully for a few moments.

As we shut the castle's great wooden door behind us, I ask if I can turn the key – I've never locked up a castle door before, never used such an old key. I don't know what the name might be for the part of the key that you hold to turn it, but this one is the size of a suitcase handle and I have to grasp it with my whole fist, though it turns as if it had been fitted only the day before.

Driving out of Sveti Vićenat we see more of the Istrian countryside, only now it is bathed in a glorious golden light. The earth that shows in ploughed fields and gulleys, and along the sides of the road, is a rich dark red that is broken up only by coarse dry grass and white stone. The fields are surrounded by ancient dry-stone walls into which little circular dry-stone houses are built, the walls a continuous spiralling course of stone. Their roofs are built up into shallow cones simply by gradually decreasing the circumference of the spiral. 'They have been here for hundreds of years,' Ozren tells us. 'No one knows how to do this any more. Their construction method is a lost art. They are for shepherds in the winter. Very strong construction.'

Everywhere there are vineyards, while some fields have alternate rows of corn and vines, and still others are scattered with more of the enormous orange pumpkins that I'd seen in the fields next to Zadar Airport. A sudden sharp smell of cabbage precedes the sight of a field where two men are cutting and piling up their bright green globes on blue tarpaulins. There are more of the tree-built hayricks, in odd-shaped little fields fringed by forests. We pass a life-sized and realistic stone Calvary that's been built by the side of the road, and then two dogs mating by a run-down wooden farm building.

'Actually,' says Ozren, looking at his watch again, torn between his schedule and his love for Istria, 'we still have time to see a very famous fresco. It's on the way. Will only take ten minutes. It's a medieval *danse macabre* – very famous.'

A few minutes later he swings the Mercedes off the main road and up a series of tight, steep, hairpin bends. At the top of the hill is the tiny village of Beram. An elderly lady appears next to the car and gets in, and we drive out of the village by another route, down a dusty track past little fields of cabbage, pumpkin and corn – flowers like tiny orange lanterns lining the side of the road – until we come to a great iron gate outside a small stone chapel. Tall pine trees shadow the road and the verges are scattered with dead pine needles, dandelion and rocket, tiny chalky-mauve flowers, and cigarette ends. A carved monument at the chapel gate, which was erected 30 years before our visit, almost to the day, by the Yugoslav Academy of Sciences and Arts (itself founded by the Croatian bishop and pan-Slavist Josip Juraj Strossmayer in 1866), commemorates the artist who painted the frescoes that we're about to see: *Majstor Vincent iz Kastva* (Artisan Vincent of Kastav).

The chapel is called St Mary of the Slate Floor, and indeed it is built upon a huge flat slab of stone that sits on the edge of a shallow hill. As we enter the chapel through a small side door I'm aware of a movement above our heads, some small shadow that darts and flutters from one end of the chapel to the other: a bat.

Vincent's paintings are quite extraordinary. Some of the paintwork is faded and the plaster has cracked here and there, but otherwise it's in a remarkable state of repair, and the *danse macabre* is the *pièce de resistance*. Against a blood-red sky we see a procession of skeletons, some dancing, one carrying a huge scythe, others playing musical instruments such as lutes, horns and bagpipes. Dancing with them, two by two, are some incredibly detailed representations of people from all strata of 15th-century Istrian society.

The documentary value of these portraits is remarkable: townspeople and nobles, in the dress of the day, carry the tools of their trades. There's a bishop, a baker, a round-cheeked wine merchant wearing a cream linen tunic and a soft, brimless felt hat with blue trim and earflaps. The detail is incredible. Around the merchant's belted waist are slung a cloth purse and a bottle, and he wears dark slippers and brown stockings. In one hand he carries a small barrel, while with the other he takes the bony hand of a grinning skeleton. Next to him is a queen who wears a blue dress with a silver hem and a crown that sits atop a white wimple, matching a purple-lined cloak. Hanging from the crook of one arm is a red, tasselled handbag. Next to her another skeleton is running and beckoning to a fair-haired king, who carries a sceptre, and is dressed in red stockings and a blue doublet, with quilted sleeves, a fur collar and a jewelled belt. He gazes impassively at the viewer as he too takes the hand of another skeleton.

None of these people seems afraid to die, though this is perhaps due to a single deficiency in Vincent's painting skills: he can't really do faces, much less use them to portray character or emotion. Consequently, all these figures – and for all their documentary value they're emphatically not characters – stare blandly out of the picture like dolls. The one exception is the wine merchant, who seems to look at the spectacle around him with an expression of purse-lipped disapproval, although this may just have been a slip of the brush, and he too doesn't resist – he's holding hands with Death as an obedient child at the side of a busy road might hold the hand of a parent.

On either side of the chapel's main door, two windows have been cut through the stone of the wall, destroying the frescoes that had been there until they were sacrificed for the sake of light. Beneath the sill of one window the knees and shins of Adam and Eve are still visible.

Beneath a more crudely painted vaulted wooden ceiling, which probably dates from the same 19th-century restoration that punched windows through the Garden of Eden, every inch of the walls is covered. Biblical scenes and the lives (or mostly deaths) of the saints are enacted in the Istrian landscape. Jesus himself enters Jerusalem on a donkey, but Jerusalem – like the towns that form a repeated motif in the background of all these frescoes – is a fortified hill-top village much like those that perch on Istria's hills to this day; and St George kills the dragon in the valley below.

On the wall opposite St George is another painting, this time of a plump-hipped and rosebud-lipped St Sebastian, whom Vincent has rendered almost feminine. His eyes are as impassive as the baker's, in spite of the fact that he's bleeding from wounds inflicted by numerous arrows that are buried almost to the flights in the flesh of his torso and legs. It's a curiously peaceful image that's completely at odds with the violence of the ragged corpse I'd seen in the church a couple of hours before. Like the faces of the townspeople dancing with Death, he is more doll than human.

It's Vincent of Kastav's inability to depict character that makes me realise how much Rebecca West's novelistic ability contributes to *Black Lamb and Grey Falcon's* power as a compelling narrative and makes it such an extraordinary book. West fleshes out her histories of the southern Slavs with believable characters rather than simple reiterations of names and dates. Furthermore, her identification and attribution of the single-most important contribution of William Shakespeare to literature and society, the invention of the modern concept of character and the understanding that people sometimes, too, act against their best interests and are subject to often conflicting motivations, gives her own portraits a three-dimensionality that is truly magnificent.

Occasionally however, these rich portraits can be so seductive that they exceed what it is possible to know, or override mere fact. West may well have felt that the urgency of her task in writing the book made such moments of licence a necessity. Her description of the 1941 coup and the accession of the young King Petar Karadjordjević II to the throne vacated by Prince Pavle is a case in point, although we can only know this now. Her telling of how the 17 year old King Petar addressed the nation on the morning of the coup, summoning a kingly wisdom far beyond his years when he must have been aware that massive Nazi revenge was imminent, is rather undermined by the more recent acknowledgement that not only was the speech written by the leaders of the coup, but also, was read out on Yugoslavian radio by an actor.

The caretaker points excitedly at another image nearby: *'Herodus i la bambini!'* I ask if I can take a photo, but she shakes her head. The frescoes are too fragile to withstand tourists' flash guns.

Just inside the doorframe, partly obscured by repairs to the plaster, is a strange cloaked and hooded figure wearing a kind of two-tiered turban that looks (at least to English eyes) like a cottage loaf. His hands are clasped as if he's praying, while radiating out around his head are eight large feathery ears of corn or barley. Blank, milky, saucer-shaped eyes are set in a wrinkled face that's not quite human, although it's hard to tell because a gouged chunk of plaster obscures the end of what might be a snout-like nose and mouth. It's an unfathomable painting, though he certainly doesn't look like a benign figure, in spite of his abundant corn headdress. I ask the lady with the key if she knows who or what the painting represents, but she just shrugs and shakes her head.

A patina of scratches covering this painting is revealed on closer inspection to be graffiti written in the Glagolitic alphabet, an ancient church script consisting of 41 letters. Many accounts claim that this was the script that St Cyril and St Methodius developed from the letters used to write a Slavic dialect of the Thessaloniki region in the southern Balkans, using a system of squares, circles and triangles, in order to write down parts of their translation of the Bible into that dialect when they came to the region as missionaries. Most accounts hold that the Cyrillic alphabet was invented, as a development from or replacement for Glagolitic, by St Clement, a pupil of Cyril and Methodius, in Ohrid, which is now in Macedonia and is one of the holiest sites in the Orthodox church, or by followers of St Cyril in the tenth century. (Others suggest that St Cyril and St Methodius invented Cyrillic, and that Glagolitic was a variant developed separately in Dalmatia.) What is apparent is that the characters of the Glagolitic alphabet are phonetic. Each has one sound and these are sounds that carry through into contemporary Serbian and Croatian. They can also be read as ideograms or symbols for more abstract words, and as numbers. The character for 'L' can be an ideogram (in this case, an abbreviation) for 'people' (*ljudi*), but (as in Latin) it can also mean '50'. There's another character for *'št'* (a root of the word 'what' in Serbian and Croatian), that has a numerical value of 800, and one that was used for '*kako*' ('how') and has a numerical value of 40. These scratched graffiti turn out to be as ubiquitous in Istria's ancient buildings as the Šahovnica is in Zagreb.

There's a monument to the Glagolitic script in Istria, the Aleja Glagoljaša, which follows the road between the villages of Roc and Hum for about seven kilometres. It's more like a series of monuments to various aspects of the history of the Glagolitic script in Croatia. The monuments are quite small and not particularly obtrusive in the landscape. They are dotted here and there along the verges, atop grassy banks or next to buildings.

Further down the road is a field, surrounded on three sides by a tree-lined bank, in which there are perhaps a dozen more of these sculptures, as well as a round picnic table with square blocks of stone for seats. We sit briefly and someone makes the inevitable Arthurian joke. I notice a small dirt footpath between two of the trees that looks as if it's been cut through the undergrowth and up the hill by use rather than by design, an example of what town planners apparently call 'desire paths' such as those that cut diagonally across any square of grass in any town. At the top, on the other side of the road that has now corkscrewed back on itself on its way up to

Hum, there is another stone monument, bigger than the others we've seen. Two long, low walls frame a central block of stone that bears the legend *'Zid Hrvatskih Protestanata Heretika'* (*'zid'* meaning 'wall'), while carved out of the block is a negative impression of the hour-glass form of what could be either the Glagolitic letter 'i' or the letter 's'. Embedded among the rough stones of the wall are cleanly dressed blocks upon which a number of phrases are engraved in a variety of different letter styles, though these words are written in Croatian using the Latin alphabet rather than the Glagolitic. The phrases are taken from one of the several books produced by the Croatian Protestants to whom this is a monument. One of them reads '*Vrime je da se imamo oda sna ustati, ne ino bog vas veseli i drago mi je da si zdrav.*' It's hard for me to translate, even with a dictionary to hand, because there are some archaic spellings. The first section means something along the lines of : 'It's time that we from dreams awaken…' The middle bit is a little harder – something about God (*bog*), an archaic version of the formal or plural form of 'you' (*vas*), and 'joy' (*veseli*). Then it ends with: 'and I'm glad that you are healthy'.

The Reformation briefly exerted a very strong influence in Croatia, before Protestantism was banned at the beginning of the 17th century. As elsewhere in Europe, the Reformation was fuelled by the advent of print technology and a Glagolitic Bible was produced here, as well as catechisms for the teaching of the new creed. This particular monument, more than any of the other ten that form the Aleja, looks rather like a war memorial, and perhaps that's appropriate since, as the Italian anarchist collective known as Luther Blissett remind us in their novel *Q,* which was published in English translation in 2003, the Reformation was far from being just a theological debate. Not only did the Reformation and the Catholic Counter-Reformation create chaos and havoc across 16th century Europe, they also more or less coincided with the juggernaut of the Ottoman Empire storming through Croatia and Hungary to besiege Vienna and threaten the rest of western Europe with occupation. The city didn't fall and, as we know, the Ottomans fell back more or less to the border marked by the Sava and the Danube. Istria itself is far less accessible over land than by sea, being largely cut off from the rest of what is now Croatia and Slovenia by a chain of high limestone mountains, and consequently the Ottomans went straight past it, just as they had Zagreb. Strategically speaking they were irrelevancies, Istria hanging off the Balkan peninsula like an appendix.

It's not clear when the Aleja monuments to the Glagolitic alphabet and the Croatian Reformation were built, beyond the fact that, to judge by the design, it certainly dates from the second half, or probably the last quarter, of the 20th century. One could equally imagine its construction being connected with the ambient and officially encouraged anti-Catholic sentiment of the Tito era, or with a stirring of Croatian separatism and/or nationalism such as the 'Croatian Spring' of the early 1970s.

Istria, with its large Italian population, was insulated to some extent from the worst excesses of nationalism during the Tudjman era and (as I've mentioned) it was never part of the fascist Croatian state (the NDH) during the Second World War. Indeed, the Partisan movement was very strong here. When we get to Motovun I see something that will, now that I've noticed it, become familiar over the next few days. In Hum, in Labin, on the walls of buildings on the edges of just about every Istrian town I visit, at least those that have not recently been repainted, can be seen faded red pro-Partisan graffiti that dates from the Second World War.

We pile back into the car and Ozren is still optimistic that we'll get to Motovun before it gets dark, but it's still a good half-hour's drive away and meanwhile even dusk seems like a memory. It's only as we crest one after another of central Istria's great hills, plunge down into deep valleys then zigzag slowly up the other sides that I realise how high up Motovun must be. 'It's amazing in the winter,' Ozren says. 'These valleys fill with mist, but Motovun is always above the clouds. It looks like an island floating there. It's really magical, like something from a fairy tale. You can look out from the city walls and see nothing but this sea of clouds.'

As we finally approach the town and drive up the winding road that leads to the floodlit village high above it's completely dark. 'I'm so disappointed,' says Ozren, locking up the car. 'I really thought we'd make it. Maybe we shouldn't have had that coffee.'

Chapter Eleven
Istria II: Motovun, Rovinj, Vrsar, Poreč (2004)

We're staying in the Hotel Kaštel, which stands at one end of Motovun's long town square. At the other end of the square everything is built from white stone, while the Kaštel is covered in a soft orange stucco. Outside, taking up this half of the square, is the hotel's open-air restaurant, its tables and chairs set out beneath half a dozen enormous horse chestnut trees.

I haven't eaten since lunchtime in Zagreb, so I practically run to my room and I'm down at a table beneath the horse chestnut trees less than five minutes later. The food is simple but good: chicken noodle soup, lamb, potatoes and gravy, with *palačinke* for desert – pancakes doused in a thick, tarry chocolate sauce. Some cats that had been sitting on a low brick wall outside the nearby post office come over to investigate almost as soon as the first course arrives. One of them rubs itself ingratiatingly around my ankles, then sits there purring. I feed it scraps of meat and the fatty bits off the bone. I learn quite quickly that it's not a good idea to stroke these cats. I wonder how long there have been stray cats here, but the answer is obvious: as long as the town.

As we eat, the warm breeze carries a magical sound of male choral singing from somewhere. For a while none of us mentions it, each assuming that it must be a CD being played in one of the many rooms that look out onto the square. Yet it doesn't sound like a recording. Something about it, the clarity of the harmonies perhaps, or some human richness in the quality of the sound, convinces us that it's a real choir, even though it's barely audible and is being carried, light as dandelion seeds, on the occasional waft of breeze.

When the waitress brings us another decanter of house red we ask her what it is. They are practising for a concert, she tells us, *'sutra uveče'* ('tomorrow evening'). Do we need to book tickets? No, it's free. *'Gde biće?'* I ask ('Where will it be?'). *'Tamo'* ('There'), she says, nodding her head in the direction of the church.

I wander over to have a look while we wait for our coffees. Inside the church of Sveti Stjepan (St Stephen) a group of ten or so men are standing to one side of the aisle as a woman conducts them. Their voices rise to fill the high dark spaces in the church roof. In a day or so *'odlično'* ('excellent') will become the most overused word in my vocabulary, prompting laughter every time I say it, but for now it seems completely appropriate: *'Odlično,'* I say, 'perfect.'

Breakfast is simple fare at the Hotel Kaštel: a buffet of milky soft white bread rolls that are so bland and puffy they remind me of the faces of those 15th-century Istrians in the frescoes at Beram, together with fruit, yoghurts, meats and cheeses. While queuing I overhear a disdainful English voice saying, 'Horrible...socialistic era...'

I take my coffee outside to breakfast with the cats instead. The main square is named Trg Andrea Antico, after one of Motovun's most famous sons. I discover, thanks to an exhibition in the hotel bar, that Antico (who was born in Motovun some time between 1470 and 1480, and died in Venice in 1540) was the first Slavic composer to have his musical compositions published. Not only that, but he was, according to one notice, 'the second-known printer, after Petrucci': he published his first book in 1510. He was also the first known engraver in Croatia and the first to publish musical notation for organ music. Granted a printing charter by Pope Leo X, he published books of madrigals in four languages – Italian, Latin, French and Spanish – all without using moveable type.

There's an alleyway between the church and the hotel that leads out to the town's 13th-century walls. The height of Motovun is quite a shock by daylight. The town nests atop a single, almost conical hill that's set in a wide valley. Far below, the River Mirna (which means 'calm') follows the line of the main road out to the west, its fortified banks as straight as a canal, while two minutes' walk around the walls to the other side of town, past fig and chestnut trees, and a little black cat asleep on the path, the view is of winding tracks and tiny farmsteads, a jumble of fields and woods, vineyards, wisps of morning mist. The hills on the far side of the valley are hazy in the morning light, while below the walls the town tumbles down the side of the hill in a mess of treetops, rooftops, church towers and cottage gardens, growing pears, figs, peppers and tomatoes. The landscape and architecture of these medieval hill towns remind me of central and southern France. I'll get used to this over the next few days: mountain villages that are more beautiful than St Paul de Vence near Nice, but that are completely unspoilt by tourism.

Croatia, of course, had a thriving tourist industry in the 1980s, which is definitely returning, pragmatism gradually replacing the rhetoric about 1,000-year states and the constitutional racism that made Croatia the nation state of Croats rather than of everyone who lived there. Even while I was having breakfast that morning, parties of elderly French, German and Dutch tourists would periodically spill through the town gate into Trg Andrea Antico. Seeing this kind of architecture, these hilltop villages and the spectacular views, it's surprising not to see all the machinery of an intensive tourism industry – swimming pool centres, hotels, car hires, holiday homes – that elsewhere in Europe would go hand in hand with it.

Ozren is a little anxious about the day's schedule. We must go to Hum, the smallest town in the world; we must visit another mountain village called Labin; we will be visiting a famous truffle shop and a hilltop restaurant where we can sample the best that Istrian *agriturizam* has to offer; all this and be back in Motovun in time for the *koncert* at eight o'clock.

Hum lives up to its reputation: it's tiny. It's also another example of what – since arriving at Motovun, through craning my neck out of the car window up at walls and rooftops on top of almost every hill, and from the motifs in the backgrounds of all the Beram frescoes – I'm already beginning to think of as a typical Istrian hill village: the pale stone buildings, the cobbled roads and pavements, small town squares paved with enormous slabs that have been worn smooth and shiny through centuries of use, the spectacular views across forested limestone hills, and the empty houses.

Hum consists of two streets and perhaps a dozen buildings; it now has just 11 inhabitants. The sound of 'Sunday Girl' by Blondie is audible as soon as we've walked up the roughly cobbled street into the town. As we continue up the steep street into the main square Egle tells us that there's a legend that, while Venice used to appoint Hum's mayor each year, now the town's 11 inhabitants are responsible for this – and even visitors can put their names forward.

As we double back on ourselves and walk back down the town's one other street, I discover where the music had been coming from: the town museum. Inside, a hippy-looking woman wearing numerous silver rings of Celtic-looking design is sitting behind the cash register, while the walls are covered in display cabinets in which all manner of Glagolitic texts, printed and on fragments of stone or clay, are displayed, along with various items of the rural everyday: implements, furniture, china. Low tables in front of the windows are lined with bottles of local spirits – a locally made *biska*, the Istrian honey-flavoured clear brandy, and *travarica*, a greenish brandy that comes complete with a bunch of the herbs that flavour it, one of which is reputed to continue growing in the bottle. The local speciality here in Hum is a mistletoe-laced variant of *travarica*, and indeed there's a druidic, new-agey feel to the museum, in spite of the New Wave CD that's playing, which is to say that there is a generic sense of manufactured antiquity. I buy a booklet about the Glagolitic alphabet for a few kuna, but, like most of today's conversation, it comes only in a German translation.

Like Hum, Istria itself is tiny. It seems that even from the centre of the peninsula you're never more than half an hour's drive from the sea. From the top of just about any substantial hill you can see the coastal towns of Rovinj or Poreč, their church spires, and the dazzle of the Adriatic. In spite of this it's a long drive up into the hills – and a few phone calls to let them know that we'll be late – before we arrive at the restaurant where we're expected for lunch.

Ozren wasn't born in Istria, but he knows this region like the back of his hand. In a smaller car, with a less competent driver, these barrierless mountain roads, which offer the passenger sudden views down vertiginous slopes broken only by rock and shrub, would be terrifying. The Mercedes at least has enough power to be able to tackle just about any incline that Istria can throw at us. Ozren swings wide into one hairpin bend after another and takes us up the side of another mountain, then down into yet another valley. Finally, turning off the main road, we drive through an idyllic upland of green fields, and park with a crunch of gravel in front of a long two-storey stone house with orange wooden shutters, a red terracotta roof and a garden centre's worth of geraniums. This *seljačko domaćinstvo* (peasant household or homestead), as it says on the sign, is the restaurant Tončić.

Agriturizam is the current buzzword in Istria, picking up on the 'slow food' movements that started off in France and Italy in the late 1980s, and that champion local produce above the dubious 'fruits' of global multinational industries. *Agriturizam* gives visitors the opportunity, Ozren tells us, to stay in high-quality guesthouses in the heart of the countryside and to sample the very best that Istria has to offer.

This restaurant, high in the hills, is a prime example. Ozren points at the upstairs windows. Beneath the terracotta tiles are guest rooms with double doors that look out across some of the most beautiful scenery you can imagine – a broad green valley, sparsely scattered with weathered white boulders, trees and hedgerows, on the far side of which, at least 15 or 20 miles away, is a high mountain ridge that stretches across as much of the far horizon as we can see, culminating to our right in the forested slopes of Mount Učka. These are the mountains of the Dinaric Alps. Beyond them lies Slovenia. This great ridge continues almost unbroken down the whole Adriatic coast of Croatia. From here it has the appearance of an enormous stone wave, kilometres long, which has been petrified at the moment of breaking.

'Look,' says Ozren, drawing our attention back to the neat lines of the carefully restored farmhouse. 'They will have two, three more rooms by next summer, and they really are beautiful. You can stay here, eat the best food, wake up and see this every morning, and everywhere you want to go, Motovun, Poreč, wherever, is just half an hour away. No wonder this is so popular.'

As we take our seats at the table Ozren explains a bit more about the *agriturizam* concept. To qualify for the label the restaurant must use a minimum of 50 per cent of local produce and no less than 40 per cent of produce from other registered Istrian suppliers; this would include truffles, game, pasta and seafood. The remaining 10 per cent comprises ingredients that cannot be produced locally, such as spices, soft drinks or bottled water.

It's the truffles that we're here to sample. Istrian truffles are world-famous and everybody tells me proudly that this is where the largest truffle on record was found. Plaster casts of this monstrosity, mounted on officially branded Guinness World of Records wooden plinths and resembling nothing so much as misshapen human brains, are displayed in delicatessens, truffle dealerships and this restaurant.

There's a slight breeze, but the sun is warm and some glasses of *biska* sharpen our appetites. The food is extraordinary. First, accompanied by as much home-made bread as we can eat, comes a huge platter of domestic hams and cheeses, and by 'domestic' I'm given to understand that they mean it was produced on this very farm. There are slices of air-dried *pršut* (a variation of the Italian *prosciutto*) and a sweet belly-pork striped with fat that is as soft as butter. Conversation ceases for a few minutes as all of us are lost in the tastes and textures of the food. All of this is washed down with beautiful wine and with bottles of Istria's mineral water, a product of all the limestone, which tastes as soft and chalky as the French *Badoit*.

Moments later a vast platter of trembling scrambled eggs appears, topped with what must be several ounces, grated, of this season's truffles. The smell is astonishing, the taste more so. There must be two dozen eggs here, and the truffle is far from being a garnish, it's a layer. Five minutes later we're all wiping the platter clean with hunks of bread.

The art of conversation is remembered and forgotten again with the disappearance of each course and the appearance of the next. We have locally produced pasta with a rich stew of wild boar. More bread. We have seconds, thirds of everything. By the end of the meal, two hours later, I'm deliriously full, and so intoxicated by the freshness and the flavours that I can't even remember what was for dessert.

En route back to Motovun for the *koncert* we stop in yet another hilltop town, the idyllic and rural appearance of which is deceptive, because Labin is a post-industrial relic; a former mining town. Here we see more fading Partisan graffiti and watch a great blazing orange sun dropping into the Adriatic. The quality of the light is such that I know it will soon be the time of the evening when, as Rebecca West wrote of an evening in Dubrovnik, 'all cats are grey and all carpets are beautiful... the colours, fused by the evening, acquire richness'.[1] I enthusiastically relate this description to Josef and György as we explore the narrow streets. There is a sudden uncanny moment that almost seems to have been conjured up by this idea of Rebecca West's. Turning a corner, we arrive at a crossroads that is completely occupied by what Josef jokingly calls a 'parliament' of cats. It's certainly quite an assembly, a couple of dozen of them sitting or lying several ranks deep and facing each other across a bare circle of flagstones. All of them have heads held high and eyes half-closed in contentment. It is almost painful to realize that we've disturbed them, but by the time we've taken in the solemnity of the scene and understood the rarity of the privilege it is too late to retrace our steps. One by one they stand up, shake a paw or two and disperse down alleys, into gardens or doorways.

Near the car park at the entrance to the town is one of Istria's many monuments to the Partisan victory in the Second World War: a modernist sculpture of a winged star that was erected in 1956 to the victims of fascism and those who fought against it. These monuments are everywhere in the towns and cities of the former Yugoslavia, and, here in Istria at least, most are intact. Elsewhere that isn't so. In Kumrovac, Tito's birthplace in northern Croatia, a small bomb beheaded his commemorative statue at the end of 2004,[2] while in Kosovo almost all the monuments from that era have been destroyed.

Ozren gets us to the church on time, but only just. The place is packed and no sooner have I found a seat than the choir, ten young men in their 20s and early 30s, all shapes and sizes, stand up and take a bow. All dressed smartly in shirt and trousers, they line up beneath the huge chandelier that is the only source of light in the enormous church. As I look around I notice that the walls are covered in a yellow wallpaper bearing a heraldic badge and the initials 'JHS'. Here and there it's torn away and you can see fragments of the frescoes beneath.

The conductor introduces the parish priest for a few words of introduction. Then she steps to one side and, still standing, plays the opening bar on a piano and counts the choir in. When they start singing the sound is magnificent. The harmonies are incredible, soaring from a gentle doo-wop to a full-throated sound that fills the huge space of the church and reverberates for a second or so.

They sing 20 or more songs before taking their final bow. I'm just getting ready to stand up and leave when I realize that the *koncert* is by no means over, for another choir is taking their place. Dressed in black suits with white shirts, and a full generation older than the first choir, they come with bald heads, glasses, bellies and grey beards, and their voices are more fragile too. The leader of the choir (they have no conductor) produces a mouth organ from his waistcoat pocket and, after a brief introduction and a couple of jokes, he gives the choir their opening note, to which they tune their voices. Only then do they start to sing. What strikes me is the sheer effort that performance demands of them. These older men visibly wince and grimace as they hit, and sustain, the higher notes. There's something about this performance that was missing in the first choir's, for all the ease of their youth, and that I can't quite grasp for a while because I'm concentrating on the music. This feeling, whatever it is, seems to be forming on the periphery of my vision, in the shadows of the church, as ephemeral as the harmonies themselves, but it's that there's something more valuable about this second choir, something about surviving and still seeing the importance of holding a high note, even though it costs more to do it. These sentimental songs about lost loves simply count for more when they come from the mouths of people who have more experience of life.

Even as I think this, I know that I'm being hopelessly romantic. I'm well aware that folk music is often adopted by the far right in Croatia, just as it was in Milošević's Serbia. I've seen nationalistic and right-wing political parties holding numerous demonstrations or rallies in Zagreb, in Split, and in Rijeka, and almost always these events are accompanied by some kind of regional folk music. Stand around and enjoy the music for too long, and someone will press a leaflet into your hand.

Later, still replete from the wonderful lunch at Tončić, we all pick at dinner in the square. As we do so we become aware of more music being carried on the breeze above the hubbub of a post-concert party that's being held in the square: 'The Flight of the Bumble-bee', played on what sounds like a glockenspiel. At first it sounds a bit cloying and twee, as popular classics played on inappropriate instruments often do, but as one piece follows another Josef suddenly drains his glass of wine and says, 'That's it, I have to see what's happening.' A few minutes later he reappears, animated with excitement: 'You have to come and see this. It's a bottle orchestra! Come!' The others demur, make noises about going to bed, but I'm not tired at all, for the excitement of the choirs has revived me.

The scene that awaits us is truly something to behold. A tiny café, called Bar Antico of course, nestles behind the bell tower of Sveti Stjepan, and the courtyard outside is packed. Every seat is taken and people stand in any remaining space. Beneath a flight of stone steps that climb to a door halfway up the church tower, lit by the lights of the bar and by two flaming torches set on the steps, is a bohemian scene that is reminiscent of a Fellini film. 'No, a Kusturica film,' Josef corrects me. Well, we are both correct. For all that the sound is precise, precious and delicate, like the tinkling of a chandelier in the breeze from an open window, the energy needed to call it forth is showing on the perspiring form of a burly, red-faced man, dressed in a shabby brown suit and checked shirt, with two sticks in each hand, who is running up and down and hammering out, by now, the overture from Bizet's *Carmen* on a huge and unwieldy xylophone, longer than the keyboard of a grand piano, which is made up of scores of wine and spirit bottles, set in two ranks one above the other and each two bottles deep. Next to him a more precise-looking man, with a tidy black ponytail and a goatee beard, is strumming neat chords in accompaniment. Together these two make up an 'orchestra' called Spirits from the Bottle.

I'm kicking myself for not having a camera, but since that means I can't stand here taking pictures, Josef and I go to the bar, try to remember the name of the drink with the herbs in it and buy the first of many rounds. Every song is applauded loudly and noisily. Mozart, Bach, Vivaldi, Ravel: it's the kind of chocolate-box classical music that easy-listening radio stations play for people who don't like classical music, but something about the setting, this little bar, the flaming torches, the rowdily appreciative audience, the warm night, or these two bohemian-looking musicians themselves has a bit of rock and roll about it. For a start, you can imagine that these two musicians may well have chosen to drink their way through all those bottles, rather than simply using empties. Moving closer, I'm delighted to see that the highest note on the xylophone is a tiny 25cl bottle of my old favourite red wine from Belgrade, T'ga za Jug.

Josef and I buy another round of *travarica* and talk to the musicians, Zoran Madžirov and Saša Dejanović, once they've finished and taken their bows. They tell us that they started playing together in the late 1980s, when they were in the army together, just for something to do to while away the time, but now they're joining a long tradition of 'medieval jugglers and vagabonds' who've played the bottles; that Mozart wrote a work for glass harmonica shortly before his death; that there's a reference to musical instruments made of bottles in a 15th-century manuscript, the *Theoria Musicae* of Gaffurius; and that a glass-instrument concert was held in London in 1746 by one Christopher W. Gluck. It turns out that they've performed and appeared on television countless times around the world. Zoran starts packing up the xylophone as he chats, but the musical entertainment isn't over yet. While the concert was finishing the two choirs also turned up at Antico and took over a whole section of the courtyard. They're being treated like celebrities, people are offering them their seats, and while they applauded Sprits from the Bottle they were also acknowledging the greetings and the praise that was being directed their way for their earlier performances.

It's as if no part of this evening could be complete without music. It doesn't take much encouragement before a couple of the more senior singers strike up the first notes of a song, which quickly turns into the third concert of the evening. While the performances in the church had been wonderful, this impromptu concert, which goes on until two o'clock in the morning, is the best of all. Josef and I chat with a couple who have been standing next to us, friends of Zoran and Saša. Jonathan and Dragana are on their way to Bosnia, where they will attend her sister's wedding in Bihać. They live in Amsterdam and just happened to be here tonight: they didn't know about the concerts beforehand, but they are very glad they came. Dragana tells us about *klapa* music, which is what the choirs have been singing. *Klapa* is the name of this kind of choral music, but the word means something like 'bunch' or 'company' and, in this context, something like 'glee club'. The music originates in Dalmatia and it's an oral tradition: the songs are not written down, just passed from generation to generation by mouth and ear. Dragana stops wondering, as she had been, whether they were going to sing her favourite song, a big hit by a group called Klapa Greben, and decides to go and put in a request. The choirs are happy to oblige and it is a beautiful song, slower than the others. Dragana comes back to join us and stands there completely enraptured while they sing: 'Listen to that! It's so beautiful!' she says. 'It's almost like being in love.'

Dvigrad is a town that's been deserted since it was hit by the plague in the 14th century. After morning coffee in the square I drive there with a local designer and photographer called Mauro. Since I first heard about Dvigrad I've tried to imagine what such a ghost town might look like. In addition to towns abandoned centuries ago, what's struck me during my travels, even in the brief period I've been in Istria, has been the number of empty houses I've seen that have been abandoned more recently. Some of this may be due to a natural depopulation of the countryside, as fewer can be sustained by poorly paid agricultural work, but I've also assumed that some of them must have belonged to Serb families who'd chosen, or been forced, to leave during the wars of the 1990s. There's a *Mary Celeste* quality about these empty houses when you see them. None is in a significant state of disrepair; they all look as if they'd been deserted in a hurry about 10 or 15 years before.

While we drive, we chat. Long before he was a designer, before the war even, Mauro did his national service in the old Yugoslav National Army (the JNA), which, thankfully, he said, ended about three days after the first violent incidents in Lika that led to war. A bit further down the road I happen to mention friends in Serbia. I'm not sure how the subject came up; perhaps he'd asked me why I speak the language. As soon as I mention Belgrade I notice him stiffen slightly. This isn't quite the reaction I'd experienced at the festival in Zagreb and in fact Mauro isn't unaware of his reaction. He laughs and says, 'Listen, I'm sorry. I didn't mean to do that, but we grow up in "Brotherhood and Unity" with all Yugoslavs, then suddenly we are at war with Serbs and with Bosnians, and this was not something that my generation caused, you know. So excuse me if I behave strangely, but it's like we were married to Serbs and now we are not, but it was very messy divorce! It's like me telling you that your ex-wife is not bad in bed, or something! You would maybe react strangely; is a kind of reflex… I mean, forgive me, I don't know if you are even married, but speaking generally. Anyway, Istria was not so involved as the rest of Croatia, we are so mixed you know, so many Italians, that it's not the same here as in other parts of the country anyway.'

I've read that many Istrians rejected the nationalism of Franjo Tudjman, even when he'd demanded they declare themselves Croatians first and Istrians second, but I'm still aware of those empty houses. The war must have made some impact here.

'Ah look,' Mauro says, pointing off to the right at another hilltop village. 'This is Draguc, you know "*draga*" means…'

'Dear, darling.'

'*Da!* Of course! Well, Draguc is like diminutive, you know, like "little darling", I always like this as a name for a town. There is beautiful church, maybe we can find the key.'

Draguc is set on a tiny spur of land that juts out into a deep valley, so rather than have to drive up some winding road to get to it we just turn off and follow the unmetalled road across what seems like a natural drawbridge, and park in a little square outside a café, which is closed.

As we stroll through Draguc, which is not so much bigger than Hum and where perhaps a third of the houses stand empty, Mauro tells me about a protest that's happening the next day – which happens to be 11 September, although the protest is nothing to do with the atrocities in New York and Washington in 2001. The second Sunday of September, here in Istria, is a special day for tourism, designed to promote the region's wine trade. On this day every year there is free admission to all of Istria's vineyards, and a free wine tasting in every one. The protest is to do with new traffic laws that have been introduced across Croatia. One states that car headlights must be switched on at all times of the day. Remembering to switch them on in the daytime is not the problem, it's remembering to switch them off when you park the car in daylight that's proving difficult: everyone's getting flat batteries. The other new law, the one that has provoked the protest, was introduced in a bid to clamp down on drunk driving. This law states that driving with anything above 0.0 per cent of alcohol in the bloodstream is a criminal offence. I keep hearing about this new law from various people while I'm in Istria. 'Is crazy,' one person tells me. 'Even priests are now criminals, because the sip of wine taken during mass puts them over the limit.' The feeling is that the government is overcompensating in an attempt to prove how progressive it is compared to its predecessors of the Tudjman era; that this is an ill-thought-out attempt at overcompliance with the kind of legislation against drunk driving that exists in the European Union, part of a raft of measures designed to prove that Croatia is ready for membership. What no one disputes is that the new law certainly spells difficulties for the yearly wine day, if not for '*agriturizam*' generally.

Tomorrow's protest is called 'The day without wine', and it is being heavily promoted across Istria. I have seen posters advertising it, printed over a parodic copy of Edvard Munch's 'The Scream'. All the vineyards will be open to the public as usual, but the only thing available for tasting will be water. The priests are joining in too: water instead of wine will be served at Mass across Istria.

Right at the end of the promontory on which Draguc is built we come to a tiny chapel. Mauro tries the door, but it's locked. An elderly man is taking some washing off a line nearby, so Mauro goes over, as is the custom, and asks him who has the key, then disappears for a few minutes to get it. As with many of these small Istrian churches, there is a loggia built around the door to provide shelter. I sit down on a bench and notice a tiny graffito: 'Silvo 1930'. There is a glassless window set in the old wood of the church door, and through it I can see that the interior of the church is built as one continuous arched vault, and that frescoes cover every inch of the plaster.

The interior walls are also covered in graffiti, a patina of tiny scratches in Glagolitic, Croatian and Italian. The figures that appear time and again in the frescoes are those of St Sebastian and another saint whom I haven't seen before. Dressed in simple peasant clothes and pointing at a wound on his thigh, visible through torn hose, he appears above the simple block of stone that forms the altar. Mauro tells me that this is St Roko, the patron saint of plague victims. Roko was, the story goes, a French nobleman who cared for the sick, including a whole townful of plague victims whom he supposedly met while on a pilgrimage. He is said to have performed some miracles, but then contracted the plague himself, though he didn't die because he was befriended by a dog that brought him food. Charged mistakenly with spying when he returned to France, he died in prison five years later. His patronage extends from bachelors, dogs and, as Mauro suggested, plague victims to falsely accused people and those with skin rashes. The wound that's visible on his leg, which all the iconic images show him pointing to, is of course a sore caused by the plague. On the right-hand wall St Roko and St Sebastian are standing in front of a pile of bodies, all of which wear crowns: they are dead kings.

St Roko didn't save the people of Dvigrad from the plague, I suppose, or perhaps he interceded and saved enough of them that those hundred or so who survived were able to move ten kilometres further inland and build themselves a new village.

It's not far from Draguc to Dvigrad. We drive past a brickyard and over a level crossing, then come to some half-built tollbooths. Soon you'll have to pay to make this journey. Mauro is pantomime-furious about the state of the road. All the roads and tunnels here in Istria, as elsewhere in the former Yugoslavia, were built under Tito's heretical (from Stalin's point of view) version of Communism, that created new forms of 'social ownership' and 'workers' self-management'.

'Look,' says Mauro, 'my grandfather's generation paid for this road, they built it, all the tunnels and everything, by self-management system. Now some privatization happens and a French company come into partnership with the government to rebuild the road, and they want to charge us for it! The contracts cover percentage of the tolls, advertisings, the rights to all petrol stations, everything! It's ridiculous! We've already paid for it, now they want us to pay for it again and not even make any money out of it ourselves! I wouldn't mind, you know, but it's a useless road. It's a dangerous road, single lane all the way, so you can't overtake, and what is more it doesn't go to any cities! What exactly is this road for? You tell me!'

Mauro lives in Pula and loves it there. 'I've lived in Zagreb, but look at this,' he says, gesturing out of the window at a distant hilltop town. 'You don't get this in Zagreb. When I get stressed I can just get in the car and in a few minutes I am out here. I can just drive down the white roads, listen to some music and I'm happy.'

Dvigrad means 'two towns' and apparently at one time that's what it was, two towns, each with its own church, squatting at either end of a single hill. Eventually the towns joined up and were fortified, creating a tiny maze of steep stone streets around a jumble of two-storey houses. We walk up to the town through a narrow street that's enclosed by the town walls on one side and the high walls of houses on the other, then turn up a side street into the town itself. The stones that form the road are as polished as the ones in Hum had been.

There is much more of the town left than I'd imagined, far more than just foundations and a course or two of stonework. The houses are overgrown, some completely filled with brambles, while wild asparagus really does grow in sunny nooks and crannies throughout the steep maze of cobbled streets. The stone floors of some of the houses are formed from the naked rock of the hill, while elsewhere this same naked rock is used to form one or two of the walls. There are small niches set into the interiors of those walls that remain. Some of them are obviously retaining holes for wooden beams and rafters, while others look big enough to hold small statues of saints. Apart from one or two buildings that are practically rubble, all that's missing from most of them are their roofs.

At the summit of the hill, in front of one of the churches, the town square itself is formed from one enormous slab of rock. Walking through this muddle of streets and houses it's easy to imagine the place teeming with life. We climb through rooms and out of front doors to reach what's left of the town's fortifications, from where we have a good view of a solitary market trader who's set up stall in the tourist car park at the foot of the walls to sell bottles of local olive oil, flavoured with slices of orange and lemon, and bottles of *biska*. Ours is the only car in the car park. He's reading a book.

Clambering around this ghost town is gruelling exercise in this heat, and it's not long before the needs of the living take over from thoughts of those who died hundreds of years before. Mauro suggests that we try some of the local seafood, which, he tells me, is amazing. The waters of the Adriatic are very clean and the coastline is rocky, full of craggy inlets, one even being big enough to be called a fjord. It's a little more leafy and tranquil than a

Norwegian fjord, and not even as rocky and dramatic as some of the coves and bays further south from here, in northern Greece or on Corfu, but it's a fjord nonetheless.

Mauro's taking me to his favourite restaurant, but we are going to take the scenic route. I'd assumed that when Mauro mentioned 'white roads' earlier he'd meant roads that are marked white on the map, but when we turn off the main road and onto a rocky, bumpy track that winds down between the trees into the river valley I say, 'Ah! This is what you meant by a white road.'

'Of course! What did you think? It's really white! There are three types of soil in Istria. Down in the south around Pula it's red, here it's white, and further north it's grey.'

High, very high, above us a concrete viaduct takes the new road across the valley from one mountain to the next, but down here time has slowed down and so has Mauro's car. He has to steer round rocks in the road, trying not to completely wreck his suspension or knock the exhaust pipe off. In fields to the side of the road there are wooden shacks on top of scaffolding towers, which are built for the spotting and shooting of wild boar. A crested bird flies up from the road as we approach. Distinctive and beautiful, it has a pink body, black-and-white striped wings, and a long curved bill. It perches in a tree beside the road, and flicks its crest up and down in alarm. I remember this from *The Observer Book of Birds*, which I had as a child: 'Ah,' I say, 'a hoopoe.' 'Here is called "*žuna*",' Mauro says. 'They are everywhere.'

We bounce sedately along the track. 'We all learned these routes when we were young,' Mauro tells me. 'When we wanted to drink we had to drive home on these white roads to avoid the police.' He pauses for a second. 'Maybe with the new law this will come back into fashion!'

The fields on either side of us are unkempt. Much of this land was once used for subsistence agriculture, but now of course it's cheaper to buy produce in the shops than to grow it. We bounce along the road for maybe four or five miles, though it seems much further.

The restaurant is called the Viking, named after some Norse epic or other shot in the fjord that it overlooks. We take a table on the large verandah. There's a breeze and, though it's September, the sun is bright and hot. It's another Indian summer, or, in Croatian, a *babije ljeto* ('Grandma's summer'). Mauro generously offers me the seat overlooking the fjord, so as we eat I have an astounding view, beyond a few souvenir stalls that line the quay and a handful of off-season tourists who wander between them, of the brilliant turquoise water.

We order shellfish from the fjord. Plump oysters, the best I've ever tasted, sit on shells so thick and flat that I wonder if there are some unique mineral properties to the water in this cool fjord, some calciferous process that's accelerated by the water that leaches out of these great limestone hills. We also order *dondole* (cockles), which, eaten off the shell, are meatier and more compact than the oysters but just as delicious. As a treat the waiter brings a small plate on which four fat shelled scampi sit, the raw translucent flesh doused only with lime juice.

I look around me, wondering if I've found the best seafood restaurant in the world, and can think of none that I've been to that can compare.

The main course is a grilled gilt-head bream. It's huge, more than enough for the two of us. We split it and slice one half off the bone for me, one for Mauro. It's accompanied by a buttery mixture of sweet, crumbly boiled potatoes and a kind of wilted fresh spinach served in a jumble on one plate – the traditional accompaniment to sea food in Istria.

We hunt out the seafood restaurants over the next few days, and some of them really do take some finding. You'd need a knowledgeable local to take you to Bepo, which is hidden half a mile and four or five turnings off the main road, in a residential area in the suburbs of Poreč. We tuck into enormous scampi, langoustines in fact, cooked in their shells this time, and served with more potato and spinach. While we eat I notice that a hush has fallen over the restaurant. Looking up I see a giant of a man, perhaps in his mid-40s, with a salt-and-pepper beard and neatly trimmed hair, dressed in baggy jogging trousers and a blue T-shirt that belie his straight-backed military bearing. Everyone watches him walk to his table. Some stand to shake his hand and even the restaurant owner comes out for a respectful chat. Seeing the hushed deference of both diners and staff I can't help wondering if this giant of a man is some kind of soldier, a war hero. The fugitive General Ante Gotovina, perhaps, on a rare day out. Ozren leans over and whispers: 'That is Vinko Jelovac – one of our greatest ever basketball players.'

The one break from Istria's regional specialities of seafood, wild boar, *pršut* and truffles comes with a late-night visit to a Macedonian restaurant called Lav (Lion). 'Have you ever tasted Macedonian food?' Ozren asks. 'Is a little like Serbian, lot of meat, but they also do beans which are very good.' It's dark by the time we reach the restaurant, but as we draw nearer it is revealed to be a vast and floodlit redbrick palace, a great ostentatious architectural monstrosity. Above the portico is a great stone statue of a lion, while off to one side of the building is a vast floodlit swimming pool. The light pollution generated by Lav is sufficient that the night sky over Istria has almost completely disappeared. Just inside the gate are two enormous brick-built barbecue ovens that are obviously designed to cater for hundreds of diners, but inexplicably the vast array of tables and benches set out under an expanse of grape vines is completely deserted. Normally the restaurant would be packed, Ozren tells us. An elderly woman bustles out to meet us and is almost embarrassed to ask where we want to sit. Someone asks if we can go inside and we all breathe a sigh of relief. It seems like a good compromise, a way of ensuring that the human warmth of our little gathering will not be lost in this sea of empty tables and the starkness of the floodlighting.

The interior is as lavish as the exterior, though built on a more human scale, with heavy dark wood furniture and mantelpiece set against the brick and stone walls, which themselves are covered in brass and iron agricultural kitsch, as well as antique guns, swords, and old black-and-white photographs of Macedonian warriors from the early 20th century and women wearing the kinds of embroidered peasant dresses that Rebecca West rhapsodized over.

In one corner of this cosy room, opposite the huge fireplace, are a group of men, who look up when we come in and then go back to an intense *sotto voce* conversation.

The Lion is owned by the kind of politician who might need a bodyguard. Ljube Boškoski was born in 1960 in Tetovo in Macedonia, but fought with the Croatian army in the early 1990s. He's the focus of some confusion, even regarding how his name is spelled (his 'name has often been rendered incorrectly as Boškovski'[3]). Having joint Croatian and Macedonian citizenship, he arrived on the Macedonian political scene when his party VMRO–DPMNE (the Internal Macedonian Revolutionary Organization – Democratic Party for Macedonian National Unity) came to power in 1998. At that point Boškoski was in command of a fighting squad called the Lions (after his restaurant, apparently, rather than the other way around), but when he was made Minister of the Interior in Macedonia, in 2001, he legitimized his 1,000-strong fighting force by putting it under the command of the Ministry.

On 15 May 2002 a host of Macedonian politicians and journalists were summoned to the village of Leunovo, in the Maurovo region of Macedonia, to witness the Lions on a tactical exercise. Boškoski showed off his own fighting skills to the assembled dignitaries, operating a heavy machine gun, then a 'froggy' mine launcher. However, when shrapnel from one of the resulting explosions ricocheted off a nearby rock the exercise turned from a display of military skill into a dangerous kind of farce that left a journalist, a French translator and two policemen injured, and needing to be rushed by helicopter to the Macedonian capital of Skopje for treatment.

The ugly farce turned even uglier later in 2002 when Boškoski announced that seven 'Islamic terrorists' had been killed in an ambush while on their way to attack foreign embassies in Macedonia. He publicly berated other governments for leaving it to Macedonia and the USA to fight the 'war on terror' alone. As further details of the incident emerged, the story changed. First it had been stated that these 'terrorists' had ambushed the police, but when someone pointed out that not a single police officer had been injured in this 'ambush' the roles were reversed: the police had ambushed the terrorists before they could put their plans into action.

In May 2004, however, Ljube's immunity from prosecution was cancelled and he and three senior police commanders were charged with murdering the seven men. Far from being terrorists, it seemed, the seven were illegal immigrants, six from Pakistan and one from India, who had paid various agents enormous sums of money to be smuggled overland to Greece, where they hoped to find work on the construction sites for the 2004 Olympic Games in Athens. The charge is that the seven men had been picked up when they entered Macedonia from Bulgaria, then shot somewhere on the road to Skopje, their bodies arranged to look as if there had been a gun battle. Allegedly the whole thing was staged, and bags containing guns and uniforms that were found near the bodies were placed there afterwards to corroborate the story.

Faced with imminent arrest, Boškoski disappeared, only to resurface in Croatia running his restaurant. For some reason, presumably related to his dual Croatian and Macedonian citizenship, the Macedonian authorities were unable to seek his extradition to face these charges and it wasn't until September 2004 – indeed, the night before we arrived at his restaurant – that the Croatian authorities finally detained him. Boškoski was now imprisoned in Pula.

I suddenly understand why the place is deserted, why a group of men are huddled in conference, in what they'd probably hoped would be the quietest corner of the restaurant, until we blundered in, and why the small blonde woman who takes our orders looks completely shattered and as if she's been crying all day. This is Boškoski's wife. I feel sorry for her nonetheless and say so, thanking her warmly for her generous hospitality and for the food, which, in spite of everything, is absolutely delicious.

Several months after our visit, on 24 March 2005, even before he could be returned to Macedonia to face charges relating to the alleged murders of the economic migrants, the Croatian authorities transferred Boškoski over to The Hague, following his indictment on 9 March for his participation in a joint criminal enterprise (JCE) that resulted in the murder of ten ethnic Albanian civilians in the village of Ljuboten in August 2001, during the brief civil war in Macedonia. Together with Johan Tarčulovski, the high-ranking police officer who was in charge of the unit that carried out the operation, Boškoski is now part of case number IT-04-82 at The Hague, which at time of writing has yet to come to trial.

The Istrian coastal town of Rovinj was built on a tiny round island. At some point in its past they ran out of space within the town's walls and the buildings spilled over onto the causeway linking the island with the mainland, while on the island itself they built right down to the water's edge, where there's now a clutter of tall, brightly painted five- and six-storey houses that ring the island, and from the lower floors of which you could step straight out onto a boat.

Mauro and I walk up the narrow streets, and find a wedding party following a clearly drunk accordion player up the broad, white stone steps into the enormous church of Sveta Eufemia. Down below the terrace, in a small enclosed garden, the remains of an earlier wedding party are loudly and tunelessly singing *klapa* songs. On top of the church's huge baroque tower there is an enormous statue of St Euphemia that also serves as a weather vane. The whole thing, which is big enough to be seen from far out at sea and must weigh several tons, turns in the wind. There's enough of a breeze that a flotilla of tiny white sailing boats are out in the bay, but the wind doesn't change in the ten minutes that we spend here, so I don't get to see this miracle of engineering in action.

On the quay, next to fishing boats that are either coming in for the day or going out for the night to catch more gilt-head bream, there's the usual monument to the Partisans, although this one is spectacular. It's set on a flat field of marble 30 feet across and 50 or more feet deep. At one end a flat stone screen, which must itself be 40 feet high, contains three highly stylized figures. There's an image of a screaming woman, with a face that could have come from Picasso's 'Guernica', her stylized hair blowing in the wind and the faint suggestion of a bandolier slung across one shoulder. A man with a pistol on his belt throws his hands up, while another stands with legs apart and points a rifle off to the right somewhere. There's something dynamic about the image, even though it's solidly architectural and created from dressed blocks of stone that are slotted together in a system of arches created by the figures' stylized limbs.

At the opposite end of the marble field stands an emblematic stone sarcophagus. Down one side of this, carved very simply with just a single line, a group of men and women, heads bowed, trudge at gunpoint before a soldier who, even though he's drawn almost diagrammatically, is recognisably a Nazi. On the opposite side six bodies are depicted, while three birds fly overhead. At one end of the sarcophagus, facing the street, is the five-pointed star of the Partisans. A group of children from Rovinj, dressed in brightly coloured T-shirts and bermuda shorts, are playing on the flat stone slabs of the memorial. None of them can be more than ten years old, and I'm conscious that they've never lived in Yugoslavia, but were born in an independent Croatia. This monument, which was built to commemorate, and to sanitize the myths about, the sacrifices that were made to create a country that no longer exists, means no more to them than any other conveniently flat playing surface. They have a football and the stone screen depicting the heroic Partisans serves as their goal.

The events that these monuments were built to commemorate have not been forgotten by everyone, however. The next morning we pass a large crowd as we drive over a country crossroads at Tican, on the road from Motovun to Vrsar. Men in shirtsleeves, baseball caps, jeans or suits are standing and sitting on chairs that have been laid out on a large area of dry grass facing a row of large standing stones. These roughly hewn slabs, which stand perhaps ten feet tall, are carved with simple representations of workers' tools: a fork, a scythe, an axe, a hook, a spade. The monument was built in 1965 to commemorate 84 Partisan fighters from this area who died in 1943. A lot of people have turned up for some kind of ceremony at which there will be speeches and, while everyone waits, music is being played over a public address system.

There are no young children of Croatia using these stones as goalposts, and I wonder if the mainly elderly people gathered here are perhaps the children and grandchildren of the fighters who died here at Tican. Flags are flying behind three granite slabs on which the names of the fallen comrades are engraved. Someone has placed a bouquet of red and white flowers, tied with a red, white and blue ribbon, in front of this roll of honour.

We're on our way to a sculpture park just outside the town of Vrsar, where Casanova lived. I found out on the way that this is not just any old sculpture park, but the home and the studio of a venerable artist called Dušan Džamonja, who was responsible for many of the most spectacular monuments to anti-fascism that were built in post-war Yugoslavia.

The park is surrounded by a white stone wall and beyond this its pristine lawns must cover several acres. Dotted around the lawns and on terraces sunk into their gently rolling slopes are numerous geometric sculptures, jarringly bisected spheres, ovoid exercises, prototypes for a Sydney Opera House that had yet to be designed when these were being made. On closer inspection the precise and solid-looking forms are made from nails, chains or small slices of stainless steel – hollow and, like the Partisan monument at Rovinj, made as much from air, from the spaces between the materials, as from the material itself. On the flat lawn nearer some buildings is a sculpture formed from a clutter of shallow arches, similar in shape to quartered car tyres and made from rusted steel.

A light shower, the first rain in six months, fills the air with the scents of pine and parched grass. As we walk around an elderly man slowly makes his way toward us with the help of a walking stick. This is Dušan Džamonja himself. A perfect gentleman, he apologizes for the weather.

Some of the sculptures, plinth-mounted, are more organic-looking, with looping folds and shadowy apertures formed from the chains. Džamonja, old enough not to care too much for false decorum, slowly raises his walking stick at one of them: 'Is like a pussy, no? A lovely pussy!' His frail and watery laugh reminds me of my late paternal grandfather in Bentley, Hampshire. He'd been a bear of a man in his prime, and would have to have been, since he was a farm labourer, but by the end of his life he could do little more than sit in his wooden armchair, hat on in the daytime, off in the evening, and cry with pleasure at the family life that continued around his chair.

Džamonja was born in Strumica, Macedonia, in 1928. 'Dušan' is a Serbian name: Stefan Dušan ruled the medieval Serbian empire at its fullest extent. This contemporary Dušan, however, has lived in Croatia most of his life and studied in Zagreb immediately after the war. When, later, I mention to a journalist in Zagreb that I've visited Džamonja, I'm told that he'd once offered to build this foundation in the city of Zagreb, but that it had been refused because of his Serbian background.

Whatever the truth of that story, it's doubtful that these sculptures would have looked as remarkable in Zagreb as they do here in Istria. While we slowly shadow him around the park, making our way towards the house and the studio complex at its centre, I wish that we had a film crew with us, so that we could spend some time here to properly document this artist. Džamonja saw and commemorated the re-formation of Yugoslavia after the Second World War. He was internationally celebrated for using new materials in sculpture in the 1960s and 1970s, and has works in almost every major collection around the world. He also knew that other great sculptor of the former Yugoslavia, Ivan Meštrović.

Slowly we get closer to the house, which is built of the same pale stone and dark wood as the walls and the gatehouse, those typical Istrian materials that Ozren pointed out on our first evening here. Inside we pause in a glass-walled office, full of drawing boards and rolled-up papers, with a long, dark wood desk lit by starry little lamps. Džamonja's wife comes to meet us and asks us if we'd like to join them for a glass of wine. First, though, we follow him through a central courtyard to further complexes of buildings: Džamonja's studios, each progressively more concerned with the actual making of his work. Last of all we arrive in a large metalwork shop, undecorated, where more of the arched structures are being made, where every surface is covered with maquettes, small models of larger sculptures, in card, paper and metal. There are vices, chains hanging from the ceilings, lifting gear and plastic buckets, as well as plastic moulds of some of the hemispheric shapes that we'd seen on plinths outside in the park. All of it looks as if it's used or at least cleaned daily, but I can't imagine that Džamonja himself, as he slowly guides us round, has the strength any longer to deal directly with the actual making of his great sculptures. I get the feeling that the small dark office space that we'd seen when we first came in is where Džamonja spends most of his time these days, making phone calls, working on the computer, doing technical drawings and proposals for architecture competitions.

Stacked against the walls in another studio are several huge drawings, six feet by four feet, in browns, ochres and black, of the same arched forms. They have the air of having been assembled more than drawn or painted; there are overlays of complex textures, spray paint, printing, cross-hatching. There are sculptures on plinths by the floor-length windows that line the corridors between buildings. Several more are installed in a clean stone-floored gallery space. Džamonja stops in front of one and slowly lifts his walking stick to point at it: 'Another pussy!'

Džamonja's wife brings us some beautiful white wine when we eventually take our places around a long wooden table on a verandah that overlooks a courtyard garden with a Hockney-ish swimming pool. As we say 'Cheers', 'Prost' and 'Živeli', and take a sip, each of us, Ozren, György, Josef and I, is handed a pile of publications, catalogues of shows and literature about the sculpture park. I leaf through a thick and expensive-looking hardbacked monograph that was already on the table, and look at more photographs of the kinds of sculptures that we'd seen in the park and in the studios, but there are some other works that catch my eye, and it's an eye that by this time has become unavoidably attuned to Tito-era anti-fascist monuments.

One of the monuments illustrated in the book commemorates Partisan and civilian deaths at the hands of Nazi and NDH troops, and is sited on a mountaintop called Mrakovica, in Kozara National Park in Bosnia-Herzegovina. According to the literature, which as we know tends to be disputed, anything up to 60,000 people died here during the Second World War and 12,000 people are buried beneath the monument, which was built in 1972 and has somehow survived the wars of the 1990s. It would dwarf even the huge monument in Rovinj, and is on a scale altogether different from that of the small street-corner sculptures and town square war memorials that I've seen everywhere in the past few days. The monument on Mrakovica is a skyscraper-like concrete structure, perhaps eight or ten storeys tall. Roughly cylindrical, it's formed from a succession of radial sections that arch out of a central core like highly stylized flowers one atop the other, or a series of stacked and elongated cogwheels. They're also slightly reminiscent of the milled steel plates that form the casing of a hand grenade. It resembles a cross between a high-tech water tower and a science fiction fortress, and is set in parkland surrounded by trees.

During the 1990s British troops stationed in the area as part of SFOR (the Stabilisation Force for Bosnia-Herzegovina, a NATO-led multinational force designed to uphold the Dayton Peace Agreement from 1996 to 2004) apparently used the monument as a decorative backdrop for a souvenir photograph of their posting. They turned up one day, en masse, to pose next to the monument, complete with tanks and guns on the ground and helicopters hovering either side of the central structure. It was an act of unthinking insensitivity that incensed local residents and would be analogous to an international power driving tanks over the British war graves in northern France.

Mrakovica is an extraordinary piece of modernist sculpture, and I wonder to myself whether there's a serious study to be made of some Yugoslav split from Soviet-style socialist realism in statuary commemorating the Second World War that might be mapped against Tito's split with Stalin. There are realist statues of Partisan leaders here and there, of course, such as the one of Joakim Rakovac in the grassy town square in Poreč, but monuments like Mrakovica mark a striking contrast to social realism, even to the neoclassicism of pre-war Yugoslav sculptors such as Meštrović.

Ozren complements Džamonja on the chilled white wine that we're drinking. It's the product of a wine-maker called Matošević, who's brought so-called 'new world' wine-making technology to Istria in order to rediscover the best of Istria's two indigenous wines, *malvazija* and *teran*. What we're drinking is a *malvazija* and it's delicious. I want to talk about the monuments.

'You must have been very proud,' I venture, pointing at the pictures, 'to have been chosen to build these.'

Džamonja shakes his head, as if to acknowledge the importance of the task. 'Very proud,' he says, 'but unfortunately there is always a need for monuments.'

We talk about them a little, but there's not enough time to ask him what they represented then, let alone how they're perceived now, although I read later that another of Džamonja's monuments to anti-fascism – a huge, abstract concrete structure that resembled a winged globe – at Podgarić, in an area that before the war was home mainly to Serbs, was completely destroyed and replaced with a Catholic chapel in 1996, following the Croatian army's occupation.

Džamonja describes a more recent proposal of his for the '9/11' memorial on the site of the World Trade Center in New York, his being one of

5,000 or so entries. This was to have been another structure on a grand scale, using one of his arched motifs, but inverted, so that as one approached the whole thing might look like two huge towers falling on either side of you, and at the apex of these two forms would have been a temple for contemplation. I do a scribble in my notebook.

'Like this?' I ask.

'No,' he says, holding his hand out for my pen. He turns my notebook around and does his own quick drawing: 'Like that.'

Secretly delighted, I'm tempted to ask him to sign it.

Later we visit the home of the wine-maker whose *malvazija* we tried at Džamonja's house. The annual wine day may have been cancelled earlier this week, but Ozren has arranged for us to visit for a private tasting.

It's still raining and almost dark as we turn off the road, somewhere between Vrsar and Pula. Ozren phones ahead on his mobile and when we pull up alongside what appears to be a small house there's someone standing in the driveway waiting for us. This is Ivica Matošević himself.

'Is the rain good for the wine?' I ask as we follow him round the back of the house and into a large kitchen.

'Well, some rain to wash the dust off is good, but not too much. Two days of rain right now is just what the vintage needs, any more than that will lead to problems. Anyway,' he says as he beckons us to a large round table covered with a checked cloth, 'please have a seat.'

Matošević can't be much older than his late 30s and looks like any smartly dressed young European professional, which of course is exactly what he is. Fashionable country-tinged music plays over small loudspeakers fixed high on the walls and an apron is tied around a pillar next to the table.

Before he takes us on a tour of the operation he tells us that he didn't set out to be a wine-maker. He trained as a landscape architect and did a PhD in ecological studies, but gradually become more interested in wine. He started out by taking a series of *sommelier* courses in Italy, in order to develop his knowledge and appreciation. It seemed to him that there was something very attractive about the lifestyle, that wine-making might be a way for him to combine his knowledge of land management and sustainable development with an opportunity to do something, one thing, very well.

There had been wine growers in his family and a certain acreage of slightly neglected vineyards, so after Ivica had spent a year or so planning what he might need to start doing this seriously, using modern technology, he approached his father to see if he was interested in investing in the business. Matošević senior took the plans away and studied them, but then came back and told him to spend another two years planning. Then he would make his decision.

'Listen,' he says, 'wine industry here turned to mass production during Tito's time, of course. This was part of the process of industrialization that went on across Yugoslavia. Unfortunately, this meant that the quality of the wine went right down. For the few of us who are now doing this seriously, each in our small way, it's not about selling in huge quantities, but about creating and telling a story, about making something of real quality. That took a lot of work even before I started growing. And my father was absolutely right – I wasn't ready. Without those additional two years, which seemed so unfair at the time, I would certainly have failed.'

When we set off on our tour I'm amazed that we don't even have to leave the building. What had looked from the road to be an average-sized house in fact leads into a cavernous brick annexe, in which half a dozen towering stainless steel vats stand silent apart from a faint hum of machinery. This is the heart of the operation, where the previous year's vintages are nearing completion. While he's talking to us Ivica looks at the dials and gauges that monitor the wine's progress.

'It is about passion,' he says. 'And without that you're nowhere as a wine-maker. You can learn everything from books, you can learn how the technology works, but that gives you a false kind of security and a half-knowledge, because every single vintage is different. There's not one mystery to making excellent wine, but hundreds of mysteries, hundreds of little steps. It's like jumping obstacles on a horse. Showjumping. It isn't just about completing the course quickly, there's handicaps, time, penalties, poise – hundreds of ways to score, hundreds of tiny steps – but each year, with each vintage, the course is entirely different.'

Leading off the main winery are smaller rooms and corridors, lined with barrels. 'If it's a perfect grape, we're ready to pay double price for this good oak,' he says, caressing one of the barrels. 'Croatian barrels are good, but these are French oak and we can be more certain of the consistent quality. It's worth it.'

'Quality' is a word that Ivica Matošević uses a lot. 'We few new Istrian wine-makers are rivals in a way,' he continues, 'but that competition produces quality. And each of us would rather produce small quantities of exceptional wine than return to the bad old days of industrial production. When you make wine in small quantities there are only so many bottles you can sell in any case. We each have a few good restaurants that champion our vintages.'

You sense that a lot of what drives Matošević is co-operation as well as competition. One of the reasons he started in the wine trade was a desire to rediscover the strengths of some of the old regional varieties, the *malvazija* and the *teran*, which he felt had become debased, simply labels that were attached to any old wine anywhere in Europe. *Malvazija* in particular, he tells us, is a noble variety, with a fruity, easy-drinking style, but almost any mass-produced white wine can now bear the name, even those that have no relation or connection to the variety. Originating in the Peloponnese, he tells us, it was introduced to Istria about 700 years ago, but it was good enough for William Shakespeare to mention it in *Richard III*, while in 14th-century Italy there were shops that sold nothing else.

In order to reclaim *malvazija* as a quality wine Matošević has had to make contact with the few real *malvazija* growers left in the Balkans, in Italy, and in Hungary and Austria. He wants to begin to organize a community, a network. He's planning the marketing already, he says. He'll sail to the Peloponnese, to Monamvazija – 'the Gibraltar of the Levant' – where the variety originated, then to Sicily and Madeira. The next step in this plan, he tells us, is to produce a cross-national badge of quality – a sort of '*apellation controlée*' – so that wine drinkers will be able to identify the quality vintages, of which there are perhaps only 25 or 30 each year, rather than the mislabelled plonk.

I tell Ivica that Dušan Džamonja offered us a glass of his *malvazija* that very afternoon.

'Džamonja? Really?' he says, delightedly. 'Well, I'm flattered. And did you enjoy this?'

Teran, on the other hand is a wine that is indigenous to Istria. It's mentioned in Roman literature: Pliny called it an elixir. It's not harmonic, though, Matošević tells us when, back at the kitchen table, he pulls the cork from a bottle for us to try some. 'If you bring it to someone, it will either be loved or hated. It's high acid, high in tannins, and has a kind of astringency.'

There's something about Ivica Matošević that makes me think of the Gospodin Mac, the Scottish mining engineer in Kosovo whom Rebecca West so admired. If she were here, sitting around the table with us, I feel sure that she'd have been very taken with Matošević too, as she'd been with the 'Gospodin Mac', with his combination of the level-headed and the visionary, his intellect, and his ability to both create something, and to inspire and motivate others. She would certainly, as we all did, have fallen in love with his wines, even with the *Teran*, which despite his warning, is absolutely delicious.

It's also certain that visionary entrepreneurs like Matošević are essential to the process of reconstruction here in Croatia, as in Serbia and the other Yugoslav successor republics. Yet for every Matošević, ploughing his own quality furrow, it's the big international public-private partnerships that are bringing the real money into Istria now, such as the French road-builders that had so incensed Mauro.

It's in Poreč that I gain some small insight into the scale of foreign investment in the region. On the boardroom table in the tourist office in Poreč I'm shown a huge ring binder: 'Tourism Development Master Plan 2002–2003, Final Draft'. The plan deals with the areas of Poreč, Tar-Vabriga and the 'Kastelir–Labina Cluster', and it makes fascinating reading. I learn, for example, that Istria has 35,000 hotel beds, 25,000 campsite places and 10,000 beds in private accommodation. As Ozren has already told us, the general trend is away from the mass tourism of the package holiday towards the 'quality' (that word again) end of the spectrum, with innovations such as *agriturizam*. In order for any of this to be possible, however, money has to be spent on infrastructure. Consequently the plan mainly consists of page after page of financial spreadsheets that show the range of investments currently shaping the area. On just one page (and this is a thick file) some 73 projects are listed. Of these ten are wholly public, such as 'Poreč Town Entrance' ('Concept: upgrading plan for an attractive town entrance', cost 300,000 euros). Of the remaining 63 projects, 12 are public-private partnerships, including golf courses, hotels and the upgrading of sewage systems, and 51 are wholly private-sector, which will mean in a lot of cases that they are internationally financed.

Something about this mode of travel, the official guided tour, has meant that we've seen a lot more churches than I would normally visit, whether the church with the frescoes at Beram, the tiny barrel-vaulted chapel at Draguc or the architectural and historical wonder that is the Eufrazijeva Basilika in Poreč, our next port of call. It also means that your experience can, sometimes, be only as good as your guide. Luckily, the Poreč tourist office has entrusted us to one of their best: a gruff-voiced, moustachioed man who storms up the polished stone street with real gusto. At one point he motions towards one of the inevitable Venetian lions of St Mark, each of which rests a paw on a Bible ('If the book is open, it meant that you had friendly relations with Venice. If it was closed, you didn't!'). Elsewhere he shows us evidence that the streets of the entire town – the polished stones we're walking on – were raised by one metre in the 17th century.

As we turn down the street and enter the compound of the basilica, past a bunch of tourists who stand and read the plaque denoting that this is a UNESCO-designated World Heritage Site, the huge doors open and hundreds of worshippers make their way back into the bright daylight of the 21st century. This church, our guide proudly tells us, was the second Byzantine basilica to be built in Europe, after Ravenna and before St Mark's in Venice.

It's a wonderful privilege to see such an old church, even if all that's left of the very first building on this site, following an earthquake, are the fifth-century foundations, two or three courses of stonework and some mosaic pavements, the most celebrated of which depicts a ragged and gnarly fish, all whiskers and fins, the early Christian symbol for Jesus (a pun involving the initials 'J C' – 'I Ch' in Greek – and the Greek word for 'fish', *ichthyos*).

The basilica that now stands on the site of the first church, though shifted a dozen metres further inland from the original, dates from the sixth century. Fragments of a beautiful Byzantine mosaic are still visible high on the exterior wall, but this doesn't prepare you for what's inside. Behind the altar and reaching up to the half-domed ceiling some 50 feet above it are the most unusual mosaics. At ground level it takes the form of geometric designs picked out in coloured tiles and huge discs of mother of pearl, which must have come from oyster shells the size of tea plates. This section was salvaged from a huge Roman temple of Neptune that once stood 100 metres or so further along the shore from the original fifth-century church but was destroyed in the same earthquake. The mosaics were then adapted slightly, to incorporate some small cross-shaped motifs made from the same mother of pearl, and re-set here.

The higher up the walls you go, moving through the massed ranks of the saints to Jesus himself, the more gold there is. The church was designed in Constantinople, and the enormous marble columns that still hold it up were made there and brought here by sea; the Italians raised – and here the guide stamps his foot – the wooden floor in the 20th century, to protect the mosaics beneath. More recently, during the 1990s, the basilica was boarded up and surrounded by a protective scaffold, after it was rumoured to have been discovered on a target list of Croatian national monuments singled out for shelling.

Opposite the front entrance is a tall octagonal tower, a baptistry, which was built, like the basilica, in the sixth century. Inside, set in the middle of the floor, is a hexagonal pool, some four feet deep. There's no water in the font today, but 14 centuries of baptisms, of feet walking down the stone steps into the water, have worn completely through the stone that lines the bottom of the font. 'All still original materials,' says our guide, pointing up at the wooden beams high above our heads, 'even the roof!'

Our brisk walk through the rest of the town passes in a blur. Still more stray cats are feasting on a pile of fish bones in an overgrown garden next to a restaurant; some fragments of stone columns and pediments from a temple of Mars have been reconstructed to form a collaged impression of how a tiny fragment of the portico may have looked; two grand hotels stand boarded up and empty among the mature cypress trees on either side of a large semi-circular lawned terrace.

The hotels are deserted now and one of them, the Hotel Rivijera, is partly covered by new hoardings. It has just been bought by an international consortium based in Germany in order to be turned once again into the luxury waterfront hotel it once was. Work will shortly also begin to restore the old Austro-Hungarian Villa Adriatic to its former glory. For the past 12 years, until only relatively recently, both these hotels, and others like them all along the coast from here down to Dubrovnik in the south, have been home to Croatian refugees who fled here from Vukovar, from Osijek, from all over Slavonia.

I peer through a crack in the boards that have been nailed across some French windows facing onto the lawn. Inside there is nothing more dramatic to tell the story of who might have lived here than a shabby room leading, through an open door, to a tiled bathroom.

Talking about this later with people we run into in a bar, I'm surprised to hear someone voice a lack of sympathy for what others in Croatia might call the 'plight' of these refugees, Croats after all, who were made homeless by the actions of Bosnian Serbs or Bosnian Muslims, but who have now had to move on. 'Well, you know,' he says, 'it's good riddance as far as I'm concerned. We've had enough of them. A lot of them are not poor at all. They still have homes and properties where they're from. They're making money from them, renting out their houses back home, and making money here as well. They could not stay here forever.'

Chapter Twelve
Istria III: Pula (2004)

The brief aerial view of Pula that I'd been afforded when the plane was coming in to land has been preying on my mind. I've been trying to imagine what goes on down in between that clutter of rooftops around the amphitheatre, what the streets are like.

I'm staying in the Riviera, a huge and evidently once palatial hotel dating from the latter days of the Austro-Hungarian Empire that's tucked a few hundred yards beyond Pula's amphitheatre, near the railway station. It's comfortable enough, and is possessed of a kind of kitsch retro charm that I'm now becoming accustomed to. This has nothing to do with the original architecture, but rather with a refurbishment, some time in the 1960s, that obliterated the original Austro-Hungarian plasterwork with modern touches: featureless, dark wooden panelling, black suspended ceilings and radios set into headboards. This hotel was presumably something of a Tito-era tourist flagship. Admittedly, the phone in my room doesn't work for some reason, but whenever I do get a call the receptionist simply asks them to ring back in ten minutes while, marvellously, he actually runs up to my room to fetch me.

My hotel room looks out over the apartment building next door, onto small balconies where old men in vests grow tomatoes. Being on the fifth floor, I'm high enough up that I can also look out over the flat roof, with its mass of chimneys and television aerials, and, beyond that, right across the calm bright waters of the bay to the hills on the other side. This is a grand sweeping view, but it's one that doesn't quite come into its own until late one night, when there's a huge thunderstorm. All the old men over the way close their shutters, but I have my face pressed up against the glass, watching the enormous forks of lightning growing closer and closer until there's practically no interval between the flashes and the claps of thunder that rattle the windows.

In the morning the streets are awash with thick and sandy orange mud that's been washed down from the hills above the town. Finding no storm drain adequate to contain it, the mud has found the quickest route downhill through the streets, forming great sticky pools at road junctions and along the gutters.

I pick my way towards the amphitheatre and wonder if I should have a swim, but to do so I'd probably have to get a bus, or walk across to the other side of town. The hotel is a stone's throw from the sea, but this part of the bay forms the northern end of Pula's harbour rather than a beach. Between the hotel and the quayside there's a small park, which is full of palm trees and in which, to judge by the sharp smell, the people of Pula walk their dogs. Further still there are railway lines and shunting yards. The railway comes all the way down through Istria to Pula, and presumably this is why the hotel was built where it was, but since Pula is situated at the southern tip of the peninsula, this is the terminus, the end of the line.

Situated where it is, Pula may not have had much strategic value when the Ottomans ploughed through Croatia on their way to besiege Vienna. This is perhaps the reason why so much of the city's ancient architecture has remained so wonderfully intact for so long. Old engravings of the town, framed on the walls of the hotel's landings and corridors, show a tiny fishing village that's dwarfed by the amphitheatre, the triumphal arch and the fortress. A lot of the stone, particularly from the amphitheatre, must have been used to build half of the old town, but it was mainly taken from the interior walls, so it doesn't really show. It's as if these great vestiges from a time when Pula was important enough to warrant such an impressive infrastructure were left alone deliberately, in case some later great power decided that the town should become important once again. Eventually, that is exactly what happened.

Julius Caesar created the Roman colony of Pula in 46 BC. He had it built on the site of an Illyrian town that had existed there for the previous 500 years or so. One of the families appointed to oversee its construction was that of Cassius, who joined the plot to assassinate Caesar just two years after Pula was officially founded. In the political and military turmoil that followed the assassination, Pula fought on the losing side, with Cassius against Octavian and Mark Antony, and the colony was demolished on the order of Octavian.

Once the dust of civil war had settled, however, Octavian saw some benefit to having a colony at the tip of Istria and ordered that the town be rebuilt. It was during this period, 2 BC to AD 14, that buildings such as the triumphal arch of the Sergius family and the Temple of Augustus were constructed. The temple, which after the Roman period became, among other things, a church and a granary, was destroyed by a bomb in 1944 and was subsequently rebuilt. The amphitheatre, which is known in Pula as the Arena, is reputed to be the sixth largest remaining Roman amphitheatre.

Rule from Venice, by Ostrogoths, Franks and Slavs, followed the eclipse of the Romans, but in the mid-19th century, during the days of the Austro-Hungarian Empire, Pula became a naval dockyard and garrison. It's not as big a port as Rijeka, which nestles into the armpit where the Istrian peninsula meets the main Croatian coast, but it's important nonetheless. One of the slum districts to the south, which is called Barake, is actually just street after street, block after block, of big stone barrack buildings dating from this period, though at some point since they were built they were turned into tenements.

Barake may have an air of terminal decreptitude about it, but I suspect that it would still be a better place to live than the former holiday camp beyond it. This village of little wooden chalets is now home, all year round, to a community of several hundred refugees who have yet to be pushed out by the promise of foreign investment and a regenerated tourist industry, although most people in Pula itself seem not to know it's there. Having been driven past it one evening, and seen signs of life – washing on lines and food cooking on fires outside the chalets – I mention it to somebody and they say, 'No, that's not true. No one lives there. Who told you that?'

There's still some industry in Pula. On one side of the road that swings down towards Barake are the entrances to a vast network of tunnels, used as air-raid shelters during the Second World War and, more recently, in a stroke of agricultural ingenuity, for the cultivation of mushrooms. On the other is a high brick wall, beyond which are the old naval docks and a huge commercial shipbuilding yard.

Walking across town to find a particular restaurant late one night, I'm taken on a shortcut across a little park on top of a hill, from which we can see down into the shipyards, which are floodlit at night. The distant hum of machinery is carried on the wind from the hulk of an enormous ferry that, I'm told, is being built for a Scandinavian line.

Elsewhere, down the hill from the Viennese villas of the vanished imperial middle class, which are now, after nearly 100 years of neglect, starting to be renovated and converted by a new, domestic, professional and middle class, there is another huge military building, complete with overgrown parade ground and high spiked fence. It had some unspecified penal function during the Tito era, but is now a squatted community centre and artists' studio, where concerts are held and exhibitions put on. It presents quite a contrast to the white-stuccoed splendour of the Casino, the former Austro-Hungarian officers' club that's now the town's main venue for exhibitions and trade fairs. The Casino stands amid palm trees in its own walled garden, on one of the town's most prominent hills.

Pula's old town is built around a central fortified mound. It's possible to walk around the town in 15 minutes, and it doesn't matter which way you walk: at some point you will find yourself standing on the Roman pavements of the Forum. This is remarkable: a great paved square that was built on land reclaimed from the sea. This is the site of the beautiful Temple of Augustus (though no trace remains of another temple that once stood in the centre of the forum). Next to it stands the Romanesque Communal Palace, which dates from a period when Pula was a self-governing municipality and was originally built around the ruins of the Temple of Diana, of which only one wall remains. Children play tag and kick a football up and down the steps of the temple.

It's a five-minute stroll from the Forum to Giardini, Pula's *corso*, its pavement four times wider than the road, where café tables are laid out four or five deep beneath the usual Jamnica-branded awnings, and where ice cream parlours compete for your attention with market stalls selling sunglasses, postcards and replica football shirts. Street vendors stand around with handfuls of the kind of cheap flashing electronic gizmos that must be available in just about every city in the world. Up until lunchtime, someone tells me, the cafés of Giardini and a few others on and near the Forum are packed:

> No one does business in the office in the mornings. Between nine o'clock and 11 is when you must go to bank, do shopping. Besides, most work takes place over a coffee, you know? Everyone you need to meet will be at a café.

Joining the Forum and Giardini is Ulica Sergievica, a narrow lane that's lined with souvenir shops, *pekare* (bakeries), grocers, pizza stands and tobacconists. This is a place to pass through, rather than to loiter or enjoy a slow beer or a few coffees.

Where Giardini and Ulica Sergievica meet is Trg Portarata (Portarata Square), the site of one of Pula's other great Roman ruins, the triumphal arch of the Sergius family. It stands in the middle of the little square and looks perfectly at home among the café tables, the shoe shops, the restaurants and the old Austrian tearoom that took five years to turn into a shopping centre and rooftop bistro, because all building work ceased when it was found to have been built over a Roman treasure trove.

There's a tourist ritual that must take place at least several times a day in Pula, and even more often during the summer. It's a ritual that I'm determined to perform myself while I'm here.

Right next to the Sergius family's arch, and the seat, literally, of this strange ritual, is a single round café table and chair that's set slightly up from the street, outside a flashy bar and restaurant called Uliks. This means 'Ulysses': a small flat behind an upstairs window in the building opposite, one that's close enough to throw a pebble at, is where Pula's most famous adopted son lived, albeit briefly.

James Joyce and Nora Barnacle arrived here in October 1904, but only through a series of chance events. After Joyce's mother died he and Nora left Ireland in the hope that there would be a job for him at the Berlitz School in Zurich, but on arrival the job turned out to have been taken by someone else, so he was posted instead to Trieste. However, their first stay in Trieste lasted for only ten days and he was quickly sent on to Pula, where he taught English not only to Austro-Hungarian naval officers, but also to the director of the Berlitz School himself. Joyce and Nora hated Pula, calling it 'a naval Siberia', and moved back up the coast to Trieste in March 1905, but they didn't stay anywhere long in those days. They moved from room to room in Trieste too, being evicted by successive landlords whenever her pregnancy – increasingly hard to conceal – was discovered.

These days Pula likes to remember James Joyce. Luckily, one doesn't need to wait until 16 June, the date of the internationally celebrated 'Bloomsday' festival, to participate in this municipal display of pride. To join the celebration one needs only to take a seat at this table outside of Uliks bar and restaurant, and take a drink with Joyce, or at least with the life-sized bronze statue that sits at the table, cross-legged, walking stick held loosely to its lap. With left hand clenched to its lapel, it – or shall we say he? – gazes up and away, to the arch and beyond. Behind the statue a plaque is fixed to the wall: '*Irski Pisac* [Irish writer] James Joyce, 1882–1941'. Made by an Istrian sculptor named Mate Čurljak, the statue is basically realist, although geometric planes and curves are used to render the face or the sweep of a knee. The result of this is a slightly 'Vorticist' styling, which means that, with his jaunty, broad-brimmed sun hat this James Joyce looks more like Wyndham Lewis's 'Self-Portrait as a Tyro'.

It's impossible to perform this Joycean ritual without feeling slightly self-conscious. I'm sitting on what practically amounts to a plinth, after all, having a drink with a statue, but to complete the proceedings – and I feel a certain obligation to do this – I hand the waiter my camera. He knows what to do. The odd passer-by can't help but nudge their companion and laugh at yet another fool who's having his photo taken with James Joyce. But what the hell, I think to myself, I've read *Finnegans Wake* from cover to cover. I've earned this.

Chapter Thirteen
Istria IV: Pula, Brijuni (2004)

Just off the coast to the north of Pula is the island of Brijuni, where Tito had his official residence. In fact it's a small archipelago in its own right, consisting of the islands of Veli Brijuni and Mali Brijuni (Big Brijuni and Small Brijuni) as well as numerous even smaller islands. James Joyce apparently spent his 23rd birthday on Veli Brijuni, in 1904, shortly before he and Nora moved to Trieste.

Brijuni is not very far offshore, perhaps two or three miles, and is clearly visible from the mainland. It's a popular tourist attraction, so an all-inclusive ticket buys a boat trip, a sightseeing tour and admission to the main island's Tito Museum.

I'm not the only one who wants to see Brijuni. There's a large crowd on the dock in the small fishing village of Fažana when I arrive, waiting to get on a little steamer with scallop-edged awnings over the upper decks and standing room for perhaps 50 or so. The trip takes less than half an hour, and I can quickly start to make out the buildings that cluster against a backdrop of pine trees around the island's tiny harbour. As we draw closer the gradual differentiation and sharpening of detail reveals a 19th- or early 20th-century brick boathouse with a gently sloping tiled roof, which squats upon and overhangs four slender stone arches. Behind this are the long clean lines of a 1960s hotel, which is partly screened by pine trees and outside which several dozen golf buggies have been parked. A large crowd waiting on the pier also gradually sharpens as we approach, to reveal a group of 50 or so soldiers from the Croatian Army, very much at ease, standing around or sitting on their kitbags. When we get off the boat they get on.

Veli Brijuni proves to be a strange island. With its gentle hills and forests, its tangerine plantations and olive groves, it feels gentler and more hospitable to life than some of the other islands along Croatia's Adriatic coast. This is illusory, or at least a recent development, because until the early 20th century this island, which at the time was the fiefdom of one Paul Kupelwieser, an Austrian industrialist, was full of malarial swamps. At Kupelwieser's invitation, Robert Koch came here and eradicated the malaria, enabling the island to be transformed into a luxurious holiday resort. This was an entrepreneurial move, rather than any great leap of the imagination, since the Austrian imperial family took their holidays on the island of Lošinj, just a few miles further south. There's a monument to Koch, a relief carving of a woman and child, which is set against a quarried rockface next to the harbour. To either side of the monument are two great green metal doors, behind which is a system of tunnels. Formerly an ammunition store, these are now (no surprise) given over to the cultivation of mushrooms.

A sightseeing 'train' such as you'd see in any French town – a steam-driven, locomotive-shaped truck pulling little 'carriages' – takes visitors around the island. On a flying visit like this the train is the only way to see very much of it.

I get on board, joining tourists from around the world, and we clatter off past barrack buildings and tenements that are hidden away in the pine woods of the northeastern coast, workers' accommodation evidently not being part of the fantasy on this island. Quickly we climb uphill, across the parched grassland of a golf course, and then a large gate opens to allow us into Tito's safari park. This is a large enclosure in which zebra, antelope, llamas and (sacred) cows roam. The safari park predates Tito, having been founded by Kupelwieser in 1911, as a staging post where exotic animals could acclimatize before being moved to zoos in European cities. Most of the animals here now, however, are descendents of those given as gifts to Tito by visiting heads of state. I've read that there were once lions, tigers and pumas on Brijuni, but there has evidently been quite a lot of natural wastage since Tito's death. The collection must surely have dwindled. Though some older residents still survive. Two elderly Asian elephants, Soni and Lanki, were gifts from Indira Gandhi.

After leaving the safari park the train rattles along a road that is lined with dense and tangled shrubbery. We are now on the island's west coast, but the land that rolls down to the sea beyond these woodlands is hidden behind a high green chain-link fence. We pass a single checkpoint manned by two soldiers from the Croatian army: beyond this, though we're not permitted to enter, is Tito's former private residence. This is now owned by the Croatian government and is still used for state events. There are several of these great villas strung along this coast, like charms on a bracelet, but disappointingly they're not part of the official tour.

The train does stop for long enough to allow us tourists to stretch our legs and briefly wander in the ruins of the Byzantine Castrum, a small fortified town that was inhabited from the 2nd century BC to the 14th century AD. Just visible from here, if you look beyond the trees that line the site, is a beautiful white stone villa with a large terrace and great arched windows overlooking the bay. A flight of great stone steps leads down to the jetty. A friend in London tells me that he and his family came to this very spot during a holiday in the 1970s. Peering across at these same steps, he'd seen an elderly and very naked man climbing up the steps from the sea. Naturally, he'd assumed that this was Tito himself.

There's something reminiscent of the cult science fiction television series *The Prisoner* about Brijuni, this self-contained little playground. The whole island, viewed from behind the plexiglass windows of the tourist train, becomes the safari park. The outdoor cinema at the top of a hill, the dinosaur footprint that you can read about but not see, the 4th-century olive tree are at once as exotic and yet pathetic as the animals most certainly seem.

An enormous private yacht is moored in the harbour. I've read that Brijuni is a favourite holiday destination of the princely family of Monaco, although this yacht is flying the British Ensign. Then there are the people – wealthy visitors and workers alike – who zoom around in their golf buggies, and shops where one can buy overpriced drinks and souvenirs – Tito's favourite brand of Cuban cigar, among other things. This all becomes as much a part of the spectacle as the few remaining animals, confined to their small section of the island. Even the ruined columns of the vast Roman country residence set on the shore of Zaljev Verige (Verige Bay, pronounced 'very gay'), on the sheltered side of the island, look more like parts of an artfully reconstructed film set, like the backdrop to some fantasy, than genuine archaeological remains.

I'm glad when the train pulls up at the harbour once again and I can wander around the Tito Museum, though this emphatically is not confined to the elegantly stuccoed cream-and-white pavilion that bears the name.

Inside, atop a flight of steps, there's a large colour photograph, dating perhaps from the 1960s, showing a white-suited Tito standing on Brijuni's jetty, which has been red-carpeted for the occasion. He's holding his hat in his hand and waving at persons unseen who, to judge from the perspective, must be somewhere off in the middle of the harbour. Lined up along the water's edge behind him are dozens of white-uniformed soldiers. At either side of this picture two legends are picked out in gold letters. On the left are the words:

ŽIVJETI ZNAČI STVARALAČKI SE UGRADITI U VRIJEME I PROSTOR U KOJEM ŽIVIŠ.

This means: 'To live means to build yourself creatively in the time and place in which you live.' The legend to the right of the picture reads:

O TEBI GOVORE TVOJA DJELA. TI OSTAJEŠ.

This is slightly more difficult to translate. It literally means: 'About you your deeds speak. You remain.' It needs a bit of a tweak to get the real sense of it in English and to make clear that it's referring to Tito rather than to 'you' the reader: 'Your deeds speak of you [and through them] you remain [with us].'

The walls of the museum are packed with dozens more photographs of Tito: here, a photograph of him turning a tap ('Thanks to Tito the inhabitants of Istrian village Peroj got the water supply in 1954'); there, a picture of him with four babies ('Tito as godfather to the first Yugoslav quadruplets from the town of Maribor'). There are pictures of him with film stars. One features Richard Burton, who played Tito in the film *Sutjeska* (1971), referring to the canyon in which one of the decisive battles of the Partisan campaign was fought (the same canyon that inspired the design of the former JNA headquarters in Belgrade that was destroyed by the NATO bombing and is now being seen as a classic of modernist architecture deserving of preservation). Another shows Tito sitting proudly next to Sophia Loren at the opening of the 17th Yugoslav Film Festival in Pula in 1970.

There are unintentional moments of humour. A stuffed dove hangs from the ceiling on a fishing line, to dangle in front of a photograph of Tito releasing a white dove. Elsewhere two photographs are accompanied by the central text, 'On Brijuni Tito was always taking care of animals.' One shows him sitting with a shotgun across his lap and a drink in one hand, while with the other he holds up the head of some great dead beast by the horn. The other photograph shows him fitting the telescopic sights to his rifle. It's hard not to imagine Tito bombing around the safari park in a golf buggy, taking potshots at the more expendable animals in his menagerie. The ground floor of the museum is given over to huge taxidermy displays that resemble grandiose trophy rooms, although visitors are assured that all the animals died of natural causes.

There's also a picture of Tito meeting the sculptor Ivan Meštrović. Tito is beaming, but Meštrović's expression is impossible to read through his great beard. Given that Tito's promises of untold wealth, artistic freedom and power in post-war Yugoslavia couldn't lure Meštrović back from his self-imposed exile, it's fair to assume that he's not smiling.

Most significantly there are photographs of Tito with a range of presidents and royals. 'He collected heads of state and animals,' someone behind me jokes. Most of these bear witness to the canny diplomatic footwork that he undertook with his signing (alongside Nasser of Egypt and Nehru of India) of the Brijuni Declaration of 1956, and the subsequent creation of the Non-Aligned Movement. This was (at that stage) a grouping of 50 countries in Africa, Latin America, the Middle East and Asia with just one European country, Yugoslavia itself, which was the hub. The Non-Aligned Movement was designed to form a power base that could become an alternative both to the Soviet bloc and to the West, and could privilege the needs and demands of the southern hemisphere and the so-called 'developing world'. In the museum on Brijuni two large illuminated maps of the world pick out the member states of this movement in (ironically enough) British Empire red.

I hear a more than likely apocryphal story about Queen Elizabeth II's first state visit to Yugoslavia. It is said that while Tito was overseeing the preparations in the days before this most important of visits he was suddenly struck with panic. The villa on Brijuni where the Queen and the Duke of Edinburgh were due to stay was surrounded by a series of ponds that were home to countless frogs. It is said that Tito, alarmed that their nightly chorus might disturb the royal sleep, called in the army, ordering a significant number of troops to exterminate the frogs. How they achieved this is not recorded, but the result was a blessed nocturnal silence, fit for a queen.

Over breakfast on her first morning on Brijuni, so the story goes, Tito proudly enquired how Her Majesty had found the accommodation. Wonderful, thank you, the Queen had replied, though she confessed to not having slept at all well. At pains not to offend her host, it is said, she told him that this was because her bedroom at Buckingham Palace over-looked the large pond in the palace garden and she'd become accustomed over the years to being lulled to sleep by the distant croaking of frogs.

An open-air theatre on Brijuni regularly stages plays, which are per-formed by a company called Ulysses Theatre. It's through two members of this company that I initially find out about another island called Goli Otok (Naked Island). I meet them not on Brijuni, however, but in a tiny bar called 'P.14' (after its address, Preradovićeva 14), which is set behind a small garden off a steep side street between Pula's central police station and the university. One of the members of the company, Rade Šerbedžija, was a huge star of the Yugoslav cinema and stage: 'Without evasion, Rade was an absolute *star*,' says his entry in the *Leksikon Yu-mitologije*, 'the personi-fication of the bohemian performer'.[1] He was also a poet and a recording artist. He has since gone to Hollywood and starred in such films as *Mission Impossible II,* as well as Stanley Kubrick's *Eyes Wide Shut.*

Šerbedžija is in Pula to promote a new memoir of his experiences during the war, entitled *Do posljednjeg daha* (*To the Last Breath*). The 1990s were a period when he seemed to find himself constantly in the wrong place at the wrong time. A Serb who was born in Croatia, and had married and had children with a Croatian woman, he had to leave his home village of Bunić in Lika, and spent time in Belgrade and in Sarajevo, where he used his sta-tus to join the vocal protests against the war. Unwilling as he was to iden-tify to the extent required with either his Serbian or his Croatian roots, he was forced to cross war zones and borders. In Belgrade he was denounced for betraying the Serbian cause and shortly afterwards he was reportedly the subject of an assassination attempt. In Zagreb he was denounced by Croatian journalists and once again attacked. He made his way to Slovenia, where he was finally given a passport, and then to London. Šerbedžija cap-tured some of these experiences in poems that he wrote at the time, and which are very accomplished, but here tonight in Pula he'll be reading from his memoir.

The bar at P.14 is absolutely packed, but a group of us squeeze in and find a table with a good view of the bar. The tall white-bearded man in a crumpled white suit and stained panama, chatting animatedly with a pony-tailed, walrus-moustached writer called Borislav Vujčić, is Šerbedžija. Rather than take the stage, he turns around and reads to us from the bar.

There's a diverse crowd here to see him. Students mix with journalists and, slightly more dressed up, Pula's cultural elite. Most incongruous are a couple standing right at the front, who are dressed in what appears to be evening wear. It turns out that they were married only a few hours earlier. It's some measure of Šerbedžija's star status that they have cut short their wedding reception in order to be here. Šerbedžija congratulates them on their wedding and, before his reading (which has everybody roaring with laughter), he invites us all to raise our glasses in a toast that has the newly weds both beaming even more than they were before. I try and work out whether the bride or the groom might be the bigger fan.

Although the Ulysses Theatre Company is staging plays on Brijuni, the play that's running at the moment is about Goli Otok. This literally means 'naked island' or 'bare lump', and apparently that's exactly what it was, a bare rocky island, although an alternative etymology has been suggested: in earlier days Goli Otok was a naturist resort.[2]

The exact antithesis of the exercise in vanity and luxury that was Brijuni, Goli Otok was a labour camp that was established by Tito in 1949. One story suggests that the decision to turn the island into a prison was hatched over celebratory cocktails on UDBA Day that year, UDBA being the Uprava Državne Bezbednosti, the former Yugoslavia's secret police.

Following the establishment of Yugoslavia as a totalitarian Communist state following the Second World War, an international association of Communist parties, the Communist Information Bureau, better known as Cominform, was set up in Belgrade. In 1948, at the behest of Stalin, Cominform and its member parties denounced Tito and his Yugoslav brand of Communism. A Soviet invasion must have seemed almost inevitable. It never came, but Tito's response was immediate. The Communist Party of Yugoslavia (the KPJ) held a great purge of anyone who still supported, or was thought to support, Soviet Communism. It's easy to imagine that people wouldn't have known if they were coming or going at this point, but laws were amended and thousands of people, who became known as the *informbiroovci* (literally 'Information Bureau people'), were arrested and given administrative (rather than judicial) two-year sentences of 'socially useful work', which could be extended at will.

These are just the readily available facts about what really constituted Tito's easily romanticized 'split with Stalin'. The estimates of how many people suffered in this way are, as ever, disputed, not least because there is no record of either the charges or the sentencing, but once Goli Otok was established many such prisoners were sent there.

As soon as they arrived on the island the prisoners (men and women, incidentally, though at some point women started to be held on the neighbouring island of Grgur) had to run a gauntlet of other prisoners, a ritual that was known as the 'hot rabbit', and were subjected to a treatment called 'choking in water'. The beating and torture of prisoners by fellow prisoners was an everyday feature of life on the island, as was the division of prisoners into classes depending upon their degree of supposed rehabilitation. Endless confessional sessions were set up, where prisoners had to take to the stage in the island's one auditorium to tell their life stories and explain what had led them to betray the people. Plays were staged here, too, but the grim theatre extended to everyday life, and is revealed in details such as that certain classes of prisoner had to wear animal tails made of rags that identified them as legitimate targets of physical violence and humiliation.

Of 31,000 *informbiroovci* (which is not to mention possibly tens of thousands of other Tito-era political prisoners), some 17,000 are estimated to have passed through Goli Otok during this period, but 30,000 prisoners may have been incarcerated there in total. In 1956 all surviving *informbiroovci* were apparently released, but it's been calculated that 3,000 or more remain buried there to this day, in unmarked graves.

It's only as recently as the early 1990s that Goli Otok has been spoken or written about in the republics that once formed Yugoslavia.[3] Judging from reports of more recent visits, the island evidently still functioned as a prison until 1989. The theatre and other buildings, apart from the cell blocks, which have been demolished, were still intact, abandoned as they'd been left, at least as recently as the mid-1990s.

A German writer known as 'Akim K', who visited the island in the early 1990s and took photographs of what remained, points out that the theatre was also used as a cinema. Posters on the wall indicate some of the films that were screened for prisoners incarcerated here during the 1980s, *Flashdance* and Ridley Scott's *Blade Runner* among them.[4]

I realise that to truly experience Brijuni you need to fill in the gaps and see what it was really a stage set for, or rather what it was hiding. To do this it's necessary to mentally superimpose Goli Otok over Brijuni, so that the prison officers' quarters merge with the Tito Museum, the exercise yards on Goli Otok where prisoners were forced to bear the weight of huge stones for hours on end with Brijuni's golf course, the foundations of ruined prison cells with Byzantine Castrum, the theatre of Goli Otok where the forced confessional sessions were staged with Tito's beautiful outdoor cinema.

Back on the mainland in Fažana, I notice a handmade sign that's set up on the balcony of a house facing the jetty, beside some potted geraniums. Next to a photograph of Tito is written: *'Druže Tito! Druže Tito! Druže Tito! i orlovi te brane!!!'* ('Comrade Tito! Comrade Tito! Comrade Tito! And eagles protect you!!!'). I'm told that on summer afternoons, as well as on significant dates in the former Yugoslav calendar (25 May, 29 November and so on), the man who lives here sets up loudspeakers on the balustrade and plays recordings of Tito's speeches. At the end of each speech he stands to attention and salutes in the direction of Brijuni.

I'm pleased to get back to the normality of the mainland. Near the car park on the edge of town I come across one of Saša Maechtig's K-67 kiosks. This one is being used by a newsagent and tobacconist. Those Dutch architects' enthusiasm for their design classic is infectious, and I take a photograph so that I can send it off to be added to the collection of images on their K-67 fansite. Later, back in Pula, near the big glass-roofed 19th-century covered market, the floor of which is slippery with melted ice from its numerous fish stalls, I see another K-67. This one is an egg stall, painted with a big chicken and the legend *'Farma "Rafaelo" Jaja'* (*jaja* meaning 'eggs'). I'm surprised to see that a catflap has been installed beneath the serving hatch.

Pula was the home of the Yugoslav Film Festival: this much I now knew, having visited Brijuni. I had also heard a rumour that the big state-of-the-art cinema that Tito had built in the centre of Pula, the Kino Beograd (Cinema Belgrade), had been turned into a car park. A film festival still takes place in Pula every year, but obviously it's no longer the Yugoslav Film Festival, and shows instead a programme of Croatian and international cinema. For a period this was at a ratio of one Croatian film for each international one shown, which must have made for quite a short programme, given the relative scale of Croatia's cinema industry. The festival, now in its 51st year, once took place in various of Pula's many cinemas, but it now happens in just one venue, the Arena.

I am keen to visit the Arena at some point during my stay. Ideally this would be just after sunset, when the city starts to cool down, and bats flutter in and out of the great stone arches beneath a darkening pink sky, but when there isn't an event happening in the amphitheatre it's closed in the evenings. One morning, on my way to buy a paper and a cup of coffee, I decide to take a quick detour and buy a ticket.

The entrance to the amphitheatre is at street level, which is several metres below the level of the Arena itself. In order to reach daylight again one has to navigate a subterranean labyrinth of tunnels and cellars, huge vaulted chambers and narrow passageways, which remind me of the vaults beneath Diocletian's palace in Split. Now no longer home to wild animals, gladiators and assorted victims in waiting, they contain an archaeological museum that displays several huge olive oil presses and numerous great terracotta oil jars discovered in the great ruined harbour villa on Brijuni. Branching off from these chambers are dark, poky tunnels that must lead off into the depths of the hill against which the amphitheatre is set.

Several flights of stairs later I emerge onto the stone terraces surrounding the Arena itself. It's clear to see that the stones of an inner wall have indeed been removed. Behind the familiar arches of this colosseum-type structure there were once great walkways, accessible from the great stone stairwells that are spaced around the structure and providing access to the uppermost seating levels. These walkways are now gone, though the staircases, or much of them, remain. Even those higher terraces themselves have long disappeared, or rather the dressed stones that faced them and made up the stone step structure. What remains are great mounds of the hardcore and concrete that the Romans employed to internally solidify and strengthen such enormous buildings.

The outer walls are complete, however, and more so than in any other amphitheatre of this type. So complete are they that it was here in Pula that archaeologists discovered that these Roman stadiums, the Colosseum among them, were built in such a way that they could be topped with huge tented awnings of canvas and wood, in order to provide both shade and shelter from the elements for the thousands of spectators. The housings for these awnings are still complete, up on top of the outer wall.

There are a few modern additions as well. Pale stone buildings containing projection booths and dressing rooms are tucked discreetly behind the original stonework, and there is some contemporary seating arranged along some of the terraces. A large screen and a temporary stage occupy part of the old arena. It's astonishing how much of the amphitheatre remains. Walking among the huge stones that are stacked here and there, I wonder how it would have felt when 23,000 noisy spectators were crowded into this enormous stadium. Pula must have been a Roman garrison of an incredible magnitude to service such a huge amphitheatre. Apart from one or two other tourists, and a handful of late-season technical staff and museum attendants, the only other living thing here now is a big black cat that has stretched out to sleep in the sun on top of a huge stone block.

That evening I ask Vesna from the tourist office if she can show me the site of the former Kino Beograd, Tito's former flagship cinema that is now a car park. 'What do you mean, "Where it *was* located?"' she says, laughing. 'I can show you the cinema itself!'

Vesna has worked in the tourist industry since before the wars of the 1990s. She even worked at one point in the big Putnik office on Terazije in Belgrade, having been to university in what was then the Yugoslav capital. I tell her that the Putnik office is still standing, but that I've never seen anyone in it, apart from the three uniformed clerks managing the front desks. 'Well, it's a shame,' she says, 'but it doesn't surprise me. Serbia and Montenegro have hardly any coast now.'

'Pula used to have many cinemas,' she tells me. 'There is an open-air cinema up on top of the old town that does special screenings during the tourist season.' She points down a side street at the end of which is a flight of steps leading up Pula's central mound. 'Then there is Kino Beograd, and Kino Partizan, Kino Zagreb, and even one other down by Arena.'

Opposite the triumphal arch on Giardini she beckons me over towards a large building, slightly set back from the street, that I hadn't noticed before. Three sets of double doors face onto the street, and one of them is open. Above them is the word 'Kino', in Art Deco lettering. Someone has obviously removed the offensive word 'Beograd'.

'This didn't used to be the main entrance, this was where you came out,' Vesna tells me. 'My friend and I used to come here, and after the film we would either go round the back, to Pula's first pizzeria, or cross over and go to one of those cafés opposite for a coffee.'

We step into the darkness and find ourselves in a cavernous space. Leaving room for access and for reversing, there's probably room for a maximum of about 15 or 20 cars to park on the black-painted concrete floor. When I'd heard that the cinema was now a car park, I'd imagined some vacant lot where it used to be, perhaps with one or two of the original walls standing as stark reminders, but as my eyes grow accustomed to the darkness I can't believe what I see. To our left, above a little white Volkswagen van, the entire upper part of the wall is taken up by an enormous white screen and great black curtains. 'That was very special screen,' Vesna tells me. 'Only the best for Tito! It was also the first cinema in Yugoslavia to have Dolby sound. It was great sound system!'

I guess that the sound system, the projectors and everything else a cinema needs are probably still here. The only things that seem to have been removed are the seats that formed the stalls. There are still curtains and house lights on either side of the auditorium. The latter are beautiful flat glass screens resembling light-boxes, the glass coloured in geometric designs like generic Mondrian-style abstract paintings. Facing the screen, above the head of a solitary security guard, is an enormous balcony whose seats climb to the far back wall, where I can see the small glass windows of the projection booth. The cars parked here now can be driven in and out through the two original sets of double doors along the back wall, which used to be thrown open at the end of the show. From there the original pedestrian ramps are broad enough to take the cars back up to the street.

This is amazing, I say eventually, but why did they close it down? They surely can't make any money out of it as a car park. Vesna doesn't know. I ask someone else about it later and they wonder aloud if maybe it's because it was called 'Belgrade', or was a reminder of the Tito era, rather than a symbol of the new Croatia.

A local journalist tells me with a scornful shrug that he understands that there are plans for some big new out-of-town shopping development, which includes a multiplex: 'Tell me why would people go to multiplex if they can go to perfectly good cinema in city centre? *Of course* it doesn't make money as a car park, it must be losing lot of money, but keeping it like this will allow someone to make much more money somewhere else! This is how business works, no?'

Crossing over Giardini, Vesna points at the pink-stuccoed apartment buildings above the café awnings and tells me that there used to be two cinemas there, just in this one block. Both were closed down for a long time, but one of them, the Kino Zagreb, has now been reopened. We go to see that one first, stepping beneath a beautiful vintage neon sign and into the cinema's circular lobby. The old ticket office has been turned into quite a stylish bar. Beyond it is a great spiral staircase, with marble steps, that climbs several stories up this circular well to the cinema itself. There are potted cacti in the windows and pictures are still hung on the walls that line the stairs, painted portrait posters of film stars that were issued by the studios: a very young James Dean, Barbara Rush, Clint Walker, Deborah Kerr, Angie Dickinson, Audrey Hepburn, John Wayne, even a Rank Organisation poster of Virginia McKenna. 'When the cinema was closed,' Vesna tells me, 'someone borrowed these portraits to show in a big art exhibition – and it was so popular because we'd all grown up seeing these faces and everyone had just assumed they'd been destroyed when the cinema closed down. We couldn't believe it.'

Next to a small door, a hatch really, marked *'Projekciona Kabina'*, and beyond padded leather double doors with porthole windows, we step into the auditorium itself. There is no balcony in the Kino Zagreb, but the seats are slightly raked. The screen is set above a bare wooden stage and the walls are lined with panels of brown hessian. It's a real period piece of mid-20th-century design, slightly at odds with the trailer for the Will Smith film *I, Robot*, which is playing on the screen before the main picture.

'Pula was big army centre,' Vesna tells me, 'but Wednesday and Sunday afternoons were when the soldiers had time off, so in those days the Zagreb always played soft porn films at those times!'

We walk the few yards along the road to where the Konditori café and bar has been built into the foyer of the old Kino Partizan. The refurbishment has been so complete that the untrained eye would have no inkling that beyond here there was once a cinema. A gleaming new cake counter and bar is set along the side of the foyer where the ticket office used to be, but beyond that some features remain. 'Look, those doors used to go up to balcony,' Vesna says, 'and these ones used to go to auditorium.' She strikes up a conversation with the barman, who, having brought the tables and chairs in from the pavement, is now wiping down the surfaces. Vesna explains that I'm visiting from England and I've expressed an interest in looking at Pula's old cinemas. *'Odlično!'* he says, smiling. 'It's still there. Please, have a look.'

Beyond the double doors we step down a short corridor and into yet another cavernous space. Much smaller than either the Beograd or the

Zagreb, the Partizan has a single vaulted roof, which is semicircular in section like an oil drum that's been cut in half. Just as at the Beograd, though, the stalls seats have all been taken out. The great white-walled space is now occupied by a couple of fridges, filled with Studena mineral water and little bottles of Pago fruit juice. There are a couple of dozen crates of Bavaria beer, three white plastic chairs and a box of rubbish set out on the tiled floor where once a couple of hundred people would have watched films every night. The screen is still intact here, too, and above us there are another balcony full of empty seats and another projection booth. 'Partizan also closed around the time of war,' Vesna tells me.

It's not so surprising, I suppose, that, if the Hotel Belgrade in Zagreb was rechristened as the Astoria, of these three great cinemas it was only the Kino Zagreb that stayed open. To put this in context, I read somewhere that the number of cinemas in Croatia generally plummeted between the 1980s and the mid-1990s from 400 to 50.

We walk down towards the Arena along the Emporor Vespasian's road, Via Flavia, and then beyond it along Istarska Street. All the shops along this particular stretch are closed down. 'We at the tourist office would like this to be regenerated,' Vesna tells me. 'It could be anything. Maybe a "creative quarter" where artists could live, and there can be craft shops and things, because this is the way all tourists come when they walk from the Arena to town centre and there is nothing here for them. It's such a waste, and these are such beautiful old buildings. It needs some kind of innovation like that to bring it back to life, otherwise it will just all get demolished and that would be such a shame.'

At the end of the row is a beautifully renovated hotel from the Austro-Hungarian era, yellow-painted, with stone balconies, while on the opposite side of the road stands a strikingly contemporary glass pavilion, which is the hotel's restaurant. The older building had been painstakingly renovated with the aim of being made into Pula's first five-star hotel, Vesna tells me, but because it is based very faithfully on the original design the rooms are not sufficiently big to qualify for five-star status within the parameters of the new tourism regulations. 'But nevertheless it is really beautiful.'

In among the boarded-up shop fronts is a slightly broader building with a white-stuccoed frontage that is still recognisable as a cinema. There are Art Deco mouldings above a clean rectangular canopy. The old cinema doors beneath have been replaced with plastic double-glazing and paper has been stuck on the inside of the glass so you can't see what they've done to the foyer. Vesna can't even remember what this cinema used to be called. 'Was maybe the Istarka, or the Istra.' It's been closed down for years.

When I talk about my cinema-viewing trip the next day even Pula residents are astonished that behind the Konditori bar the Kino Partizan should still be intact. 'Wow!' someone says, 'That is real history.' They're right. These 20th-century ruins, overlooked architectural detritus in some ways and great social spaces in their time, seem just as evocative of a vanished world as the admittedly more spectacular Roman ruins, particularly on the back of my visit to Brijuni, and the glimpse that it afforded into Tito's vanity and the star-studded splendour that was the Yugoslav Film Festival.

I'm in an old-fashioned working men's café that stands opposite the Castropola Bookshop, on Zagrebačka Street. Many people have told me that it's one of the best places to eat good plain food in the city. Over a plate of *tripice* (tripe) cooked in a tomato sauce I meet another former Yugoslavian-era movie star, Igor Galo. I write his name down in my notebook and as I do so he corrects me: 'No, it's only one "l". I lost the other one during socialism!' When I look up in surprise he tells me that 'Gallo' is a common surname in Italy and France too, but there they still spell it correctly: G-a-l-l-o. 'What can you do?' he laughs.

Galo starred in many classics of Yugoslav cinema. He also worked internationally, starring in Sam Peckinpah's *Cross of Iron* among others, with James Mason, James Coburn, Maximilian Schell and David Warner. 'He was youngest Hamlet,' Galo tells me. 'A *great* actor, truly.'

Igor Galo has lived in Pula for 35 years. His parents came from Motovun, but he was born in Serbia. 'Listen,' he says, 'I went to nine schools. In Slovenia, Croatia, Serbia, Dalmatia, you name it. You can call this the typical former Yugoslav experience, the Yugoslav *spirit*. That's how it was. If you stay in one place all your life you can't really know this, but if you move then you do, and you can speak fluent Slovenian, write in Latin or Cyrillic, know the differences between the dialects, and between Serbian and Croatian. Now children don't learn these things, so what are now our neighbouring countries are made even more foreign to them than they actually are. We need to be able to understand each other, and let's face it, that is so easy!'

A role in a new feature film is in the offing, but Igor now spends most of his time helping to run a non-governmental organization (NGO) called

Homo. He is leaving for Zagreb later this afternoon to supervise the installation of an exhibition of political cartoons from across the former Yugoslavia, all of which date from the first half of the 1990s. He suggests that this is a new way to try to understand the war, to look at how it was reported, how the different editorial stances of all the newspapers, and therefore the governments or their respective oppositions, were reflected in popular culture. Newspaper cartoons provide a barometer of ideas that have been 'mainstreamed' or of things that are impossible to say in any other editorial form.

Some of the cartoons Igor describes are emblematic visual jokes or significant puns. A famous caricature of Milošević by a cartoonist called Koraksić Predrag, known by the pseudonym Corax, published in *Borba* in 1992, shows the nationalist writer and ideologue Dobrica Ćosić sitting on Milošević's knee while the then President plays the single-stringed *gusle* and tells Ćosić 'how things used to be'.[5] Others display a more pointed humour. One shows Hitler and Ante Pavelić (the leader of the fascist NDH during the Second World War) as angels looking down at a burning Croatia. Hitler turns sadly to Pavelić and says 'Lucky you! You can go home now!'

The great thing about the exhibition, as far as Igor is concerned, is that it's taking place as part of a political conference that will be attended by three presidents of ex-Yugoslav states, from Croatia, from Serbia and Montenegro, and from Bosnia-Herzegovina: 'They are coming just to prove that they can come!' he jokes. 'But no, everyone knows that there has to be regular collaboration between the ex-Yugoslav countries, and now to an extent there is. It's just that you have to push them a little to make it happen more quickly.'

The conference will also be attended by NGOs, by ambassadors, 'the *corps diplomatique*', the Council of Europe, the OSCE mission: 'These are the usual suspects, I know, but thank goodness those organizations sponsor events like this, because from our side we could not make it happen without them. In parallel,' he continues, 'we could not exist either. For 15 years now we have been dealing with human rights protection in Serbia and Montenegro, in Bosnia-Herzegovina, and in this country.'

Homo was started in Pula in 1991 as an informal group of women who were concerned about friends and neighbours being expelled from jobs or homes. They had support from men, but this had to be clandestine as it was more dangerous for men to speak out in public at that time. Galo made many documentary films in Lika, recording what was happening during and after the war. 'When we found out what was hiding behind the hill,' he says, 'we had to try and do something about it.'

Like Drago Pilsel, members of Homo were some of the first to go into Lika after Operation Storm, but this too was dangerous. The NGO has had support from British charities that helped it to set up an office in Korenica, where it provides free advice to 'returnees' – those refugees who were displaced to other republics during the war and now want to return home. These people, Galo tells me, need 'direct protection' as much when they return home – if they can return home – as when they left. I remember something that Drago Pilsel had said over dinner in Zagreb: 'These [returnees] are mainly elderly people, and they're in a very hostile environment. They have no jobs, no social life, no way to really survive.'

I've read in the paper that morning that this year is the last in which people can reclaim property. A deadline has been set and if they don't apply before the end of September they cannot come. 'Simple as that,' Igor says, not laughing any more, telling me that his organization are doing all they can to publicize the possibility of refuges returning. 'But the catch is that they also have to realize citizenship here too before they can reclaim their property. As if that is going to be easy! These people's records are missing in some cases.'

It's easy, he tells me, for the government to say things at a high level, but at a local level it's very different because local officials are often reluctant to implement the directives, and when people do manage to return they are often the victims of violence.

While we eat I'm looking again at the day's paper, the *Jutarnji List* (*Morning Paper*). The front page story is about an investigation by the OESS. The headline reads, '85% of Serbian refugees are not coming back.'

Igor's ultimately an optimist, however, and has preserved his faith in his countrymen. He thinks that most people are still basically anti-fascist and that they buy their newspapers, which were founded by the Partisans after all, because of this vestigial anti-fascist feeling. But when it mattered they didn't realize that those same newspapers had shifted to right-wing positions over the years. They were too trusting of the information they were being given by politicians. Most people, he thinks, realized that basically Yugoslavia was over, but they didn't necessarily identify with the nationalists in any of the republics. They just thought that it was 'some people over there'. Then houses started being confiscated, or just looted and burned down.

And first of all, he tells me, it was houses of people in the public eye, TV stars, whatever. It was as if this process was very carefully planned, with an eye on the future. The nice, well-preserved houses on the main roads, the ones that might be good for business, were left alone. Others were razed to the ground, and after that there was no way to stop it. Bosnian Croats were invited to take over Serb houses, and this whole thing started between Tudjman and Milošević, fighting over their little gaps and footholds along the Sava River. Igor's organization attempted simply to document this when it was happening, and to make sure they copied their communications to people in government, so that·they could never say they didn't know.

Igor suddenly looks at his watch: we've spent a bit longer together than we had meant to. He apologizes profusely, tidies the knife and fork on his plate, and beckons for the bill. He must leave for Zagreb to supervise the installation of the exhibition and attend the conference.

I don't have to finish my meal alone, however, because others, friends of friends, have come in to eat in the meantime. Anyone you don't know in Pula will almost certainly be a friend of a friend, since Istria's village sensibility is just as tangible here as anywhere else. Finding no other seats, they'd sat down opposite Igor and me while we were talking.

Someone whose name I don't catch, and who obviously didn't get the drift of our conversation at all, forces an abrupt and wholly unpleasant end to what had up until this point been a good lunch. She achieves this in a manner so inexcusable that I cannot let it go unchallenged. Attempting to join in, or to fill some gap she'd perceived in the conversation, she laughs in a jolly way and says, 'Well, let me tell you, those Serbs. When I heard there was going to be a war, I just said to myself, "Hooray! Now we can have a holiday from them!"'

This jolly idiot, who would probably consider herself a liberal, obviously doesn't notice my increasingly horrified expression. She's too busy warming to this poisonous pet subject of hers, which is evidently just too good to keep to herself: 'Yes, and you know the funny thing about Serbs is that, wherever they go, they immediately form criminal gangs. It's true! They are all really criminals and that is how they organize themselves, with gangs like that, it must be genetic. It's just how they are. They cannot help it. Oh! I was *so glad* when they all moved away. I just thought, '*Finally* we can live on our own!'

Chapter Fourteen
Istria IV: London, Pula (2004)

I meet an artist from Belgrade called Ivan Grubanov who has been working on an extraordinary and, until very recently, secret drawing project. I miss an exhibition of his work in a gallery just off Old Street in London, because I'm travelling in Croatia, but upon my return I phone the gallery to see if I can make an appointment to see the pictures anyway. I'm shown through to a basement storeroom that is full of large wooden crates, which the director, Laurence O'Hana, starts to unpack. He burbles excitedly as he does so, telling me that the exhibition I just missed was of 158 drawings, that they are for sale as a single work and that a smaller set of 12 drawings has just been bought by the Deutsche Bank collection.

The reason for the secrecy that has characterized the project up to now is clear: Grubanov has been drawing Slobodan Milošević, from life, at The Hague. I ask how this came about and he tells me that, along with many others, he'd worked for B92 Radio in Belgrade during the war. There was nothing special about this, he says, a lot of people did, but as a result he had a press card, which he was able to use to gain access to the press gallery at Courtroom No. 1 at ICTY, The Hague, where the Milošević trial was and, at the time of writing, still is being held.

Grubanov tells me that his sitting in the press gallery at The Hague was the end result of a process that had begun on the eve of the war, in March 1991. His father had taken him to the anti-Milošević protests in Belgrade, a way to illustrate to his son that it was possible to exercise political responsibility and that part of that responsibility is to protest when what your leaders are doing is wrong. The young Grubanov had seen this as an initiation, a way for him to grow up and to learn how to make a political statement on the streets.

The initiation turned out instead to be into the certain, bloody knowledge of just how far Milošević was prepared to go to hold on to power: the protests led to opposition leaders being jailed and the needless deaths of several protesters. But the opposition movement didn't go away, in spite of that murderous denouement in March 1991, even if it might have been hard to see this from outside of Serbia. It found its outlets in Radio B92 and other media, as well as in continued street protests. Ivan tells me that, like many, many others, he'd continued to take part: 'It was the only thing that an individual was able to do.'

He also tells me that he has had to accept the fact that Milošević defined his generation's identity. Milošević has become the first thing that people think of or see or know about when they think of Serbia, and for a young Serbian artist this adds to the day-to-day problems that already exist. 'It's not like being a young British artist or a young German one. We come from what is perceived as a very weak and unreliable art community, let alone country – so Serbian artists are a very insecure investment.' Consequently, Grubanov describes the protest movement as the battle for his whole generation:

> Previous generations had no idea about real life, no space for making choices at all. The next generation were totally unprepared and just fled. My generation had to grow up in this, we were too young to do anything else, so we grew up with all that media manipulation, which led to a country that publicly at least had no faith in anyone but themselves, and no desire to be accepted or approved; quite the opposite.

While he's talking I think of that supposedly Serbian characteristic, *inat*, which I'd understood to mean some sort of 'in-spite-of-ness', and, bizarrely, of the famous slogan of Millwall Football Club's fans: 'No one likes us, we don't care!'

Faced with this, the protest movement was about having to prove yourself ethically and morally, and simply fighting for some kind of life. 'And each time, with each new wave of protests,' Grubanov says, 'we always thought that this is the final thing, the last push; this is how we'll get him away, how we'll reassert normal life.'

It was in March 2001, ten years after those first protests, that Ivan was driving through Belgrade when he heard the news on the car radio that Milošević, who had been out of power for six months by then, was under what amounted to a virtual siege of his house. One attempt to arrest him had already failed, but the uneasy stand-off between Milošević, holed up with his bodyguards, and the government of the then new Serbian President Vojislav Koštunica continued. A crowd had gathered to watch and wait, and Grubanov felt that he had no choice but to go to Topčider and join them:

> I was part of the mob waiting outside his house, because in spite of the effect he'd had on my generation, this enormous blight, I'd never seen him in public and I suddenly just wanted to *see* this man. But maybe he was as humiliated by himself as we were, because he never came out.

Milošević was eventually arrested on 30 March 2001, but it wasn't until 29 June that same year that he was transferred to The Hague, in a move that saw the late Prime Minister Zoran Djindjić deferring to international law rather than the (still, then) Yugoslav Constitution, under which there was no legal way to extradite him.

Shortly after this Grubanov was accepted on an artists' residency programme in Amsterdam. When Milošević's trial started at the ICTY Ivan still felt that he wanted or needed to actually see Milošević in person. That was when he dug out the old B92 press card. 'I had no clue about this as an art project. It just suddenly seemed important, like a ceremonial event that needed to be recorded somehow.'

When he arrived in the press enclosure for the first time Grubanov started writing just like all the other journalists, but these notes quickly began to be replaced by drawings. 'The Belgrade Art Academy was famous for life drawing,' he tells me by way of explanation:

> The models were elderly people trying to find a way to survive. Also you could go to the city zoo, where entrance was free if you were there to draw! But still, my first drawings were nervous. I just wanted to have as many images as I could. It took a while before I realized that I was producing a body of evidence. Those first drawings didn't reflect my experience of history, let alone the full complexity of events, so I decided to make them more complex, to gather as much detail as I could, as much evidence as possible.

Like the opposition protest culture in Belgrade, this for Grubanov was about being present and taking responsibility:

Not least because the charges and accusations being cited in Milošević's trial were usually addressed to Serbs generally, rather than Milošević in particular. Of course, as in any work of theatre, I also ended up identifying with him, like with an actor on the stage.

Grubanov realized that he had some important sketches, but he felt under self-imposed pressure to produce a single drawing that could capture this character, Milošević, in itself; a portrait, perhaps. 'I knew when he was angry, nervous, sulking. I felt I knew him well, but none of the drawings reflected this full complexity, so I started to just draw his face.' Far from Milošević being captured in these drawings, he was actually disappearing. 'I started adding sentences, a few words from the testimonies that were taking place at the time of each drawing, as if that was a way of bringing him back, extracting some kind of truth.'

During the second year of the trial the space for visitors was restricted. Ivan Grubanov ended up always sitting in the same place behind the glass opposite Milošević. In Belgrade his family started videoing the proceedings from The Hague from the television, because every time the camera angle shifted to show one particular prosecutor addressing Milošević, Ivan was there in the background behind the glass, in what had become his usual seat:

> I made 50 or more drawings of his face from that position, but I wasn't happy with any of them. This felt symptomatic of my unsatisfactory relationship with him, and all the different emotions (mine and his) that were impossible to capture in a single drawing. I realized that I had visually exhausted the subject. I'd drawn everything. But of course it wasn't even necessarily about the outcome, about one single work of art, but about being present and taking my share of the responsibility. It became about the personal idea of being able to clarify my own conscience, and being a draftsman allowed me to go beyond, and achieve some, I can't remember the word, it sounds spiritual… *catharsis.*

> It's very emotional. It engages all the senses, hearing all of your history like that, understanding what has become your national identity.

Still the drawings had to be made secretly, as Grubanov feared that if he were found out he would no longer be allowed into the gallery:

What surprised me most was how, even if there were only a couple of lines on the page, Milošević was there, and the representation seemed almost stronger than when I was trying to capture too many details. And that was when this process started to feel important. It was a way to begin to make sense of all those years I spent in Serbia, and to try to understand why I was identifying with him as I was. I felt that I must have been doing something wrong, because this was the man I'd been fighting against.

He pauses for a second. 'I felt ashamed. Guilty.'

Back in the art gallery crates are unpacked, and one after another of Grubanov's drawings is brought out and propped against the wall of the storeroom. They are on A5 notebook pages, mounted on white card in plain wooden frames. Here is a drawing executed with a few lines of one of the prosecutors, with his back to the viewer, the side of his face visible. There are the microphones and work stations, the patterns and designs of the high-specification office furniture that's used in the courtrooms. Headphones and gowns are captured; a camera is mounted on the ceiling. Another drawing shows the hand of a bewigged lawyer tapping on a laptop computer, his little finger delicately extended as if in that parody of taking tea.

On some of the drawings are those fragments of transcript, an occasional sentence from the proceedings: 'Everyone was afraid.' 'The KLA must have done that, I don't know.' 'Did you see them put him in the car?' 'I think it must have been an axe.' Here and there, in the background, is a faint but immediately recognizable Milošević. I suddenly understood what Grubanov had meant when he talked about Milošević disappearing, but even when the drawing of him was rendered in just one or two lines the man was instantly recognizable.

A few of the later drawings show only Milošević's hair. For all that Grubanov felt that he was approaching some kind of truth by this point in his two-year process, as I looked at it now in the back room of the art gallery, the whole project seemed to be turning into one very famous fiction. As the trial of Slobodan Milošević lumbers fitfully on, with its few days of sittings each week, and subject to repeated delays due to his ill health so that its completion is receding correspondingly into the future, here, before my eyes, Milošević was disappearing, slipping from everybody's grasp. He seemed to have become the Cheshire Cat from Lewis

Carroll's *Alice in Wonderland*, that famous hairline, rather than a smile, being all that remains of him.

Ivan Grubanov's work, the sheer persistence of it and his honesty about the conflicting emotions that it invoked within him, is deeply resonant. Both the drawings and the conversation stay in my mind for days afterwards. Something about the process – Grubanov's sustained attention to minutiae, the idea of a body of research being built up incrementally with these huge numbers of small drawings – makes concrete for me something that seems blindingly obvious, but had nevertheless been hovering just out of sight.

I'm immediately reminded of two things I'd read, which each translate this sudden thought about an artistic process into the everyday political realm. One passage is from a satirical political essay by the Serbian theorist Ivan Čolović, from the mid-1990s, and another is from a novel of the same period by Slobodan Selenić, which is set in the mid-20th century and maps the genesis of the Tito era, but which was seen as a powerful satire of Milošević.

Čolović writes with deliberately heavy sarcasm about the grand and carefully choreographed demonstrations and events that the Milošević regime engineered in place of any genuine civil and political process. They had started with his seizing control of the 500th anniversary of the Battle of Kosovo Polje, and thus seizing power, with the famous declaration: 'You shall never be beaten again.' Under Milošević, Čolović writes:

> popular gatherings… and promotional party meetings [were] a far more acceptable form of political activity than the multi-party Assembly and debate within it. For the Assembly, unlike the dignified and magnificent gathering of the people, … may be transformed into a stage for quarrels, conflict, ill-mannered attacks by deputies and other ugly things unworthy of glorious Serbian history, which only blur and compromise the clear aims of the national struggle, disturb national harmony, break up the power of the state.[1]

In his novel Slobodan Selenić describes politics as being, 'but for war, the most dangerous form of entertainment among the Serbs,'[2] but goes on: 'We need modesty and diligence … not grandiose political schemes, and even less do we need high-handed, inflammatory speeches.'[3]

'Modesty and diligence' are certainly returning to the political sphere in

Serbia, as in the other Yugoslav successor republics. They are replacing, to some extent at least, the 'grandiose political schemes' and 'inflammatory speeches' that Selenić describes.

This same reassertion of a kind of due process may be true of art. When I first came to write this book, and to travel like so many before me in Rebecca West's footsteps, the countries that I visited seemed to be places that demanded slogans to fight slogans – the grand and sometimes quixotic gestures of protest, pitted against regimes that held on to power with sound bites and subterfuge. The art works that seemed most relevant to that landscape were not Mozart's arias but Gordon Matta-Clark's measured destruction of buildings, Gordana Stanišić's walk to nowhere, the abject performance art of Stuart Brisley. In the social and political realm, in Serbia at least, the opposition movement had only just ceased to mobilize itself around one objective, ousting the man who'd almost destroyed them, as much through mass cultural demonstrations as through the steady attempts to reassert the democratic process.

These approaches to representing the wars of the 1990s (and a protest is surely also a representation of sorts, just as much as a picture might be) were still absolutely resonant when I first visited Belgrade, not least because they'd succeeded and Milošević had gone. Yet we could all feel that the power of these gestures was fading, with peace achieved and with Milošević in The Hague. Now that there is a slow return to the messiness and unpredictability of civil society, it is, arguably, the painstakingly slow and methodical self-reflection embodied by an artist like Ivan Grubanov, with his endless hesitant sketches, that may provide us with the best representation of life in the former Yugoslavia now. This process of self-reflection, his including himself in the picture so to speak, is the key. If Milošević, like the Cheshire Cat, is disappearing, he can't ultimately succeed, because there is a vast body of evidence. Those thousands of pages of transcript stop him doing so and tie him to us.

With her self-portrait of what an Englishwoman felt on the eve of war Rebecca West succeeded in demonstrating what later became the rallying cry of Carol Hanisch and other feminists: the personal is political.[4] Yet West's writing also illustrates that the inverse is true: the political is personal.

It might be hard, perhaps even impossible, for contemporary readers to empathize with West when, in the epilogue to *Black Lamb and Grey Falcon*, she writes: Often, when I have thought of invasion, or when a bomb has dropped near by, I have prayed, "Let me behave like a Serb."[5] However, in making this statement, or in saying that her book is broadly pro-Serb,[6] West was not lionizing or identifying with the likes of former general, now fugitive, Ratko Mladić, even though he might still be thought to epitomize the most widespread international image of his people (whether 'his people' is understood to mean the Bosnian Serbs in particular, the Serbs in general or, still more problematically, the multi-ethnic population of Serbia).

West's self-confessed admiration of Serbs pivots on what she learned in the then Yugoslavia about the broader human tendency towards destruction and the relative rarity (as she judged it) of the countervailing tendency to defend what is good. West saw this equation most delicately balanced in the epic Serbian poem about the defeat at Kosovo Polje, in which the grey falcon of her title presented Tsar Lazar with a choice between winning an earthly kingdom or sacrificing all for a heavenly kingdom. This seemed to West to represent a choice between the proper reassertion of love for what is good and the worship, in the name of heaven, of pointless sacrifice and suffering. She saw it too in the re-enactment of a ritual animal sacrifice in a Macedonian Easter festival that crystallized her deep mistrust of the version of Christianity that emphasizes suffering, and which she describes as 'a theory of the Universe which supposes a God capable of showering down blessings in exchange for meaningless bloodshed'.[7] Like the young married couple sacrificing a lamb as a customary means of ensuring their own happiness through the gift of children, West saw that Britain before the Second World War was 'in the power of the abominable fantasy which pretends that bloodshed is pleasing to God,'[8] and while she was confident we would not wish to wield the knife, the human belief in self-sacrifice is, she believed, so strong that we would willingly be the lamb.

Rebecca West realised in the late 1930s that this kind of death cult was all around us: not only that, but it was in its ascendancy. Her stark realization was that this death cult was epitomized not only by the Nazis, but also by the appeasers' wilful acceptance of the prospect of 'sacrificial self-immolation'.[9] But perhaps West's most important lesson, aside from the obvious one that she teaches about what it is possible for a work of literature to achieve, is also that this choice, this acceptance of a will to self-destruction and the destruction of others, is not something that was somehow uniquely visited upon the Yugoslavs at the beginning of the Second World War. Rather, it is something that we may recognize in ourselves too, in the choices that we make every day, sometimes even in spite of our best interests or our basic desires to be happy.

West's admiration was not directed at those who would wish death upon their people and manipulate that death wish to serve their own power: it was directed towards those who would *resist*. I am as certain as I can be that, if West's travels had taken place in the 1990s, she would have learned similar lessons, even if to chart the horrors of the Second World War, the Tito era and the dissolution of Yugoslavia would have resulted in a book at least twice as long as *Black Lamb and Grey Falcon*. I am also absolutely certain that her heroes would not have been Milošević, Karadžić, Mladić or any of their counterparts, but those who resisted them and who won out, however fragile and contingent that victory necessarily continues to be. Out of all this she might still perhaps – and, in my view, rightly – have been able to say, more moderately, let me behave *like that*. But she might also have learned that honour is not determined by nationality, that it is not the single God-given prerogative of one ethnic group.

I'm determined to visit the former World boxing champion Mate Parlov before I leave Pula, but I have no idea where his bar is and it's not listed in any of the tourist guides. As if this would help me to find it, I've been trying to imagine what it might look like. 'Is it old-fashioned?' I ask Vesna at one point during our cinema tour. 'Or kind of modern?' 'Oh, it's old-fashioned,' she says, and I immediately conjure an image of some old wood-panelled *kafana* like the Manjež in Belgrade, or the Austrian beer and food halls in Zagreb. This is quickly dispelled when she adds, '*Really* old-fashioned. You know, like, 1970s!'

Nataša, a highly respected journalist from Zagreb who now lives and works in Pula, agrees to take me to Mate's bar on my last evening in Pula. We don't have to go very far and I immediately realize that I've walked past it countless times. The violet neon sign that spells out 'Mate' above the door might have given it away. It's just a few yards from the old Kino Beograd, on the same side of Giardini.

The interior, we discover, is bathed in a kind of twilight that defies the senses: it's impossible to tell if it's day or night outside without checking. Vesna was right about the design, which is spectacular. Parlov must have spent a lot of money to get his little bar *just so*. A central circular table, set at standing-with-a-glass-in-your-hand height, is mounted around a big swooping chromium-plated pole that somehow also becomes a central light fitting. Everything that isn't made of chrome seems to be made from beige leather, and there's a sense that when it was opened this might have been the best kind of bar that money could buy. It's worn the intervening 20 or 30 years very well too.

The bar is deserted when we arrive, although during the hour we spend in it the regulars come in, in a steady stream, to have their nightly drink with Parlov and exchange a few words with him. Everyone seems to stop for just one, then be on their way – it's as if supping with a champion somehow fortifies the drink.

It's immediately obvious that the bear of a man who is serving behind the bar when we arrive is Parlov himself, although, apart from his size and a slightly broken nose, he really doesn't have the damaged air of a former champion. He's in excellent shape. 'Such a gentleman, too,' says Nataša later. 'What a nice man.'

Having bought the necessary drinks, we formally introduce ourselves, pay our respects and acknowledge Parlov's achievements in first winning every possible competition and honour that it's possible to achieve as an amateur – national amateur champion, European champion, Olympic champion – and then repeating the process as a professional. 'A Yugoslav Cassius Clay and Mohammed Ali rolled into one,'[10] jokes his entry in the *Leksikon Yu-mitologije*, but he really was a national hero. Even if the country that he was a hero to no longer exists, he certainly does.

While we talk I notice that there is another room down some steps beside the bar. When we've got the formalities out of the way we're invited down to take a look. *Gospodin* Parlov (I decide that 'Mr' is the appropriate form of address for a world champion) flicks on some lights and takes us down to his trophy room. There are glass cabinets lining the walls, containing dozens of trophies, plates, medals and photographs. He talks us through them, suddenly lighting upon his fight with the British boxer, John Conteh, and I suppose that he's doing this out of politeness, since I'm visiting from London (*'Da*, he was a good fighter, but I beat him!'). I point at a set of medals and ask if one of these was his Olympic gold from Munich. 'What can I say?' he ruefully admits. 'My Olympic medal was stolen.'

I ask him what he thinks of boxing now. Does he still follow it? 'Not at all,' he says calmly. 'I never watch. *Nikad!* [Never!] There are too many titles, too many different boxing authorities. How can any of them mean anything any more? Nobody can be undisputed champion as I was. It's a circus, not a sport.'

It really is a pleasure to meet someone who could easily have abused his position by aligning himself with nationalist politics during the 1990s, but didn't. I'm certain that plenty of politicians would have wanted him on, or even at, their side; for them it would have been very useful just to be photographed with this giant hero. Parlov resolutely didn't allow this to happen. I remember a quotation from a newspaper interview that he gave in 2001. Parlov was talking to two journalists in the hotel bar during the Pula Book Fair, Ante Tomić and Mile Stojić. Speaking of the 1990s he said, 'How could I be a nationalist? I was champion of the world!'

I'm left with the impression that this quiet life in Pula suits Gospodin Parlov very well. It's ironic: the door with his name above it is always open, anybody can come in at any time, yet he couldn't be living a more private life if he went and hid in the mountains. He is still a hero.

For some reason I think again of that photograph I saw on Brijuni of an impassive Ivan Meštrović meeting and yet rebuffing Tito: the artist's refusal to be instrumentalized. I remember also a small relief sculpture in the Meštrović Museum in Split. Entitled 'My People's Artist', it shows a stooped and elderly blind man in whose hand hangs a useless *gusle* and who is being gently led by a young man with a lantern. More than any other sculpture, this is the most clearly reflexive work by Meštrović. Surely paradigmatic, it evokes his romantic visions both of the role of art and of what he himself set out to achieve: to create a culture of, about and for the southern Slav peoples, the Yugoslavs, and to represent that to the world.

Now that the unified southern Slav culture that Meštrović played a part in creating and mythologizing no longer exists, his public sculptures are cast adrift to mark the boundaries of a phantom country, a map of which lies beneath the new maps and borders of the Yugoslav successor republics. Meštrović's vision and his sculptures have become just another stratum in the rich palimpsest that is the archaeology of the region.

When Mate Parlov was born, in Split in 1948, Meštrović had already been away in his self-imposed exile in South Bend, Indiana, for nine years, and the sculptor died in 1962, ten years before Parlov won his Olympic gold medal. Yet in a way they had something in common, because Parlov's sustained feat was also about creating something for the former Yugoslavia.

Thinking of the way that Meštrović brought that immanent physicality to his sculptures of the human form, but how, like Rebecca West, he also did so much to represent his subjects as psychological characters, as complex human subjects, my view is that Mate Parlov would have fascinated him, both as a man and as a subject. Possibly less when Parlov was at the height of his powers – Meštrović's sculptures are never simply celebrations of physical power or classical perfection – as *now*, when that Olympian physique is fading and Parlov has faced some fundamental choices, echoing the choices that Meštrović himself was also forced to make. To his eternal credit, Gospodin Parlov chose to reject the new kind of celebrity and patronage that could have been his during the nationalistic 1990s.

The great writer and critic John Berger suggested in a recent documentary that the dichotomy between good and evil exists at the moment of choice, not in its consequences.[11] It was precisely such a choice that Mate Parlov faced in the early 1990s, and it's the consequences of that choice that he now lives out in his quiet little bar, his very earthly kingdom, having the occasional singsong, being remembered only by a few elderly regulars and occasional visitors to Pula. I feel sure that, if he were still alive to witness *this* Mate Parlov, Ivan Meštrović would have made one hell of a statue of him.

Acknowledgements

This book would not have been possible without the generosity, friendship and hospitality of numerous people. I'm particularly indebted to Borivoj Radaković. I would also like to express my sincere thanks to the following: Gordana Stanišić and the Stanišić family, Edo Popović, Pawel Pawlikowski, Vladimir Arsenijević, Sandra Ukalović, Nenad Rizvanović, Boško Zatezalo, Zorica Radaković, Nataša Petrinjak, Svetlana Rakočević, Magdalena Vodopija, Ozren Grbavčić, Vesna Ivanović, Egle Vošten, Kruno Lokotar and friends at AGM in Zagreb, Dražen Pantić, Zoran Ferić and all the other writers who were part of the FAK movement or contributed to *Croatian Nights,* Danijela Stanojević, György Dalos, Josef Haslinger, Michael Moorcock, Fiona Sampson, Brendan Simms, Dave Watson, the British Council in Zagreb, Istrian Tourist Board, Castropola Bookshop, Pula Book Fair, Mauro Ferlin, Josip Paro, Flora Turner, Vesna Goldsworthy, Bronac Ferran, Jenny Calcutt, and the many others who provided introductions, leads, opportunities and suggestions, or helped to make these journeys and this project not only possible, but also such a tremendous and life-affirming pleasure. *Black Lamb and Grey Falcon* by Rebecca West is published in Great Britain by Canongate. Above all I would like to thank my wife Sarah, and the very great Rebecca West.

Chapter notes

Chapter One (pp. 9-32)

1 'The Trial of Adolf Eichmann, Session 46 (part 4 of 6)', *The Nizkor Project*, archived at: http://www.nizkor.org/hweb/people/e/eichmann-adolf/transcripts/Sessions/Session-046-04.html

2 Maria Todorova, *Imagining the Balkans*, Oxford: Oxford University Press, 1997, p. 26.

3 Maria Todorova, *Imagining the Balkans*, p. 183.

4 Olivia Manning, *The Balkan Trilogy*, London: Mandarin Paperbacks, 1992, p.11.

5 Kate Hudson, *Breaking the South Slav Dream: The Rise and Fall of Yugoslavia*, London: Pluto Press, 2003, p. 57.

6 Kate Hudson, *Breaking the South Slav Dream*, p. 60.

7 Rebecca West, *Black Lamb and Grey Falcon*, reissued Edinburgh: Canongate, 1993, p.406. Jan and Cora Gordon, *Two Vagabonds in the Balkans*, London: The Bodley Head, 1925, p. 120.

8 Jan and Cora Gordon, *Two Vagabonds in the Balkans*, p. 120.

9 Jan and Cora Gordon, *Two Vagabonds in the Balkans*, p. 124.

10 Jan and Cora Gordon, *Two Vagabonds in the Balkans*, p. 124.

11 Rebecca West, *Black Lamb and Grey Falcon*, p. 433 (abbreviated to West from now on).

12 West, p.20

13 Nicholas Blincoe and Matt Thorne (eds), *All Hail the New Puritans*, London: Fourth Estate, 2000.

14 Leon Trotsky, *The Balkan Wars 1912–13: The War Correspondence of Leon Trotsky*, New York: Pathfinder Press, 2001, pp. 93–4.

15 Helsinki Committee for Human Rights in Serbia (HCHRS), *Human Rights in the Shadow of Nationalism: Serbia 2002*, Belgrade: HCHRS, 2002, p. 273.

16 Davor Konjikušić, 'Sugar Re-packed in Serbia and Sold to the EU', *Southeast European Times*, Belgrade, 10 March 2004. Archived at: http://www.balkan-times.com/html2/english/040310-DAVOR-001.htm

Chapter Two (pp. 33-50)

1 Dubravka Ugrešić, *Have a Nice Day: from the Balkan War to the American Dream*, London: Jonathan Cape, 1994, p. 12.

2 Miljenko Jergović, 'The Library' in *Sarajevo Marlborough*, London: Penguin Books, 1997, p. 153.

3 George Orwell, Letter to the Duchess of Atholl, 15 November 1945, in Sonia Orwell and Ian Angus (eds), *The Collected Essays, Journalism and Letters of George Orwell,* Volume 4: *In Front of Your Nose, 1945–1950,* London: Penguin Books, London, 1970, p. 49 (first published London: Secker & Warburg, 1968).

4 Count Hermann Keyserling, trans. Maurice Samuel, *Europe,* New York: Harcourt, Brace, 1928, quoted in Maria Todorova, *Imagining the Balkans,* p. 116.

5 Misha Glenny, *The Balkans,* London: Granta Books, 2002, p. xvii.

6 Ljubo Sirc, *Between Hitler and Tito: Nazi Occupation and Communist Oppression,* London: André Deutsch, 1989, p. 21.

7 Misha Glenny and Gerald Knaus, 'Thessaloniki and Beyond: Europe's Challenge in the Western Balkans', background paper presented to the World Economic Forum, South-East Europe Meeting, Athens, Greece, 23–24 May 2003. Archived at: http://www.weforum.org/pdf/SEEurope/Glenny_Knaus_paper.pdf

8 West, p. 21.

9 Duško Doder, 'No Way Out', *Guardian* Review section, 10 December 2005.

10 Carl Rollyson, *Rebecca West: A Saga of the Century,* London: Hodder & Stoughton, 1995, p. 149.

11 Rebecca West, Letter to Henry Andrews, 15 May 1938, in *Selected Letters,* ed. Bonnie Kime Scott, New Haven, CT, and London: Yale University Press, 2000, p. 166.

12 Rebecca West, Letter to Ben Huebsch, 22 December 1938, in *Selected Letters,* p. 167.

13 Rebecca West, Letter to Aleksandar Woollcott, April 1941, in *Selected Letters,* p. 169.

14 Rebecca West, Letter to John Gunther, late April to 10 May 1941, in *Selected Letters,* p. 173.

15 West, p. 773.

16 http://members.aol.com/balkandave/frmcon.htm

17 e-mail from Dave Watson, 21 February 2004, reproduced with permission.

18 Vojin Dimitrijević, 'The 1974 Constitution and Constitutional Process as a Factor in the Collapse of Yugoslavia', in Payam Akhavan and Robert Howse (eds), *Yugoslavia, the Former and Future: Reflections by Scholars from the Region,* Geneva: United Nations Research Institute for Social Development, 1995, pp. 45–74.

19 George Orwell, 'Shooting an Elephant', in Sonia Orwell and Ian Angus (eds), *The Collected Essays Journalism and Letters of George Orwell,* Volume 1: *An Age Like This, 1920–1940,* Harmondsworth: Penguin Books 1970, p. 267 (first published London: Secker & Warburg, 1968).

20 Vesna Kesić, 'Muslim Women, Croatian Women, Serbian Women, Albanian Women…' in Dušan I. Bjelić and Obrad Savić (eds), *Balkan as Metaphor,* Cambridge, MA: MIT Press, 2002, p. 317.

21 Misha Glenny, *From Our Own Correspondent,* BBC Radio 4, Saturday 24 January 2004.

22 Leon Trotsky, *The Balkan Wars 1912–13: The War Correspondence of Leon Trotsky,* New York: Pathfinder Press, 2001, p. 203.

23 Slavenka Drakulić, *They Would Never Hurt a Fly,* London: Abacus, 2004, p. 10.

24 In the film *Pioneers in Art and Science: Metzger*, directed by Ken McMullen, Arts Council England 2004.

25 BBC Radio 4 News, 2 December 2003.

26 Slavenka Drakulić, *They Would Never Hurt a Fly*, Abacus, London, 2004, p. 135.

27 http://www.nieman.harvard.edu/reports/99-2NRsummer99/Cicic.html

28 'Bosnia Gets Tough on Sexist Humour', *Independent*, 23 August 2003.

29 Carl Rollyson, *Rebecca West: A Saga of the Century*, London: Hodder & Stoughton, 1995, p. 161.

30 West, p. 89.

31 Rebecca West, Letter to Miss G. Rotherham, 11 December 1944, from *Selected Letters*, ed. Bonnie Kime Scott, New Haven, CT, and London: Yale University Press, 2000, p. 188.

32 Rebecca West, Letter to Stoyan Pribićević, 5 June 1945, in *Selected Letters*, ed. Bonnie Kime Scott, New Haven, CT, and London: Yale University Press, 2000, p. 189.

33 West, Letter to Pribićević, in *Selected Letters*, p. 190.

34 West, Letter to Pribićević, in *Selected Letters*, p. 191.

35 West, p. 1089,

36 West, p. 1089.

37 George Orwell, 'London Letter to *Partisan Review*, March–April 1942', in Sonia Orwell and Ian Angus (eds), *The Collected Essays, Journalism and Letters of George Orwell*, Volume 2: *My Country Right or Left, 1940–1943*, London: Penguin, 1970, p. 212 (first published London: Secker & Warburg, 1968).

38 Letter from D.S. Savage, in Orwell and Angus (eds), *The Collected ...*, Volume 2: *My Country Right or Left, 1940–1943*, pp. 254–5.

39 West, p. 846.

40 West, pp. 846–7.

41 Rebecca West, Letter to Stoyan Pribićević, 5 June 1945, in *Selected Letters*, ed. Bonnie Kime Scott, New Haven, CT, and London: Yale University Press, 2000, p. 193.

42 Rebecca West, *The Fountain Overflows*, reissued London: Virago, 1984, p. 11.

43 Robert D. Kaplan, *Balkan Ghosts*, New York: Vintage, 1994, p. xiii.

44 Laura Silber and Allan Little, *Yugoslavia: Death of a Nation*, New York: Penguin Books, 1997 (revised and updated edition of *The Death of Yugoslavia*, London: Penguin Books/BBC Books, 1996), p. 287.

45 Robert D. Kaplan, *Balkan Ghosts*, p. xxvii.

Chapter Three (pp. 51-69)

1 West, p. 470.

2 www.beograd.org.yu

3 Ljubo Sirc, *Between Hitler and Tito: Nazi Occupation and Communist Oppression*, London: André Deutsch, 1989, p. 143.

4 Srdjan Jovanović Weiss, 'NATO as Architecture Critic', in *Cabinet*, New York, 2000: http://www.normalgroup.net/turbo/natocritic.htm

5 Srdjan Jovanović Weiss, 'NATO as Architecture Critic'

6 'Three Pioneers on the Electronic Frontier Honored at Internet Policy Conference', EFF Media Release, 7 April 1999, archived at: http://www.eff.org/awards/pioneer/1999.php

7 West, p. 472.

8 West, p. 383.

9 Srdjan Jovanović Weiss, Miloš Mirosavić and Jelena Masnikosić, 'Turbo Architecture and Other Stories', Normal Group, at http://www.normalgroup.net/turbo/index.html.

10 Srdjan Jovanović Weiss, 'Loss of Memory?: New Urban Condition of Belgrade', Normal Group: http://www.normalgroup.net/ turbo/tnprobe.html.

11 West, p. 918.

12 Lawrence Durrell, *White Eagles Over Serbia*, London: Faber, 1957, p. 59.

13 West, p. 483.

14 West, p. 655.

15 'The Trial of Adolf Eichmann, Session 46 (part 5 of 6)', *The Nizkor Project*, archived at: http://www.nizkor.org/hweb/people/e/eichmann-adolf/transcripts/Sessions/Session-046-05.html

16 Marcus Tanner, *Croatia: A Nation Forged in War*, New Haven, CT, and London: Yale University Press, 2001, p. 26.

17 Kate Hudson, *Breaking the South Slav Dream: The Rise and Fall of Yugoslavia*, London: Pluto Press, 2003, p. 2.

18 From 'Deaths in Wars and Conflicts 1945 to 2000', University of Maryland, archived at: http://www.cissm.umd.edu/documents/deaths%20wars%20conflicts.pdf

19 'New Figures on Civilian Deaths in Kosovo War', Human Rights Watch, Washington, DC, 7 February 2000. Archived at: http://www.hrw.org/press/2000/02/nato207.htm

20 West, p. 473.

21 Colin Woodard, 'Illegal and Dangerous: Albania's Risky New Real Estate', *Christian Science Monitor*, 12 July 2002; archived at http://www.csmonitor.com/2002/0712/p08s01-woeu.html.

Chapter Four (pp. 70-77)

1 Marko Prelec, 'The Fear of Islam in Croatian Politics', from a presentation to the East European Studies Program at the Woodrow Wilson International Center for Scholars, 1998; archived at: http://wwics.si.edu/index.cfm?topic_id=14 22&fuseaction=topics.publications&doc_i d=18872&group_id=7427.

2 See text at www.ohr.int.

3 Milovan Djilas, *Tito: The Story from Inside*, London: Phoenix, 2000, p.10.

4 Leon Trotsky, *The Balkan Wars 1912–13: The War Correspondence of Leon Trotsky*, New York: Pathfinder Press, 2001, p.122.

Chapter Five (pp. 78-95)

1 Toby Stone, *New Moment*, Belgrade and London: 2003, p. 2.

2 Leon Trotsky, *The Balkan Wars 1912–13: The War Correspondence of Leon Trotsky*, New York: Pathfinder Press, 2001, p. 95.

3 West, pp. 562–3.

4 Ann Lane *Yugoslavia: When Ideals Collide*, Basingstoke and New York: Palgrave Macmillan, 2004, p. 25.

5 http://news.gmane.org/ gmane.culture.discuss.boundary-point/ cutoff=3138

6 http://article.gmane.org/ gmane.culture.discuss.boundary-point/1492

7 Richard Beeston, 'Yugoslavia Invites Royal Family Back to Palace', *Times*, 10 July 2001.

8 http://www.royalfamily.org/ statements/state-det/state-475.htm

9 Neil Clark, 'The Quisling of Belgrade', *Guardian*, 14 March 2003; archived at: http://www.guardian.co.uk/comment/story/0,3604,913918,00.html.

10 Neil Clark, 'The Quisling of Belgrade'

11 'Mourning Djindjić – and Hoping for a Better Future', Letters, *Guardian*, 18 March 2003.

12 Information on General Export's holdings, divisions and operations taken from the company website: http://www.avio-genex.co.yu/.

13 'Early Elections in Serbia', report on Radio Netherlands, 10 October 2000. http://www.rnw.nl/hotspots/html/yugoslavia001010.html

14 West p.929

15 West p. 933

16 Ann Lane, *Yugoslavia: When Ideals Collide*, Basingstoke and New York: Palgrave Macmillan, 2004, p. 165.

17 Sandro Orlando, 'Banker Slobo is Worth $10 Billions', *Corriere economia*, 26 April 1999.

18 Sandro Orlando, 'Banker Slobo is Worth $10 Billions'.

19 'People Or Territory?: A Proposal For Mitrovica', Berlin: European Stability Initiative, 2004.

20 Gabriel Partos, 'Q&A: Kosovo Violence', London: BBC News Online, 2004; archived at http://news.bbc.co.uk/1/hi/world/europe/3523884.stm.

21 Dragomir Vojnić, 'Disparity and Disintegration,' in Payam Akhavan and Robert Howse (eds), *Yugoslavia, the Former and Future: Reflections by Scholars from the Region*, Geneva: United Nations Research Institute for Social Development, 1995, pp. 91–2.

22 'Kosovo Clashes Ethnic Cleansing', BBC News Online, 20 March 2004; archived at http://news.bbc.co.uk/1/hi/world/europe/3551571.stm.

23 K-FOR, the UN Security Council sanctioned peacekeeping force in Kosovo, formed after a vote of the Security Council on June 11 1999.

24 UNMIK press release, 'No Serbs Involved in Drowning', B92, reported on www.balkanpeace.org/hed/archive/Mar04/hed620.shtml.

25 West, p. 953.

26 Sandro Orlando, 'Banker Slobo is Worth $10 Billions', *Corriere economia*, 26 April 1999.

Chapter Six (pp. 96-115)

1 West, p. 470.

2 Dušan I. Bjelić and Lucinda Cole, *Sexualizing the Serb: Balkan as Metaphor*, Cambridge, MA: The MIT Press, 2002, p. 291.

3 Dušan I. Bjelić and Lucinda Cole, *Sexualizing the Serb: Balkan as Metaphor*, Cambridge, MA: The MIT Press, 2002, p. 281

4 West, p. 55.

5 West, p. 1127.

6 West, p. 1128.

7 West, p. 231.

8 Ann Lane, *Yugoslavia: When Ideals Collide*, Basingstoke and New York: Palgrave Macmillan, 2004, p. 31.

9 West, p. 144.

10 West, p. 252.

11 West, p. 253.

12 Duško Kečkemet, 'Ivan Meštrović 1883-1962', *Katalog Galerije Meštrović* Zagreb: Turistkomerc, 1990, p. 15.

13 West, p. 466.

14 ICTY Milošević proceedings, The Hague, 13 November 2003 (archived at http://www.un.org/icty/transe54/031113ED.htm), p. 29,000.

15 ICTY Milošević proceedings, 13 November 2003, p. 28,995.

16 ICTY Milošević proceedings, 13 November 2003, p. 28,996.

17 'Dutch Peacekeepers', Kirsten Grieshaber, *The Road to Srebrenica*, Columbia Graduate School of Journalism, 2001; archived at http://www.columbia.edu/itc/journalism/nelson/rohde/peacekeepers_dutch.html.

18 Jan Willem Honig and Norbert Both, *Srebrenica: Record of a War Crime*, London: Penguin, 1996, p. 104.

19 Jan Willem Honig and Norbert Both, *Srebrenica: Record of a War Crime*, pp.116–26.

20 ICTY closed hearing, Tuesday 21 March 2000, cross-examination of Nesib Mandžić, pp. 957–82; archived at http://www.un.org/icty/transe33/000321ed.htm.

21 'Statement of Facts and Acceptance of Responsibility' (Tab A to 'Annex A' to the 'Joint Motion for Consideration of Plea Agreement Between Momir Nikolić and the Office of the Prosecutor'; archived at http://www.un.org/icty/mnikolic/trialc/facts030506.htm.

22 ICTY Milošević proceedings, The Hague, 13 November 2003 (archived at http://www.un.org/icty/transe54/031113ED.htm), p. 29,036.

23 'Statement of Facts and Acceptance of Responsibility' (Tab A to 'Annex A' to the 'Joint Motion for Consideration of Plea Agreement Between Momir Nikolić and the Office of the Prosecutor'; archived at http://www.un.org/icty/mnikolic/trialc/facts030506.htm.

24 ICTY closed hearing, Tuesday 21 March 2000, cross-examination of Nesib Mandžić, pp. 957–82; archived at http://www.un.org/icty/transe33/000321ed.htm.

25 'New List of Srebrenica Missing', B92, Belgrade, 10 June 2005.

26 Robert Thomas, *Serbia Under Milošević: Politics in the 1990s*, London: Hurst & Company, 1999, pp.199–208.

27 ICTY Milošević proceedings, The Hague, 13 November 2003 (archived at http://www.un.org/icty/transe54/031113ED.htm), p. 29,002.

28 Ian Traynor, "Balkan Butcher" Left No Smoking Gun', *Guardian*, 28 February 2004.

29 Human Rights Watch, "Safe Areas" for Srebrenica's Most Wanted: A Decade of Failure to Apprehend Karadžić and Mladić', Briefing Paper, 29 June 2005.

Chapter Seven (pp. 116-135)

1 West, p. 705.

2 http://www.publicplan.com/K67/K67_Kiosk_Shots.html

3 'Adaptations', Craig Buckley, New York 2004: www.samplesize.ca/curatorialAdaptations.html.

4 European Boxing Championships, Pula: http://www.posta.hr/marke_det_e.asp?serija=495&brmarke=495.

5 Irwin and Eda Cufer, interviewed by Joanne Richardson, 'NSK 2000?:. http://subsol.c3.hu/subsol_2/contributors/nsktext.html.

6 Jasminka Dedić, 'The Erasure: Administrative Ethnic Cleansing in Slovenia', European Roma Rights Centre: http://www.errc.org/rr_nr3_2003/noteb2.shtml.

7 'Prime Minister Anton Rop argued on 26 January that the highest possible damages under the proposed amendments to the organic law – 150,000 tolars ($800) per person – will amount to less than the 600 million-tolar ($3.2 million) cost of a referendum': Radio Free Europe/Radio Liberty, Balkan Report Vol. 8, No. 5, 6 February 2004.

8 *Independent on Sunday*, 26 October 2003.

9 Igor Mekina, 'Slovenia from Within: Bureaucratic Ethnic Cleansing', AIM Ljubljana, 23 December 2000.

10 Aleksandar Zograf, interviewed by Chris Lanier, 'Dreamtime/Wartime: The Comics of Aleksandar Zograf', San Francisco, 2002; available on:http://www.aleksandarzograf.com/whois.html.

11 Ann Lane, *Yugoslavia: When Ideals Collide*, Basingstoke and New York: Palgrave Macmillan, 2004, p. 95.

12 Zdravko Zupan, 'Comics in Serbia During World War II', *GRRR!*, Pancevo, 2003, p. 38.

13 Kate Hudson, *Breaking the South Slav Dream: The Rise and Fall of Yugoslavia*, London: Pluto Press, 2003, p. 34.

Chapter Eight (pp. 136-145)

1 Milovan Djilas, *Tito: The Story from Inside*, London: Phoenix Press, 2000, p. 64.

2 Milovan Djilas, *Tito: The Story from Inside*, p. 21.

3 'Serbia's Changing Political Landscape', *Europe Briefing*, Belgrade and Brussels: International Crisis Group, 22 July 2004, p. 1.

Chapter Nine (pp. 146-158)

1 Rebecca West, *The Fountain Overflows*, reissued London: Virago, 1984, p. 11.

2 Laura Silber and Allan Little, *Yugoslavia: Death of a Nation*, New York: Penguin Books, 1997 (revised and updated edition of *The Death of Yugoslavia*, London: Penguin Books/BBC Books, 1996), p. 138.

3 Prosecutor v. Milan Babić: Sentencing Judgement, ICTY, 29 June 2004, p. 4.

4 Prosecutor v. Milan Babić, p. 4.

5 Prosecutor v. Milan Babić, p. 6.

6 Prosecutor v. Milan Babić, p. 6.

7 Prosecutor v. Milan Babić, p. 10.

8 Prosecutor v. Milan Babić, p. 10.

9 Prosecutor v. Milan Babić, p. 10.

10 Prosecutor v. Milan Babić, p. 11.

11 Prosecutor v. Milan Babić, p. 9.

12 West, p. 1089.

13 West, p. 1089.

14 West, p. 1089.

15 Vesna Goldsworthy, 'Travel Writing as Autobiography: Rebecca West's Journey of Self-Discovery', in Alison Donnell and Pauline Polkey (eds), *Representing Lives: Women and Auto/biography*, Basingstoke: Macmillan Press, 2000, p. 88.

16 Vesna Goldsworthy, 'Travel Writing as Autobiography', p. 94.

17 Vesna Goldsworthy, 'Travel Writing as Autobiography', p. 92,

18 Vesna Goldsworthy, 'Travel Writing as Autobiography', p. 94.

19 West, p. 1145.

20 Slobodan Selenić, *Fathers and Forefathers*, trans. Ellen Elias-Bursać, London: Harvill Press, 2003 , p. 85–6.

21 George Mallen, 'Stephen Willats: An Interview on Art, Cybernetics and Social Invention', *Page Sixty: The Bulletin of the Computer Arts Society*, London: Computer Arts Society, 2005, p. 1.

22 War Crimes Suspect was Using a False Passport', *Guardian*, 10 December 2005.

Chapter Eleven (pp. 174-204)

1 West, p. 232.

2 'Bomb Beheads Tito's Statue,' *Independent*, 28 December 2004.

3 Michael Farquhar, 'Macedonian Ex-Interior Minister Charged', Institute of War and Peace Reporting, TU No. 398, 15 March 2005; archived at www.iwpr.net/index.pl?archive/tri/tri_398_2_eng.txt.

Chapter Thirteen (pp. 211-228)

1 Djordje Matić, Šerbedžija, Rade' in *Leksikon Yu-mitologije*, Belgrade and Zagreb: Rende/Postskriptum, 2004, p. 379 (trans. Tony White).

2 Akim K at www.goli-otok.com.

3 Information about Goli Otok drawn from Boris Vujčić, 'Mala Kronika Velike Nelagode' ('A Small Chronicle of a Big Disgrace'), in Boris Vujčić and Rade Šerbedžija, *Play Beckett*, Zagreb: Kazalište Ulysses, 2004, and Akim K's excellent website at www.goli-otok.com.

4 Akim K at www.goli-otok.com.

5 See Ivan Čolović, 'The Politics of Time', in *The Politics of Symbol in Serbia*, London: Hurst & Company, London 2002 (first published as *Politika Simbola*, Belgrade: Biblioteka, 1997 and 2000).

Chapter Fourteen (pp. 229-240)

1 Ivan Čolović, 'Characters and Figures of Power', in *The Politics of Symbol in Serbia*, London: Hurst & Company, 2002, p. 202.

2 Slobodan Selenić, *Fathers and Forefathers*, trans. Ellen Elias-Bursać, London: Harvill Press, 2003, p. 92.

3 Slobodan Selenić, *Fathers and Forefathers*, p. 116.

4 The phrase 'the personal is political' is attributed to Carol Hanish in *The Oxford Dictionary of Quotations* (Oxford and New York: Oxford University Press, 2004, p. 601) and elsewhere, though this attribution remains the subject of debate.

5 West, p. 1126.

6 Rebecca West, Letter to Miss G.Rotherham, 11 December 1944, in *Selected Letters*, ed. Bonnie Kime Scott, New Haven, CT, and London: Yale University Press, 2000, p. 188.

7 West, p. 1125.

8 West, p. 1121.

9 West, p. 1145.

10 Dejan Novačić, 'Parlov, Mate' in *Leksikon Yu-mitologije*, Belgrade and Zagreb: Rende/Postskriptum, 2004 p. 294 (trans. Tony White).

11 John Berger in *Art, Poetry and Particle Physics* (DVD), directed by Ken McMullen, Arts Council England, 2005.

Bibliography

As I've already mentioned, the number of generally available books and other text resources in English about the Balkan region and the former Yugoslavia has increased significantly in recent years. However, I've limited this bibliography to works that proved to be of particular significance to this project. In addition to *Black Lamb and Grey Falcon*, works by Rebecca West that provided particular insight over and above general interest are also included in this bibliography. Readers wishing to find out more about Rebecca West (born Cicely, later 'Cicily' Fairfield, 1892-1983) are directed initially to the two excellent biographies by Victoria Glendinning and Carl Rollyson and to the website of the International Rebecca West Society.

Non-fiction Books

Akhavan, Payam, and Robert Howse (eds), *Yugoslavia, the Former and Future: Reflections by Scholars from the Region*, Geneva: UN Research Institute for Social Development, 1995

Barber, Stephen, *Extreme Europe*, London: Reaktion Books, 2001

Berger, John, *Art and Revolution*, reissued London: Granta Books, 1993 (first published London: Weidenfeld & Nicolson, 1969)

Bjelić, Dušan I., and Obrad Savić (eds), *Balkan as Metaphor: Between Globalization and Fragmentation*, Cambridge, MA: MIT Press, 2002

Brân, Zoë, *After Yugoslavia*, Footscray, London and Oakland, CA: Lonely Planet Publications, 2001

Burgess, Alan, *The Lovely Sergeant*, London: Heinemann, 1963

Chirot, Daniel (ed), *The Origins of Backwardness in Eastern Europe: Economics and Politics from the Middle Ages until the Early Twentieth Century*, Berkeley and Los Angeles: University of California Press, 1989

Collin, Matthew, *This is Serbia Calling: Rock 'n' Roll Radio and Belgrade's Underground Resistance*, London: Serpent's Tail, 2001

Čolović, Ivan, *The Politics of Symbol in Serbia: Essays in Political Anthropology*, trans. Celia Hawkesworth, London: Hurst & Company, 2002

Djilas, Milovan, *Tito: The Story from Inside*, trans. Vasilije Kojić and Richard Hayes, London: Phoenix Press, 2000

Drakulić, Slavenka, *Café Europa: Life After Communism*, London: Abacus, 1996

Drakulić, Slavenka, *They Would Never Hurt a Fly: War Criminals on Trial in The Hague*, London: Abacus, 2004

Giovanni, Janine di, *Madness Visible: a Memoir of a War*, London: Bloomsbury, 2004

Glendinning, Victoria, *Rebecca West: A Life*, London: Weidenfeld & Nicolson, 1987

Glenny, Misha, *The Balkans, 1804–1999: Nationalism, War and the Great Powers*, London: Granta Books, 2000

Glenny, Misha, *The Fall of Yugoslavia: the Third Balkan War*, third revised edition, New York: Penguin Books, 1996

Goethals, Kate (ed.), *Music and Technology*, London: Royal Society of Arts, 2004

Goldsworthy, Vesna, *Inventing Ruritania: The Imperialism of the Imagination*, New Haven, CT, and London: Yale University Press, 1998

Gordon, Jan and Cora, *Two Vagabonds in the Balkans*, London: John Lane, The Bodley Head, 1925

Grubanov, Ivan, *Visitor*, Belgrade: *Muzej savremene umetnosti*, 2005

Gržinić, Marina, *Fiction Reconstructed: Eastern Europe, Post-Socialism and the Retro-Avantgarde*, Vienna: edition selene, 2000

Hall, Brian, *The Impossible Country: A Journey Through the Last Days of Yugoslavia*, New York: Penguin Books, 1995 (first published Boston, MA: David R. Godine, 1994

Helsinki Committee for Human Rights in Serbia (HCHRS), *Human Rights in the Shadow of Nationalism: Serbia 2002*, Belgrade: HCHRS, 2002

Honig, Jan Willem, and Norbert Both, *Srebrenica: Record of a War Crime*, London: Penguin Books, 1996

Howkins, John (ed.), *CODE: Collaboration and Ownership in the Digital Economy*, London: Academia Europa/Arts Council England, 2002

Hudson, Kate, *Breaking the South Slav Dream: The Rise and Fall of Yugoslavia*, London: Pluto Press, 2003

Hyman, Susan (ed.), *Edward Lear in the Levant: Travels in Albania, Greece and Turkey in Europe, 1848–1849*, London: John Murray, 1988

Jezernik, Božidar, *Wild Europe: The Balkans in the Gaze of Western Travellers*, London: Saqi Books, 2004

Judah, Tim, *The Serbs: History, Myth and the Destruction of Yugoslavia*, New Haven, CT, and London: Yale University Press, 2000

Kaplan, Robert D., *Balkan Ghosts*, New York: Vintage, 2004

Labon, Joanna (ed.), *Balkan Blues: Writing Out of Yugoslavia*, Evanston, IL: Northwestern University Press, 1998

Lane, Ann, *Yugoslavia: When Ideals Collide*, Basingstoke: Palgrave Macmillan, 2004

Loyd, Anthony, *My War Gone By, I Miss It So*, reissued London: Black Swan, 2002 (first published by Doubleday, 1999)

Malcolm, Noel, *Bosnia: A Short History*, London: Macmillan and New York: New York University Press, 1994

Neuffer, Elizabeth, *The Key to My Neighbour's House: Seeking Justice in Bosnia and Rwanda*, London: Bloomsbury, 2003

Orwell, George, *The Collected Essays, Journalism and Letters of George Orwell*, four volumes, ed. Sonia Orwell and Ian Angus, paperback edition London: Penguin Books, 1970 (first published London: Secker & Warburg, 1968)

Poulton, Hugh, *Who are the Macedonians?*, London: Hurst & Company, 2000

Prentice, Eve-Ann, *One Woman's War*, London: Duckworth, 2000

Rollyson, Carl, *Rebecca West: A Saga of the Century*, London, Hodder & Stoughton, 1995

Selenić, Slobodan, *Fathers and Forefathers*, tr. Ellen Elias-Bursać, London: Harvill Press, 2003

Silber, Laura, and Allan Little, *Yugoslavia: Death of a Nation*, New York: Penguin Books, 1997 (revised and updated edition of *The Death of Yugoslavia*, London: Penguin Books/BBC Books, 1996)

Simms, Brendan, *Unfinest Hour: Britain and the Destruction of Bosnia*, London: Penguin, 2002

Sirc, Ljubo, *Between Hitler and Tito: Nazi Occupation and Communist Oppression*, London: André Deutsch Ltd, 1989

Stanišić, Gordana, exhibition catalogue, London: The Showroom, 1994

Stanković, Miloš, *Trusted Mole: A Soldier's Journey into Bosnia's Heart of Darkness*, London: HarperCollins, 2000

Tanner, Marcus, *Croatia: A Nation Forged in War*, New Haven, CT, and London: Yale University Press, 2001

Thomas, Robert, *Serbia under Milošević: Politics in the 1990s*, London: Hurst & Company, 1999

Todorova, Maria, *Imagining the Balkans*, New York: Oxford University Press, 1997

Trotsky, Leon, *The Balkan Wars 1912–13: The War Correspondence of Leon Trotsky*, New York: Pathfinder Press, 2001

Ugrešić, Dubravka, *Have a Nice Day: From the Balkan War to the American Dream*, London: Jonathan Cape, 1994

Virilio, Paul, *Art and Fear*, London: Continuum, 2004

Vukić, Fedja (ed.), *Zagreb, Modernity and the City*, Zagreb: AGM/Zagreb Film Festival, date not shown

West, Rebecca, *Black Lamb and Grey Falcon: A Journey through Yugoslavia*, two volumes, London: Macmillan, 1942; revised and reissued in one volume, London: Macmillan, 1955; reissued, London: Macmillan, 1977; paperback edition, 1982; reissued, Edinburgh: Canongate, 1993

West, Rebecca, *Selected Letters*, ed. Bonnie Kime Scott, New Haven, CT, and London: Yale University Press, 2000

West, Rebecca, *Survivors in Mexico*, ed. Bernard Schweizer, New Haven, CT, and London: Yale University Press, 2003

West, Rebecca, *The Meaning of Treason*, reissued London: Virago, 1982

Zograf, Aleksandar, *Bulletins from Serbia: E-mails and Cartoon Strips from Behind the Front Line*, Hove: Slab-O-Concrete, 1999

Fiction

Andrić, Ivo, *The Bridge Over the Drina*, trans. Lovett F. Edwards. London: Harvill Press, 1994

Arsenijević, Vladimir, *In the Hold*, trans. Celia Hawkesworth, London: Harvill Press, 1996

Blissett, Luther, *Q*, London: Heinemann, 2003

Brecht, Bertolt, *Threepenny Novel*, trans. Desmond I. Vesey and Christopher Isherwood, London: Penguin, 1973 (first published New York: Grove Press, 1956; trans. from *Die Dreigroschenroman*, 1934)

Durrell, Lawrence, *Esprit de Corps*, London: Faber, 1957

Durrell, Lawrence, *Prospero's Cell*, London: Faber, 2000

Durrell, Lawrence, *White Eagles Over Serbia*, London: Faber, 1993

Goytisolo, Juan, *State of Siege*, trans. Helen Lane, London: Serpent's Tail, 2003

Jergović, Miljenko, *Sarajevo Marlboro*, trans. Stela Tomasevic, London, Penguin Books, 1997

Kiš, Danilo, *A Tomb for Boris Davidovich*, London: Faber, 1985

Kiš, Danilo, *Hourglass*, London: Faber, 1992

Manning, Olivia, *The Balkan Trilogy*, London: Mandarin, 1992 (first published as one volume, London: Heinemann, 1987)

Ming, Wu, *54*, trans. Shaun Whiteside, London: William Heinemann, 2005

Narayan, R.K., *Mr Sampath – The Printer of Malgudi*, London: Eyre & Spottiswode, 1949. (Reissued in the collection *More Tales From Malgudi*, London: Minerva, 1977)

Saint-Exupéry, Antoine de, *The Little Prince*, London, 1943

West, Rebecca, *The Fountain Overflows*, reissued London: Virago, 1984 (first published London: Macmillan, 1957)

West, Rebecca, *The Return of the Soldier*, revised edition, London: Virago, 1980 (original edition first published London: Macmillan, 1918)

Articles and Reports

Beeston, Richard, 'Yugoslavia Invites Royal Family Back to Palace', *The Times*, 10 July 2001

Clark, Neil, 'The Quisling of Belgrade,' *Guardian*, 14 March 2003

Dedić, Jasminka, 'The Erasure: Administrative Ethnic Cleansing in Slovenia', Budapest: European Roma Rights Centre, 2003

European Stability Initiative, 'People or Territory?: A Proposal for Mitrovica', Berlin: European Stability Initiative, 2004

Free Serbia, 'All President's (Dead) Men' : Free Serbia, 2000, archived at http://www.xs4all.nl/~freeserb/feuilleton/assasinations/e-todorovic.html

Glenny, Misha, and Gerald Klaus, 'Thessaloniki and Beyond: Europe's Challenge in the Western Balkans', Davos: World Economic Forum, 2003

Grieshaber, Kirsten, 'Dutch Peacekeepers', The Road to Srebrenica, New York: Columbia University Graduate School of Journalism, 2001

Gubbins, Ed, *Wireless Review*, 1 April 2003, archived at http://www.wirelessreview.com/ar/wireless_drazen_panticcodirector_location/

Human Rights Watch, *New Figures on Civilian Deaths in Kosovo War*, New York: Human Rights Watch, 2000

Human Rights Watch, *'Safe Areas' for Srebrenica's Most Wanted: A Decade of Failure to Apprehend Karadzic and Mladic*, New York: Human Rights Watch, 2005

Jovanović Weiss, Srdjan, 'Loss of Memory?: New Urban Condition of Belgrade': Normal Group

Jovanović Weiss, Srdjan, 'Nato as Architecture Critic', *Cabinet*, 2000

Jovanović Weiss, Srdjan, Mirosavić, Miloš and Masnikosić, Jelena, 'Turbo Architecture and Other Stories': Normal Group

Konjikušić, Davor, 'Sugar Re-packaged in Serbia and Sold to the EU,' *Southeast European Times*, 2004

Lessig, Lawrence, 'Getting the Law Out of the Way', *Music and Technology*, London: Royal Society of Arts, London, 2004

Nicklanovich, Michael D., 'Rebecca West's Constantine the Poet', *Serb World USA*, 1999

Orlando, Sandro, 'Banker Slobo is worth $10 Billions,' *Corriere Economia*, 1999

Partos, Gabriel, 'Q&A: Kosovo Violence,' BBC News Online, 2004

Prelec, Marko, 'The Fear of Islam in Croatian Politics': Woodrow Wilson International Center for Scholars, 1998

Radio Netherlands, 'Early Elections in Serbia': Radio Netherlands, 10 October 2000

Reindl, Donald F., 'Signs of Intolerance, or Just Legal Wrangling in Slovenia', *RFE/RL Balkan Report*, 8:8, 2004

Richardson, Joanne, 'NSK 2000?', *Subsol* (Ljubljana), 2000

Stone, Toby, *New Moment*, Belgrade, 2003

Traynor, Ian, "Balkan Butcher" Left No Smoking Gun', *Guardian*, 28 February 2004

Woodard, Colin, 'Illegal and Dangerous: Albania's Risky New Real Estate', *Christian Science Monitor*, 2002

Zupan, Zdravko, 'Comics in Serbia During World War II,' *GRRR!* (Pancevo), 2003

Web Resources

Balkan Military History: http://members.aol.com/_ht_a/balkandave/frmcon.htm

Balkan Peace: www.balkanpeace.org

Beograd: www.beograd.org

Electronic Frontier Foundation: www.eff.org

European Roma Rights Centre: www.errc.org

Human Rights Watch: www.hrw.org

International Criminal Tribunal for the Former Yugoslavia: www.un.org/icty/

Nizkor Project Holocaust Archive: www.nizkor.org

Organization for Security and Cooperation in Europe: www.osce.org

Radio Free Europe/Radio Liberty, *Balkan Reports*: http://www.rferl.org/reports/balkan-report/

The International Rebecca West Society: www.rebeccawestsociety.org

World Economic Forum: www.weforum.org